RNIN UNIVERSITY OF
GLOUCESTERSHIRE

Avatars in Networked Virtual Environments

Avatars in Networked Virtual Environments

Tolga K. Çapin
Computer Graphics Lab, EPFL, Lausanne, Switzerland

Igor S. Pandzic
MIRALab, University of Geneva, Switzerland

Nadia Magnenat-Thalmann
MIRALab, University of Geneva, Switzerland

Daniel Thalmann
Computer Graphics Lab, EPFL, Lausanne, Switzerland

JOHN WILEY & SONS, LTD
Chichester · New York · Weinheim · Brisbane · Singapore · Toronto

Copyright © 1999   John Wiley & Sons Ltd
                    Baffins Lane, Chichester,
                    West Sussex PO19 1UD, England
                    National 01243 779777
                    International (+44) 1243 779777
e-mail (for orders and customer service enquiries): cs-books@wiley.co.uk

Visit our Home Page on http://www.wiley.co.uk or http://www.wiley.com

Other Wiley Editorial Offices

John Wiley & Sons, Inc., 605 Third Avenue,
New York, NY 10158-0012, USA

WILEY-VCH Verlag GmbH, Pappelallee 3,
D-69469 Weinheim, Germany

Jacaranda Wiley Ltd, 33 Park Road, Milton,
Queensland 4064, Australia

John Wiley & Sons (Canada) Ltd, 22 Worcester Road,
Rexdale, Ontario M9W 1L1, Canada

John Wiley & Sons (Asia) Pte Ltd, 2 Clementi Loop #02-01,
Jin Xing Distripark, Singapore 129809

Library of Congress Cataloging-in-Publication Data

Avatars in networked virtual environments / Tolga K. Çapin...[et al.]
       p.   cm
    Includes bibliographical references and index
    ISBN 0-471-98863-4 (alk. paper)
1. Interactive multimedia. 2. Virtual reality. I. Çapin, Tolga K.
QA76. 76. 159A99 1999
006. 7—dc21   99-13561
                                         CIP
British Library Cataloguing in Publication Data
A catalogue record for this book is available from the British Library

ISBN 0-471-98863 -4

Produced from PostScript files supplied by the author.
Printed and bound in Great Britain by Bookcraft (Bath) Ltd
This book is printed on acid-free paper responsibly manufactured from sustainable forestry, in which at least two trees are planted for each one used for paper production.

Contents

Preface

Telepresence is the future of multimedia systems and will allow participants to share professional and private experiences, meetings, games, parties. Networked virtual environments (NVEs) is a key technology to implement this telepresence. NVEs are systems that allow multiple geographically distant users to interact in a common virtual environment. One of the particularly important research challenges in NVEs is the user representation or avatar, the way that participants are graphically represented in the VE. This can range from a very simple block-like representation to highly realistic virtual humans with articulated bodies and faces. We believe that real-time realistic 3D avatars will be essential in the future, as better user representation can improve a user's sense of presence in the environment and their ability to communicate with other users. We also need autonomous virtual humans to populate the virtual worlds.

The objective of this book is to explain the techniques for integrating virtual humans into virtual environments. The first chapter introduces the basic concepts of NVEs. Chapter 2 surveys different factors and design decisions while developing networked virtual environment architectures, and it surveys previous work based on this perspective. Chapter 3 introduces our solution: the Virtual Life Network (VLNET), a flexible framework for virtual humans in networked collaborative virtual environments. Chapter 4 describes the design philosophy and elements of VLNET. As VLNET is the most advanced NVE in terms of realistic virtual humans, we emphasize this key issue. We also discuss the motivations and challenges behind including virtual humans (VH) in the NVE systems. Based on the VLNET system, Chapter 5 describes the different means of facial communication we have developed. It also looks at gesture and non-verbal communication. Chapter 6 is dedicated to all problems of handling virtual human data across the network. Chapter 7 considers the potential relation of the future MPEG-4 standard to NVEs, based on experience from our active participation in the MPEG-4 ad hoc group on face and body animation. It also discusses the standardization of virtual humans in VRML. Chapter 8 presents several applications, including a virtual tennis game. There is also an extensive study of the experimental results and achievements.

The research in VLNET has been financed by the Swiss Priority Programme for Information and Communication Structures (SPP ICS) of the Swiss National Science Foundation. Our participation in the work of the MPEG committee is in the framework of the European ACTS projects VIDAS and COVEN.

We are also grateful to all people of MIRALab, University of Geneva, and LIG, EPFL, for their cooperation and support during this work and the development of VLNET.

Tolga K. Çapin
Igor S. Pandzic
Nadia Magnenat Thalmann
Daniel Thalmann

1 Concepts in Networked Virtual Environments

1.1 Virtual Environments

Ivan Sutherland introduced the concept of inserting people in computer-generated worlds in 1965, and made the first realization in 1968 with a tracked head-mounted stereoscopic display drawing wireframe models. Since then, together with the development of computer graphics knowledge and technology, various systems containing virtual environments have been developed.

Steve Ellis has presented an important introduction to virtual environment concepts (Ellis 1991). He defines *virtualization* as 'the process by which a human viewer interprets a patterned sensory impression to be an extended object in an environment other than that in which it physically exists'. He further categorizes virtualization into three levels: *virtual space*, *virtual image* and *virtual environment*. An example of the virtual space is a flat surface on which the image is rendered, and the observer can visualize three-dimensional objects through this space. Virtual image refers to perception of the object in depth, for example through stereoscopic images displayed on helmet-mounted displays. The third level, virtual environment, embodies the participant as part of the virtual world, so that his/her viewpoint and actions in this world correspond to those of the physical (real) world.

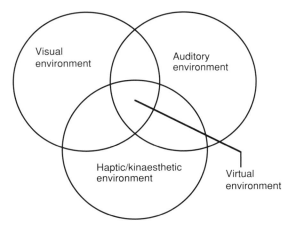

Figure 1-1. Elements of a virtual environment

In a virtual environment, the sensory impressions are delivered to the senses of the human participant through computer-generated displays. Ideally, a virtual environment has to provide three elements to immerse a participant: visual, auditory, haptics/kinesthetics. As shown in Figure 1-1, the virtual environment is an intersection of these elements. This intersection is important because it shows a fully interactive environment including all elements. However, this definition is general, and smaller virtual environments can be created by using subsets of the three components.

Kalawsky (1993) defined virtual environments as 'synthetic sensory experiences that communicate physical and abstract components to a human operator or participant. The synthetic sensory experience is generated by a computer system that one day may present an interface to the human sensory systems that is indistinguishable from the real physical world'.

Virtual environment refers to a technology which is capable of shifting a subject into a different environment without physically moving him/her. To this end, the inputs into the subject's sensory organs are manipulated in such a way that the perceived environment is associated with the desired virtual environment, not with the physical environment. The manipulation process is controlled by a computer model that is based on the physical description of the virtual environment. Consequently, the technology is able to create almost arbitrarily perceived environments.

There are other definitions of a virtual environment. However, most definitions agree that support of a totality of senses is necessary to make the participant feel present in the virtual surrounding. This book deals with virtual environments, where the participants are represented by 3D virtual human embodiments within the computer-generated world. This can be achieved by high-end configurations with magnetic trackers attached to the body, but also by desktop configurations where the participant sees their virtual embodiment interacting with the virtual objects.

1.2 Networked Virtual Environments

Until recently, the majority of virtual worlds have been single-user systems (Singh and Serra 1994). Compared with traditional systems, single-user systems provide tremendous benefit to the user but their utility in the real world is quite limited. This is because they do not support collaboration among a group of users. Networking coupled with highly interactive technology of virtual worlds will dominate the world of computers and information technology. It will not be enough to produce slick single-user, standalone virtual worlds. These systems will have to connect people, systems, information streams and technologies with one another. The information that is currently shared through file systems or through other 'static' media will have to be exchanged through the network. This information has to reside 'in the net' where it is easy to get at. Developing virtual worlds that support collaboration among a group of users is a complex and time-consuming task. In order to develop such virtual worlds, the developer has to be proficient in network programming, object management, graphics programming, device handling and user interface design. Even after gaining expertise in such diverse specializations, developing network-based virtual worlds takes a long time since network-based programs are inherently more difficult to write and debug than standalone programs.

Trends towards networked applications and computer supported collaborative work, together with a wide interest for graphical systems and virtual environments, have in the recent years raised interest for research in the field of networked virtual environments (NVEs) (Durlach and Mavor 1995). NVEs are systems that allow multiple geographically distant users to interact in a common virtual environment. The users themselves are represented within the environment using a graphical embodiment.

Figure 1-2 schematically presents the basic principle of the NVE. Each workstation has a copy of the virtual environment.

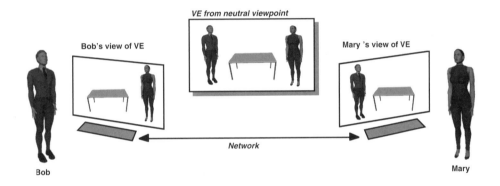

Figure 1-2. Principles of networked virtual environments

The user can evolve within the environment and interact with it. All events that have an impact on the environment are transmitted to other sites so that all environments can be updated and kept consistent, giving the impression for the users of being in the same, unique environment. The users become a part of the environment, embodied by a graphical representation that should ideally be human-like.

Networked virtual environment systems are suitable for numerous collaborative applications ranging from games to medicine (Doenges et al. 1997; Zyda and Sheehan 1997), for example:

- Virtual teleconferencing with multimedia object exchange
- All sorts of collaborative work involving 3D design
- Multi-user game environments
- Teleshopping involving 3D models, images, sound (e.g. real estate, furniture, cars)
- Medical applications (distance diagnostics, virtual surgery for training)
- Distance learning/training
- Virtual studio/set with networked media integration
- Virtual travel agency

Networked virtual environments have been an active area of research for several years now, and a number of working systems exist (Barrus et al. 1996; Carlsson and Hagsand 1993; Macedonia et al. 1994; Ohya et al. 1995; Singh et al. 1995; Zyda et al. 1993). They differ largely in networking solutions, number of users supported, interaction capabilities and application scope (Macedonia and Zyda 1997), but share the same basic principle.

Several aspects of NVE systems have been subject to thorough research with interesting results: scalability and network topologies (Macedonia et al. 1994; Singh et al. 1995; Funkhouser 1996), efficient space structuring (Barrus et al. 1996; Benford et al. 1995), real-time simulation (Rohlf and Helman 1994), feeling of presence in NVEs (Benford et al. 1995; Welch et al. 1996, Hendrix and Barfield 1996; Tromp 1995).

There is also an increasing interest in shared graphical spaces that allow people to interact with each other in remote locations, or with programs and virtual objects. Here are some different perspectives:

- *Science fiction vision:* William Gibson's *Neuromancer* (1984), a popular science fiction novel, envisions the computer network as an immersive virtual space, with people interacting with each other. Another science fiction novel is *Snow Crash* by Neal Stephenson (1992); this involves a computer-generated 3D large-scale space and people performing business with their virtual embodiments.
- *MUDs:* A MUD is defined as a networked, multi-participant, user-extendible environment in which the user interface is entirely textual. Participants communicate with each other and input commands for their actions (e.g. go east, smile) by textual messages (Curtis 1992). Several MUDs involve a large number of participants, and later systems such as Internet Relay Chat (IRC) have received a wider popularity; in IRC, participants create channels for various subjects and distant participants can join the same channel for chatting. An improvement to these systems is Palace from Palace Corporation, which is a multi-user virtual environment where the participant representations are 2D.
- *Successful virtual reality applications:* There have been an increasing number of successful applications that make use of virtual reality. Most of these applications benefit from sharing the experience with other people.

Until recently, networked graphics applications were prototype systems, demonstrating the effectiveness of the technology. However, a current effort is to provide real applications, manifested by the 3D graphics interchange standardization efforts such as VRML 2.0 and MPEG-4. The main contributors to these standards are companies hoping to diffuse their application content.

1.3 Virtual Environments for Interaction

Increasing hardware and network performance together with the software technology make it possible to define more complex interfaces for networked collaborative applications. Exploiting a virtual environment is an increasingly popular method as a natural interface for this purpose. An NVE can provide a more natural shared system, by supporting interactive human collaboration and integrating different media in real time in a single 3D surrounding. It provides a powerful system as it supports awareness of and interaction with other users; and it provides an appropriate mechanism for interaction with the VE by supporting visual mechanisms for actions, data sharing and protection.

Providing a behavioural realism is a significant requirement for systems that are based on human collaboration, such as computer supported cooperative work (CSCW) systems. Networked CSCW systems also require that the shared environment supports an appropriate interface for gestural communication, awareness of other users in the environment, mechanisms for different modes of interaction (synchronous vs. asynchronous, the ability to work at different times in the same environment), mechanisms for customized tools for data visualization, protection and sharing.

Virtual environments can support powerful mechanisms for networked CSCW systems, as they provide a more natural interface to the environment. This can be accomplished in several ways:

- Representing the users and special-purpose service programs by 3D virtual humans in the virtual environment.
- Mechanisms for the participants to interact with each other in the natural interface via facial interaction and body gestures of their virtual embodiments.
- Mechanisms for the participants to interact with the rest of the virtual environment through complex and realistic behaviours such as walking for navigation, grasping, etc.
- User-customized tools for editing the picked objects, depending on the object type (e.g. images, free-form surfaces).

1.4   Virtual Humans in NVEs

Realism not only includes believable appearance and simulation of the virtual world, but also implies the natural representation of participants. This representation fulfils several functions:

- The visual embodiment of the user
- The means of interacting with the world
- The means of feeling various attributes of the world using the senses

The realism in participant representation involves two elements: believable appearance and realistic movements. Realism becomes even more important in multi-user networked virtual environments, as participants' representation is used for communication. The local program of the participants typically stores the whole or a subset of the scene description, and they use their own avatars to move around the scene and render from their own viewpoint. This avatar representation in NVEs has crucial functions in addition to those of single-user virtual environments:

- *Perception (to see if anyone is around)*: the participants need to be able to tell at a glance who else is present in the same VE, and this should be done in a continuous manner. The realistic embodiment makes it easy to distinguish embodiments from other virtual objects.
- *Localization (to see where the other person is)*: the position and orientation of other participants can convey different meanings. In particular, orientation of the embodiments may convey a special intention related to non-verbal communication.
- *Identification (to recognize the person)*: the embodiments make it easy to differentiate different participants in the NVE. Using this embodiment regularly, the participant has a bounded, authentic and coherent representation in the virtual world. In addition, by changing decoration of the body through clothes and accessories, the representation has an emergent identity.
- *Visualization of others' interest focus (to see where their attention is directed)*: to understand where the other participants' attention concentrates, this may be critical to supporting interaction. For CSCW applications, it may make it easy to focus the discussion. Or, for non-verbal communication, the gaze direction helps to control turn-taking in conversation, as well as modifying, strengthening or weakening what is said verbally.
- *Visualization of others' actions (to see what the other person is doing and what they mean through gestures)*: an action point corresponds to where in the virtual world a person is manipulating. This is crucial in applications where synchronous collaboration among participants is important (e.g. modifying different parts of an object). Figure 1-3 shows the importance of individual and general views.
- *Social representation of self through decoration of the avatar (to know what the other participants' task or status is)*: the decoration of the avatar can convey meanings which shape the interaction. This decoration can be constant, such as a uniform; or it can change from day to day or even within one day, such as accessories that the avatar wears.

Although networked virtual environments have been around as a topic of research for quite some time, in most of the existing systems the embodiments are fairly simple, ranging from primitive cube-like appearances (Greenhalgh and Benford 1995), non-articulated human-like or cartoon-like avatars (Benford et al. 1995) to articulated body representations using rigid body segments (Barrus et al. 1996; Carlsson and Hagsand 1993; Pratt et al. 1997). Ohya et al. (1995) report the use of human representations with animated bodies and faces in a virtual teleconferencing application, as described in Chapter 2.

Using virtual human figures for avatar representation fulfils these functionalities with realism, as it provides a direct relationship between how we control our avatar in the virtual world and how our avatar moves related to this control. Even with limited sensor information, a virtual human frame that reflects the activities of the user can be constructed in the virtual world. Slater and Usoh (1994) indicate that using a virtual body, even if simple, increases the sense of presence in the virtual world.

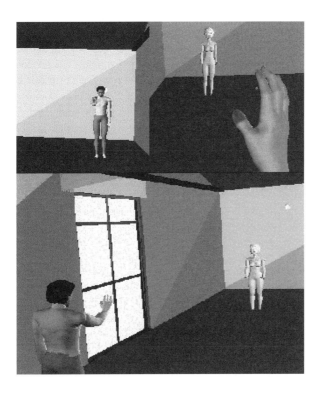

Figure 1-3. Two individual views (above), and the overall view of the scene (below)

We believe that the simulation of highly realistic virtual humans for participant representation in NVEs can fulfil these functions. However, in most existing systems the participant representation is rather crude, often using non-articulated objects as embodiments. It is necessary to provide a framework for including highly realistic, articulated and deformable virtual humans into the NVE, capable of both body and face animation. This framework should include the following items:

- *Virtual human simulation* involving real-time animation and deformation of bodies and faces.
- *Virtual environment simulation* involving visual database management and rendering techniques with real-time optimizations.
- *Networking* that involves communication of various types of data with varying requirements in terms of bit rate, error resilience and latency.
- *Interaction* involving support of different devices and paradigms.
- *Artificial intelligence* (in case autonomous virtual humans are involved) through decision-making processes and autonomous behaviours.

Each item represents a separate area of research. When they are combined, it is important to consider how they interact. Development of the proposed framework is therefore a complex task and requires careful design of the software architecture.

The networked virtual environments are often described as systems that permit the users to feel as if they were together in a shared virtual environment. Indeed, the feeling of 'being together' is extremely important for collaboration. Probably the most important aspect of being together with someone, either in the real world or a virtual world, is the ability to communicate. A function that virtual humans can fulfil, and that we find particularly interesting, is allowing more natural communication through facial expressions and gestures. Facial expressions, lip movements, body postures and gestures all play an important role in our everyday communication. Therefore we believe they should have their place within the NVE systems.

In most of the existing NVE systems the communication between participants is restricted to text messages and/or audio communication (Barrus et al. 1996; Greenhalgh and Benford 1995; Singh et al. 1995). Some systems (Carlsson and Hagsand 1993; Pratt et al. 1997) include a means of gestural communication by choosing some predefined gestures or simple behaviours. The natural human communication is richer than this. Recognizing this problem, Ohya et al. (1995) present a virtual teleconferencing system where facial expressions are tracked using tape markers while body and hands carry magnetic trackers, allowing both face and body movements to be synthesized.

We propose a flexible framework for including virtual humans in networked virtual environments, and we use this framework to explore different means of communication in such environments. Table 1-1 defines a few keywords.

1.5   Problem Domain

NVEs with virtual humans are emerging from two threads of research having a bottom-up tendency. First, over the past several years, many NVE systems have been created using various types of network topologies and computer architectures. The practice is to bring together a variety of earlier monolithic applications within one standard interface; it consists of building multiple logical or actual processes that handle a separate element of the NVE. Second, at the same time, virtual human research has developed far enough to provide realistic-looking virtual humans that can be animated with believable behaviours in multiple levels of control. Inserting virtual humans in the NVE is a complex task. There are four main issues:

- Selecting a scalable architecture to combine these two complex systems.
- Realistic modelling of the virtual human with believable appearance for interactive manipulation.
- Animating it with minimum number of sensors to have utmost behavioural realism.
- Investigating different methods to decrease the networking requirements for exchanging complex virtual human information.

Table 1-1. Definitions and concepts

Agent	A software process that has autonomous behaviour. It does not necessarily have to be represented by a graphics entity
Autonomy	Quality or state of being self-governing
Avatar	A graphical representation of a real person in a networked virtual environment, together with its behaviours
Directly controlled virtual human	A virtual human whose body and face geometric representation is directly updated by the user or program controlling it
Embodiment	*See* avatar
User-guided virtual human	A virtual human whose control is in the form of tasks to perform (e.g. go to a location, sit), and which uses its motor skills to perform this action by coordinated joint movements
Participant	A real person that participates in the networked virtual environment, and is represented by an avatar
Representation	*See* avatar
Virtual human	A graphics entity that is totally represented by computer and looks like a real human

In this book, we survey problems in and solutions for inserting virtual humans in networked virtual environments. We have built an architecture, VLNET (Virtual Life Network), and we tried to integrate artificial life techniques with virtual reality techniques in order to create truly virtual environments shared by real people, and with autonomous living virtual humans with their own behaviour, which can perceive the environment and interact with participants. Figure 1-4 shows some applications of the system.

1.6 Immersion and Presence

Immersion is a key issue in virtual reality systems as it is central to the paradigm where the user becomes part of the simulated world, rather than the simulated world being a feature of the user's own world. The first 'immersive VR systems' have been the flight simulators where the immersion is achieved by a subtle mixture of real hardware and virtual imagery. Cockpits are real with their instruments, joysticks, levers, switches, buttons and sliders. Each instrument possesses individual mechanical characteristics. Pilots are constrained to floor-mounted chairs, and during take-off and landing scenarios they are restrained by seat belts. It would be ridiculous to build all the instruments and chairs in the virtual world.

The drawback is that monitors are used, and the pilot and co-pilot cannot share each other's images, as each is looking at their individual display. This could be resolved by using a system of projectors and a panoramic spherical mirror, as in WIDE system made by Rediffusion simulations. Typically, three projectors form a seamless coloured image on the back-projection screen, with each projector forming an image of 50° horizontal field of view.

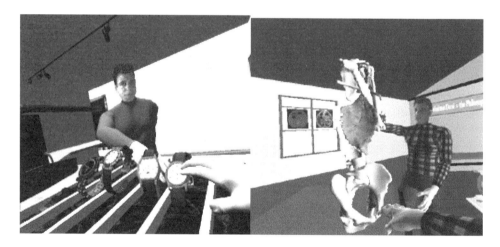

Figure 1-4. VLNET applications

According to Slater et al. (1994), the human participant is 'immersed' in the virtual environment in two ways. First, through the VE system displaying the sensory data depicting their surroundings. Part of the immediate surroundings consist of a representation of the participant's body and the environment is displayed from the unique position and orientation defined by the place of the participant's viewpoint within the environment. Body-tracking devices, such as electromagnetic sensors enable movements of the person's whole body and limbs to become part of the dynamic changes to objects in the VE under their immediate control. This is the second aspect of immersion: proprioceptive signals about the disposition and dynamic behaviour of the human body and its parts become overlaid with consistent sensory data about the representation of the human body, the virtual body (VB). These environments are called *immersive virtual environments* (IVEs).

The term 'immersion' is a description of a technology which can be achieved to varying degrees. A necessary condition is Ellis's notion (Ellis 1991) of a VE, maintained in at least one sensory modality (typically the visual). For example, a head-mounted display with wide field of view, and at least head tracking would be essential. The degree of immersion is increased by adding additional and consistent modalities, greater degree of body tracking, richer body representations, decreased lag between body movements and resulting changes in sensory data, and so on.

Astheimer et al. (1994) define 'immersion' as the feeling of a VR user, that their virtual environment is real. Analogous to Turing's definition of artificial intelligence: if the user cannot tell which reality is 'real', and which one is 'virtual', then the computer-generated one is immersive. A high degree of immersion is equivalent to a realistic virtual environment. Several conditions must be met to achieve this: the most important seems to be small feedback lag; second is a wide field of view. Displays should also be stereoscopic, which is usually the case with head-mounted displays. A low display resolution seems to be less significant.

We perceive the world through a continual stream of visual, auditory, tactile, kinesthetic and olfactory sensory data. The rendering of this external sensory data is not enough to create immersion. The human body must itself be tracked, so the changes in the displays are driven by movements of the human body.

Consider the example of turning one's head around. The perceiver experiences a change in the ambient optic array corresponding to the turn. Objects on one side become occluded by the head and go out of view, and others come into view. There is a translation of the whole, and a rearrangement of object occlusion relationships. Objects (and parts of the body too) now occlude different parts of other surfaces, and become occluded in a different way themselves. And the perceiver can voluntarily cause significant changes in the scene. For example, a movement of an arm will cause a change in the occlusion structure.

We may say that immersion requires the overall body to be tracked with movements resulting in changes transmitted to the display systems. For a greater degree of immersion, head tracking is essential.

According to Slater, an immersive virtual environment may lead to a sense of *presence* for a participant taking part in the experience. Presence is the psychological sense of 'being there' in the environment based on the technologically founded immersive base. However, any given immersive system may not always lead to presence for all people. Presence is so fundamental to our everyday existence that it is difficult to define. It does make sense to consider the negation of a sense of presence as the loss of locality, such that 'no presence' is equated with no locality—a permanent flux in the sense of where self is.

There is a link between immersion and presence, but this is not a simple function. In fact, different individuals have different requirements for sensory data in order to construct their models of the world. The following criteria seem to be crucial:

- Presence is the sense of 'being there' in the environment specified by the displays.
- The participant is likely to momentarily 'forget' about the external physical world, and treat the virtual world as real.
- The participant would exhibit behaviours that are the same as those they would carry out in similar circumstances in everyday reality.

Flight simulators provide a very high degree of presence for their users, but they only provide presence in one relatively fixed environment—the airplane cockpit. VR systems should be capable of providing presence in an arbitrarily large number of environments, limited only by the imaginations of the environment designers.

For the human participant to be immersed within the virtual environment, they should be a part of the environment. Immersion is achieved through an individualistic view of the world. That is, the environment is rendered from the participant's point of view in the virtual world, and they have mechanisms to interact with the environment using their embodiment. Slater defines immersion like this: 'An ideal *immersive* virtual environment is one where totality of inputs to the participant's senses is continually supplied by the computer-generated displays'.

Immersion will probably lead to the degree of presence of the participant. Presence refers to 'the participant's sense of "being there" in the world created by the virtual environment system. Immersion describes a kind of technology, and presence describes an associated state of consciousness' (Slater and Usoh 1994). Besides immersive technology, some other factors that contribute to presence are interaction with the environment, correlation between the performance of everyday activities in the physical world, and how they are replicated in the virtual world (e.g. walking for navigation).

Personal presence has two indications: *subjective presence* and *behavioural presence*. Subjective presence refers to what the participant thinks about being present in the virtual world; behavioural presence describes the measured behavioural parameters through observations of the participant. Slater et al. (1996) discuss how subjective presence and behavioural presence are logically orthogonal, but related in practice.

Slater et al. (1996) introduced the notion of *shared presence* in NVEs, and proposed two elements to consider. First, the sense of presence of other individuals in the same VE, and the sense of being part of a group 'which is more than just the sum of individuals'. They again separate the subjective and objective aspects of each of these elements. The subjective aspects consider how each individual feels, and the objective aspects relate to the observable behaviour of the overall group and the individual group members.

Personal presence is a prerequisite for shared presence (Slater et al. 1996). And the following statements hold:

- The virtual body is more important in shared presence than in personal presence. The body is used as a medium to obtain spatial, acoustic and ideally tactile information for sensing the presence of others in the same VE.
- Sense of interaction and exchange of information is necessary with others, rather than static existence of others.
- Representation of others is important in order for shared presence, and different people might respond differently to different embodiments: some find just crude

representations of virtual bodies sufficient, while others might require high-quality bodies.
* Immersive technology of the NVE affects shared presence.

Figure 1-5 illustrates the concepts of personal presence and shared presence.

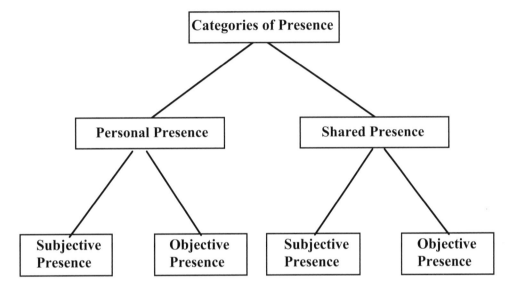

Figure 1-5. Categories of presence

1.7 Fidelities of NVEs

Stytz (1996) defines a number of fidelities required from NVEs:

1. *Visual realism fidelity*: the environment should look realistic, as much as possible.
2. *Sensory fidelity*: visual, aural and haptic/kinesthetic information presented to the participant should replicate the real world as much as possible.
3. *Physics fidelity*: the NVE should incorporate the effects of gravity, electromagnetic spectrum emissions, motion (including friction), energy consumption and conservation.
4. *Modelling fidelity*: objects should have correct scaling and move in realistic speeds, and this should be replicated at remote participants' hosts accurately.
5. *Actor behaviour fidelity*: the behaviour of computer-generated actors (autonomous actors) should mimic the behaviour of human-controlled actors faced with the same circumstances.
6. *Time fidelity*: there should be minimum amount of time between one entity's action and the other's notification of it (latency and lag).

7. *Information fidelity*: the amount and timeliness of information should be sufficient to develop situation awareness and support decision making of actors:

   • Complexity fidelity: this is the type, amount, and arrival rate of information
   • Nuance fidelity: this concerns the presentation of any detail unnecessary for decision making but essential for a realistically complex presentation (throwaway detail).

8. *Input device fidelity*: this includes two fidelities:

   • Fidelity of framework for interaction: the input devices should replicate the real-world framework for interaction. For example, steering wheel, pedals, and gears for virtual car driving simulation.
   • Fidelity of the type of interaction to support the system's purpose.

9. *System fidelity*: concerns the activities and responses of actors in the NVEs, when considered as a whole, through coordinating the system and aggregates of actors.

Stytz (1996) discusses how the requirement from each type of fidelity depends on the objectives of the NVE, the architecture and the potential applications. Typically, the NVE architecture will sacrifice one type of fidelity to increase another type. In addition to the fidelities listed here, the NVE software (like all types of software) should give favourable results when evaluated by general extent: generality, usability, portability, understandability and efficiency.

1.8   Human Communication

NVE systems are basically communication systems, so communication and collaboration between people are their primary purposes. Actually, the fact that the users share the same virtual environment and can interact with it simultaneously enhances their ability to communicate with each other. However, the means of communication that are taken for granted in real life—speech, facial expressions, gestures—are not necessarily supported in NVE systems due to technical difficulties. Most systems support audio communication, and very often there is a text-based chat capability (Barrus et al. 1996; Greenhalgh and Benford 1995). Some systems (Carlsson and Hagsand 1993; Pratt et al. 1997) include a means of gestural communication by choosing some predefined gestures. The natural human communication is richer than this. Facial expressions, lip movement, body postures and gestures all play an important role in our everyday communication. Ideally, all these means of communication should be incorporated seamlessly in the virtual environment, preferably in a non-intrusive way. Ohya et al. (1995) recognize this need and present a system where facial expressions are tracked using tape markers while body and hands carry magnetic trackers, allowing both face and body to be synthesized. In this book, we propose further improvements in the area of facial communication.

2 A Taxonomy of Networked Virtual Environments

There have been several networked virtual environments (NVEs) described in the literature. However, a framework for understanding NVE components is missing. In this chapter, we provide a reference frame for different NVE components. We summarize the issues to consider while developing complete NVEs, and we compare the most characteristic solutions in the literature for each discussion. In order to discuss the issues to be considered in NVE development and analysis, we can divide our taxonomy into three elements (Table 2-1):

- *Preconditions* are the facts that NVE system designers have minimum control of. These typically include the target application requirements, constraints of the network, computing and interface equipment.
- *Design decisions* include the tools and parameters that NVE system developers can control, such as the protocol for communication and the client architecture.
- *Further issues* include the further tools and techniques that NVE system designers can exploit in order to run the NVE system more efficiently, and to increase the quality of the feedback to the user.

Table 2-1. Elements of NVE taxonomy

Preconditions	• Target applications • Underlying network • Projected number and quality of participants' hosts • Type of input devices
Design Choices	• Host program architecture • Data and task distribution scheme • Network topology • Participant embodiment • Communication protocol
Further Improvements	• Collisions among objects and participants • Access rights for manipulating objects • Finer picking resolution • Force-feedback • Level of detail • Filtering • Dead reckoning • Message compression • Distributed virtual world simulation synchronization

2.1   Preconditions of NVEs

2.1.1   Target Applications

There have been a number of pilot or working applications constructed in the literature. Table 2-2 demonstrates a set of applications developed with the current NVE systems.

Table 2-2. Successful virtual world application domains (Mine 1997)

Domain	Example applications
'Being there' experience for the sake of experience	Phobia therapy (Rothbaum et al. 1995) Aesthetics (Davies and Harrison 1996) Entertainment (Pausch et al. 1996)
Training and practice of different skills	Surgery (Hunter et al. 1993) Military (Macedonia et al. 1994) Maintenance (Wilson et al. 1995) Way finding
Visualization of unrealized or unseeable objects	Architecture (Brooks 1986) Fluid flow (Bryson and Levit 1992) Nanosurfaces (Taylor et al. 1993)
Design	3D models (Butterworth et al. 1992) Cityscapes (Mapes 1995)

Although the theoretical approach of the early systems tried to provide a general-purpose virtual environment for any type of application (Bricken and Coco 1993), it was later realized that these systems lack efficiency, one of the principal requirements for NVE systems. Recent efforts concentrated on characterizing applications for different dimensions. Slater et al. (1995) proposed three such dimensions:

- The number of participants and entities simultaneously involved in the same world.
- The complexity of the objects and their behaviours, ranging from static data to those responding to participant interaction, and on to dynamically changing objects without user intervention.
- The degree of interaction among participants, ranging from low (users can see each other), through medium (users can be involved in complex activities), to high (synchronized activities to achieve a common task).

Each of the applications will need different network requirements and interentity synchronization; this will affect the development of the NVE system. The system design is also affected by the application's required amount of accuracy, visual display quality, and simulation environment. Thus, the NVE system design should consider the target application characteristics.

2.1.2 Underlying Network

Essentially, communication among the entities will pass through the lower layer, the network layer. Therefore, the communication component of the NVE system should take into account the underlying network preconditions.

SIMNET (Pope and Schaffer 1991) used a dedicated network for message communication, hence the broadcast property of the network was used for efficient communication. However, with public networks, the broadcast mechanism overloads the network with sent messages, if ever this operation is permitted. Therefore, especially over wide area networks, other methods should be considered for communication.

The network characteristics underlying the NVE system can have a wide range. Funkhouser (1996) classified the network characteristics of wide area networks into three types:

- *Connection*: this allows two workstations to send data unidirectionally over a connection-oriented link. An example is the modem link using a standard telephone line, with two-way, connection-oriented, unicast data transport with low latency and bandwidth.
- *Unicast*: this allows a message to be sent to each other entity on the network for distributing messages. An Internet connection without the multicast capabilities is an example. This distribution of one update message requires $O(N)$ separate communications.
- *Multicast*: a subset of workstations can communicate with each other using connectionless messages. The underlying network should support the multicast operation. The MBONE (Multicast Backbone implemented over the Internet) is an example. This requires one update message for distributing a message.

For generality, heterogeneous networks can be constructed using a combination of the different network types. For example, modems can be attached to communicate clients to servers in the client–server architecture; and multiple copies of the servers handling different parts of the environment can communicate using multicast. Internetworking can be performed using routing over the network layer. In this way, geographically dispersed sites, using different local network topologies, can communicate together while providing robustness and optimization of routes for minimizing latency (Macedonia et al. 1995).

2.1.3 Projected Number and Properties of Connecting Hosts

The projected number of connecting hosts is an important factor in developing efficient NVE systems. Although the number of connecting hosts is expected to increase with the concurrent developments in network and CPU technology, we can postulate that some applications will require smaller numbers of participating hosts than others. These applications will typically require better display quality and representation than large-scale NVEs (e.g. teleconferencing).

In addition, it is also important to consider the properties of the connecting hosts. The processing power of the workstation should be sufficient to cope with the messages received, and to perform the environment simulation and processing of remote entities without degrading the performance and quality of the simulation.

A number of research groups studied medium- to large-scale virtual environments. Among them, NPSNET was reported to be successfully simulated with 300 entities, theoretically shown to grow to thousands (Macedonia et al. 1995).

2.1.4 Input Devices and Rendering Systems

Many different types of input device are in current use. In their number of tracked degrees of freedom, they range from the ubiquitous mouse to a large number of magnetic trackers attached to the body. Similarly, the display systems can be as simple as a desktop display, or a more complicated set of helmet-mounted displays. The input devices and rendering systems are expected to depend on the type of application, among other factors. The CAVE system has been successfully used for scientific visualization problems. CAVE is a nine-foot cube, where the walls are rear-projected video screens. The user wears a pair of liquid crystal shuttered glasses and a tracking device on the top of their head, and carries a little wand as a navigation tool.

Although the listed preconditions are logically orthogonal to each other, in practice they must be related for developing efficient NVE systems.

2.2 Design Decisions for NVEs

The design decisions of NVEs are the parameters under the control of NVE system developers. Different than the preconditions of NVEs, these are the elements that can be changed during software development, in order to have an efficient simulation of the virtual world.

2.2.1 Host Program Architecture

An NVE is defined as a single environment shared by multiple participants connecting from different hosts. Each host typically stores the whole or a subset of the scene description, and lets the participant use their own avatar to move around the NVE. Additionally, the local program simulates the behaviour of a set of entities in the world, and also handles the real-world sensing using a set of input devices.

The primary task of an NVE system is to immerse the participant. This is achieved through participant-oriented development of the system, something described by the *participant-in-the-loop* concept. Here the participant is the centre of the system, and the goal of the NVE system is to immerse the participant inside the virtual world naturally.

An NVE system is a complicated piece of software that integrates all components, ranging from input devices to animation techniques for objects and embodiments. These components have been researched in the past, and research is continuing to have more favourable results in terms of efficiency and quality. NVEs are emerging from these research areas with a bottom-up tendency. The practice is to adopt a modular design, bringing together earlier monolithic applications within one standard interface by building multiple logical or actual processes to handle separate elements of the VE.

NVE software shares similar design goals as the other types of software:

- *Generality*: the system should be used for general applications.
- *Usability*: the system should be easy to use by both users and programmers.
- *Portability*: the system should work on different platforms.
- *Understandability*: the system should be easy to understand by both participants and programmers.
- *Efficiency*: the three overheads for the system should be low: display, CPU, network processing.

In addition, there are other characteristic goals of NVEs:

- *Rapid development of applications*: one of the main motivations for using VR technology is because it allows simulations to be built rapidly and at a lower cost. Therefore, the virtual environment system should let the users create applications rapidly.
- *Modularity*: the system should be modular so it can incorporate new applications and configurations rapidly and easily, by replacing components with new ones.
- *Decoupling of main VE tasks from the application*: most of the VR applications share similar requirements, such as general NVE tasks display and collision detection. The applications should be able to specify a subset of NVE components for use in the simulation, building on the system to perform other NVE tasks.
- *Immersion and embodiment of the participant*: the environment should provide a natural representation of the participant to perform main tasks such as navigation or object interaction. It should also allow the participants to communicate easily.

Figure 2-1 shows an integrated NVE system and its relationship with the participant. The NVE software provides input to and receives output from the participant, while integrating independent simulation programs and communicating with remote hosts serving other participants. Embodiment is the key element as it bridges between the participant and the virtual world.

There are two main approaches for NVE development systems: *toolkit-based* and *integrated software-based*.

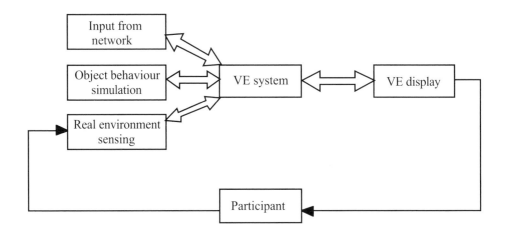

Figure 2-1. An integrated NVE system

2.2.1.1   Toolkit-Based   Architectures

Toolkit-based architectures provide tools and libraries for creation and interaction with virtual environments. Here are some of the functions they provide:

- Controlling the objects in the environment
- Moving the body representation
- Changing viewpoint
- Object relationships
- Display
- Management and synchronization of resources
- Networking multiple participants
- Obtaining statistics

WorldToolkit

WorldToolkit (WTK) is developed by Sense8 Corporation. It provides a complete VE development environment with an object-oriented structure. The WorldToolKit API currently consists of 1000 high-level C functions; it is organized into over 20 classes, including the universe (which manages the simulation and contains all objects), geometrical objects, viewpoints, sensors, paths and lights. Functions exist for device instancing, display set-up, collision detection, loading object geometry from file, dynamic geometry creation, specifying object behaviour, and control of rendering.

WorldToolkit uses the single-loop simulation model, which sequentially reads sensors, updates the world model and generates the images. Therefore, the latencies for every operation are accumulated, affecting the simulation performance of the environment and the virtual body. During the simulation loop, individual objects can have task functions executed.

Geometric objects are the basic elements of a universe. They can be organized in a hierarchical fashion and interact with each other. They may be stationary objects or exhibit dynamic behaviour. WorldToolKit provides a 'level of detail' process which corresponds to a method of creating less complex objects from the detailed object. When objects are too far in the distance for their detail to be seen, WorldToolKit uses a simpler version. This makes it possible to achieve something as close as possible to real-time performance. It results in objects that are indistinguishable at an appropriate distance. Geometric objects can have a behaviour associated with them, such as velocity. Once a behaviour has been associated, it is called continuously throughout the simulation loop.

The majority of virtual environment applications require objects in the universe to be able to interact with other objects. These objects may be under the control of the user or completely autonomous. When they collide with one another, WorldToolKit performs collision tests to work out the intersection points. A collection of mathematical functions are available to manage the dynamic behaviour of objects.

Each universe is a separate entity and can have different rules or dynamic behaviour imposed on its objects. Moving between different universes in WorldToolKit is achieved by portals (Section 2.2.2.8), which are assigned to specific polygons. When the user's viewpoint crosses the designated polygon the adjacent universe is entered. The idea of a portal is rather like walking through a door into another room. With this approach, it is possible to combine several smaller universes together to make one large virtual environment.

MR Toolkit

MR (Minimal Reality) Toolkit was developed by researchers at the University of Alberta (Shaw and Green 1993). The MR Toolkit is in the form of a subroutine library that supports the development of VR applications. In addition, the toolkit supports various tracking devices, distribution of the user interface and data to multiple workstations, real-time performance interaction and analysis tools. The subroutines are called from a C program.

The MR toolkit has three levels of software. The lowest level is a set of device-dependent *packages*. Each package consists of a client–server software pair. The server is a process that continuously samples the input device and performs further processing such as filtering; the client is a set of library routines that interface with the server.

The middle layer consists of functions that convert the 'raw' data from the devices to a format more convenient for the user interface programmer. Routines such as data transfer among workstations and workspace mapping also reside in this layer.

The top layer consists of high-level functions that are used for the average virtual environment interface. For example, a single function to initialize all the devices exists in this layer. The top layer also contains routines to handle synchronization of data and operations among the workstations.

The programs that use MR Toolkit are divided into two sections, the configuration and compute sections. The toolkit configuration section initializes the MR Toolkit and processes the configuration file for the application. Each data structure in the system is shared by at most two programs, the master program and the slave program. There is a one-way transfer of data between programs: one program produces the data and the other consumes it. The configuration file is used to make changes to the device configurations without recompiling programs, such as replacing a mono viewing station to stereo viewing. The compute section is the section that performs the actual processing. The slave program waits for a packet of information coming from the master program, then it produces the next set of results and transmits them to the master program.

The MR Toolkit gives a low-level interface to develop NVE applications, so it has advantages of generality. Furthermore, the configuration file and the mechanism of connecting processes in a master–slave manner, give the advantage of modularity.

The drawback of the MR Toolkit is that it does not address rapid prototyping. The application programmers have to use the C, C++ or FORTRAN language toolkit to develop complex programs. Additionally, the only support for high-level mechanisms for immersing the participant and decoupling the main NVE tasks and application are left in the application program, at the low level.

Other Three-Dimensional Toolkits

Other toolkits, such as IRIS Performer from Silicon Graphics, Java3D and OpenGL Optimizer also support the development of virtual reality applications; however, they are low-level libraries for manipulation of the environment, viewpoints and display parameters. They do not address support for I/O devices, participant representation, motion systems and networking. Therefore, they do not address rapid prototyping of NVE applications. Consequently, we regard these toolkits as instruments to develop NVEs, rather than architectures.

2.2.1.2   Integrated Software-Based Architectures

Integrated software-based architectures, in contrast to toolkit approaches, provide a complete system that implements basic VE tasks. This is similar to thinking of implementing the NVE system as a distributed database access problem, therefore the details of the main NVE tasks and synchronization of data are transparent to the application developer. The new applications are developed either by using the previously developed components, or by replacing them with new programs. The shared database typically contains these elements:

- *Position* of the entities in the virtual environment
- *Behaviour* of the entities
- *Constraints* related to object representations and their relationships
- *Visual* elements such as polygons comprising the models
- *Audio* elements attributed to objects and participants
- *Tactile* information
- *Force* parameters of the objects
- *Collision* detection and avoidance data among elements

VEOS

VEOS (Virtual Environment Operating Shell), developed by the University of Washington, was one of the first complete NVE architectures to provide an integrated software to develop general applications. VEOS uses a tightly integrated computing model for management of data, processes, and communication in the operating system level, hiding details from the applications as much as possible.

The basic building block for the VEOS programming model is called an *entity*. An entity is a coupled collection of data, functionality and resources. It can function asynchronously and independently of others. Every item in VEOS (environment, participant, hardware devices, programs) is an instance of an entity. Entities differ from the objects in an object-oriented model: while the objects are static data and responsive functions, entities additionally contain interface resources and computational resources which can be accessible. Each entity contains a unique name, a private partition, processes defining its behaviours, interaction with other entities expressed as perceptions accompanied by external reactions and internal models. The entity connections are dynamic during run-time (links and parent–child relationships are reconstructed during simulation). This allows flexibility in managing entities for different behaviours.

The main elements of VEOS are as follows:

- *KERNEL* provides low-level database, process and communication management; it also handles OS details. Kernel consists of three components:
    - *Shell* handles initialization of processes on different resources, connections among nodes, and management of the external LISP interface with the external application.
    - *Talk* provides a standard way of communication among components.
    - *Nancy* allows a uniform data structure to be shared by VEOS Kernel and external applications. As internal data structure, Nancy uses an extension of the LINDA language.
- *FERN* provides functionalities for distributed entity management. For example, distribution of virtual memory and handling of multiprocessor shared memory are two of this module's responsibilities. In addition, FERN facilitates lightweight processes, called threads. Threads are defined as cooperating tasks specified by a sequential program, and share single address space for clearer data-sharing semantics and better context-switching performance.
- *SENSORLIB* provides a library of device drivers for commonly used VR devices.

Two languages are the central data-sharing mechanism between components. Application programmers using VEOS communicate with the system through LISP programs with generality, but with low speed. LINDA language is used to provide more general and template-based object representations, and is used for storing the data.

The VEOS system is general, modular and it decouples the various tasks in the NVE. However, there is little information relating the system's support for rapid development of applications, understandability and immersion of participants. The most important drawback of the system is its lack of support for efficiency, in order to support a general solution. Furthermore, it requires a good knowledge of the LISP and LINDA languages.

dVS

dVS, developed by Division Ltd in the UK (Grimsdale, 1991), is one of the commercial VE development tools commonly used today. The system aims to provide a modular line for creating and interacting with virtual prototypes of CAD products. The architecture is based on dividing the environment into a number of autonomous *entities* and processing them in parallel. It is designed to suit a range of different parallel architectures. It supports loosely coupled networks, symmetric multiprocessors and single-processor systems. An entity represents high-level 3D objects, which encapsulate all the elements of the object. Here are some of them:

- Rendering
- Sound spatialization
- Collision detection
- Dynamics
- 3D position tracking (body management)
- Input device handling

Each element in the virtual environment is processed in parallel, e.g. the system processes visual elements of the environment in parallel with audio elements. Therefore, the processing is divided according to the elements of the VE.

The run-time system (Figure 2-2) is structured as a collection of cooperating server processes, attached to one central process, simulation engine. The server processes' responsibility is to provide the synchronization of their multiple copies in different hosts. The synchronization is achieved by communicating the events generated by the user, among the simulation engines at each host.

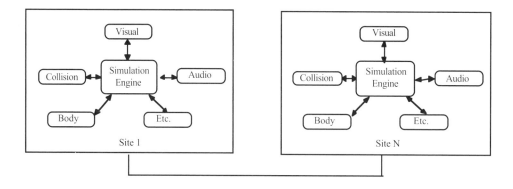

Figure 2-2. dVS run-time components

The designer of the application configures and makes use of the existing servers, but there is the possibility of providing extra functionalities by adding new servers (Figure 2-3).

The advantage of dVS is that the user, a CAD model designer, can easily operate the system by using supplied functionalities. However, the system has a few disadvantages: although it provides an integrated solution to CAD model development, the support for general applications is limited. The system is usable (a few configuration files need to be modified to use it), portable (it works on SGI workstations and PCs), understandable and efficient (the elements are optimized for the underlying computer system; for example, the visual element uses IRIS Performer on SGI workstations). And here are some other drawbacks: the current version of the system is not designed for multi-user applications with a dynamic number of participants and integration of different applications. The environment designer creates an application by writing a program that includes all the simulations and object behaviours in the application, and then they connect it on their host to the other clients. The remote participants then connect to this server to animate their local copies of the virtual world database. Therefore, it is not possible for two application developers to connect their animation programs within the same world. Additionally, there is no mechanism for the participants to distribute their bodies to the remote participants: the body files have to be uploaded to the remote hosts by using ftp protocol explicitly before connecting to the virtual world. Finally, the body configuration file may be too limiting for animating the body with general-purpose gestures.

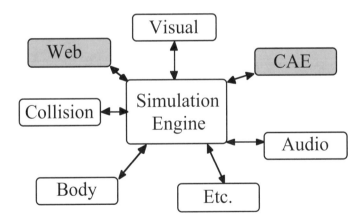

Figure 2-3. Adding new functionalities in dVS through simulation engine

NPSNET

NPSNET-IV, developed at the Computer Science Department of the Naval Postgraduate School (NPS), is an experimental test bed for developing NVEs.

NPSNET can be used to simulate an air, ground, nautical (surface or submersible) or virtual vehicle, as well as human subjects. A virtual vehicle, or stealth vehicle, is a vehicle that can navigate in the virtual world but has no graphical representation and is therefore not seen by others. The standard user interface devices for navigation include a flight control system (throttle and stick), a SpaceBall with six degrees of freedom, and/or a keyboard. The system models movement on the surface of the earth (land or sea), below the surface of the sea and in the atmosphere. Other entities in the simulation are controlled by users on other workstations, who can be human participants, rule-based autonomous entities, or entities with scripted behaviour.

The virtual environment is populated not only by users' vehicles or bodies, but also by other static and dynamic objects that can produce movements and audiovisual effects.

NPSNET uses the *Distributed Interactive Simulation* (DIS 2.03) protocol (IEEE 1993) for application-level communication among independently developed simulators (e.g. legacy aircraft simulators, constructive models, and real field-instrumented vehicles). The DIS protocol attempts to provide a basis for communication between different hardware and software platforms involved in a simulation. DIS is a group of standards being developed by the US Department of Defense and industry that addresses communications architecture, format and content of data, entity information and interaction, simulation management, performance measures, radio communication, emissions, field instrumentation, security, database formats, fidelity, exercise control and feedback. A second purpose is to provide specifications to be used by US government agencies and engineers that build simulation. The main application target has been battlefield simulation.

The system has also been used for investigating how to integrate these techniques:

- *IP Multicast* to support large-scale distributed simulation over internetworks.
- *Heterogeneous parallelism* for different tasks of NVE simulation at the client level.

The participants configure the type of participation and input device before connecting to the NVE from a set of predefined node types: air, ground, nautical or virtual vehicle.

NPSNET conveys simulation state and event information in 27 protocol data units (PDUs), defined by the IEEE 1278 DIS standard. Only four of the PDUs are used for actual entity interaction, the remaining PDUs for transmitting information for actions and simulation control.

NPSNET uses dead reckoning for decreasing communication. Dead reckoning is a predictive extrapolation technique, where the next positions of entities are computed based on their last received position, velocity and acceleration. It is described in Chapter 6.

The underlying NPSNET-IV software architecture is based on a multithreaded approach (Figure 2-4). The system takes advantage of the multiprocessor architecture and heterogeneous parallelism offered by the SGI Onyx computers with Reality Engine graphics, and the SGI Performer graphics library. On a four-processor computer, NPSNET-IV maps the draw, cull, application and network threads into the Performer processes, using IRIX shared arenas for communication among threads.

NPSNET succeeds in providing an efficient large-scale networked virtual environment using general-purpose networks and computers, with the standard communication protocol DIS. Using a multithreaded approach facilitates efficient computation over multiprocess architectures. In addition, the user can select a set of input techniques for interaction and they can select a role in the VE. However, NPSNET lacks the properties of generality and modularity (as the target application, battlefield simulation, is a special case), portability (works on SGI computers and predefined input devices), and rapid development of new applications. Additionally, the DIS traffic handling at the application level creates complexity, demanding more computational power (Macedonia et al. 1994).

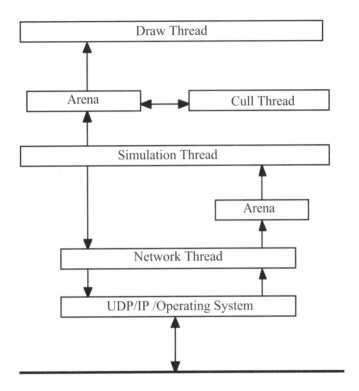

Figure 2-4. NPSNET software architecture (Macedonia et al. 1994)

DIVE

Dive (Distributed Interactive Virtual Environment) (Carlsson and Hagsand 1993; Hagsand 1996; Frécon and Stenius 1998) has been developed at the Swedish Institute of Computer Science. The Dive system is a toolkit for building distributed VR applications in a heterogeneous network environment. The networking is based on peer-to-peer multicast communication (reliable multicast is used, except for the continuous data streams, i.e. video and audio, that use non-reliable multicast).

The Dive run-time environment consists of a set of communicating processes, running on nodes distributed within a local area network (LAN) or wide area network (WAN). The processes, representing either human users or autonomous applications, have access to a number of databases, which they update concurrently. Each database contains a number of abstract descriptions of graphical objects that together constitute a virtual world. Associated with each world is a process group, consisting of all processes that are members of that world. Multicast protocols are used for communication within such a process group.

Each member of a process group has a copy of the world database or parts of it; when a process joins a certain group, it copies the world data from another member of that group. The information in this replicated database is kept by using reliable multicast protocols. When the last group member exits a world, the state is lost unless a persistence manager is used. A process may enter and leave groups dynamically. In VR terms this means that an object (e.g. user representation) can freely travel between different worlds.

It is possible to distinguish between several different types of processes in the Dive environment. We will now briefly present the most important ones.

A *user process* is a process that interfaces directly to a human user, and is therefore often responsible for managing the interaction between the user and the virtual environment.

The *visualizer* is a specific example of a user process that is responsible for a large part of what a Dive user encounters in the interface; it manages the display devices, different input devices, navigational aids, etc.

Application processes typically build their user interfaces by creating the necessary graphical objects, after which they listen to events in the world and react to them according to some control logic.

Users in Dive are represented as actor entities. An actor is a user or an automated process, representing a process-bound entity that performs actions within a world.

Dynamic behaviour and interaction of objects, user interface support and audio are implemented using the DIVE/TCL interface: an event in the system triggers a DIVE/TCL script, resulting in actions.

Figure 2-5 shows an example of DIVE/TCL script.

```
proc move_up {id type actor srcid}          {
        for {set i 0}{$i < 100}{incr I}{
                dive_sleep 100
                dive_move $id 0 0.5 0 LOCAL_C
        }
}
dive_register select move_up
```

Figure 2-5. A TCL script for moving objects in DIVE

The move_up procedure is registered by *dive_register*, which is invoked when a Dive *select* event occurs at the object containing the script. With this approach, powerful event- and timer-driven behaviours can be specified by having access to the complete Dive functional interface. Therefore, new behaviours have to be programmed using Dive/Tcl scripts, necessitating the application programmers' knowledge of the Dive/Tcl language based on Tcl (Tool Command Language) (Ousterhout 1994)

In addition to object and participant management, a set of visualization programs exist for different display devices ranging from normal monitor displays to head-mounted displays. This allows participants to be connected to the NVE simulation, and enables easy configuration for different display devices.

MASSIVE

MASSIVE (Model, Architecture and System for Spatial Interaction in Virtual Environments) (Benford et al. 1995; Greenhalgh and Benford 1995) was developed at the University of Nottingham. The main goals of MASSIVE are scalability and heterogeneity, i.e. supporting interaction between users whose equipment has different capabilities and who therefore employ radically different styles of user interface, e.g. users on text terminals interacting with users wearing head-mounted displays and magnetic trackers.

MASSIVE supports multiple virtual worlds connected via portals (Section 2.2.2.8). Each world may be inhabited by many concurrent users who can interact over ad hoc combinations of graphics, audio and text interfaces. The graphics interface renders objects visible in a 3D space and allows users to navigate this space with six degrees of freedom. The audio interface allows users to hear objects and supports both real-time conversation and playback of preprogrammed sounds. The text interface provides a plan view of the world via a window (or map) that looks down onto a 2D plane across which users move (similar to multi-user dungeons). Text terminal users may interact by typing messages to one another or by invoking emotions (e.g. smile, grimace).

These interfaces may be arbitrarily combined according to the capabilities of a user's terminal equipment. Thus, at one extreme, the user of a sophisticated graphics workstation may simultaneously run graphics, audio and text clients. At the other, the user of a dumb terminal (e.g. a VT-100) may run the text client alone. It is also possible to combine the text and audio clients without the graphics, and so on. This allows users of radically different equipment to interact, albeit in a limited way, within a common virtual environment. The spatial model of interaction allows the mapping of real-world interactions to the interactions between participants.

SPLINE

SPLINE (Scalable Platform for Interactive Environments), developed by Mitsubishi Electric Research Labs, is a software platform that allows the creation of virtual worlds featuring multiple, simultaneous, geographically separated users; multiple computer simulations interacting with the users; spoken interaction between the users; immersion in a 3D visual and audio environment; and comprehensive run-time modifiability and extendibility. The system's main application theme is *social virtual reality*, where people interact using their embodiments.

An important feature of SPLINE is the support for both pre-recorded and real-time audio. Volume attenuation is used to indicate distance of sound sources, and differential attenuation of left and right channels to indicate direction (it is planned to incorporate better audio rendering algorithms to create a more detailed auditory environment).

SPLINE introduces a new synchronization algorithm for synchronizing sound with other events in the environment. Sound synchronization demands millisecond precision for composing sound samples. On the other hand, virtual environments may persists for days and months. Unfortunately, time stamps with millisecond resolution and such long time span would require a lot of bits, making them impractical to use. SPLINE introduces modular time stamps with 1 ms precision and 1 week modulus using a quotient-normalized modular time stamps algorithm (Waters et al. 1997) to avoid the complexity of the usual modular arithmetic.

The SPLINE data-sharing mechanism is managed by a *world model* that mediates all the interaction, so instead of communicating directly with each other, applications rely on the world model to send updates to remote world models in other participants' hosts (Figure 2-6). This mechanism allows applications to be integrated without considering the underlying networking details. The applications communicate with the world model through an application programming interface (API), and the world model passes this data to the interprocessor communication module below it (Figure 2-6). The task of the IPC module is to maintain approximate consistency between the world-model copies, through sending and receiving messages with the remote IPC processes. The network interface specifies the format of these messages.

The main application can be connected to SPLINE together with a visual renderer, and audio renderer, lifting the constraint to implement every task in the application process. Figure 2-6 demonstrates the configuration of SPLINE processes and their relationship with the application process. The application programming interface is through a special language, called Scheme; however, the designers of the system plan to use Java for specifying behaviours (Waters et al. 1997).

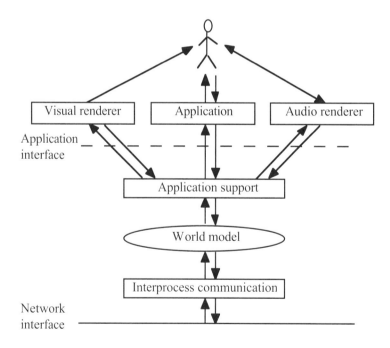

Figure 2-6. Elements of the SPLINE system (Waters et al. 1997)

The MERL group, developers of SPLINE, have created an application called Diamond Park. The park consists of a square mile of detailed terrain with visual, audio and physical interaction. The participants navigate around the scene through bicycling, using an exercise bike as physical input device; and their embodiment moves on a virtual bicycle with speed calculated from the force exerted on the physical bicycle. SPLINE uses a simple articulated body representation composed of rigid body parts (Section 2.2.4.6). Audio communication is supported, but there is no support for facial or gestural communication. Figure 2-7 shows a Diamond Park session.

Figure 2-7. A Diamond Park session (Reproduced by permission of MERL, Mitsubishi Electric Research Lab)

The advantages of the SPLINE system are as follows: the system proved to be effective on a pilot application, efficiency is achieved by trading off complex data consistency computations among participants' hosts. The Diamond Park application could be developed using the system in a short time and integrated without major problems. Additionally, using an exercise bicycle interface and mapping it to virtual bicycles increased the relationship between proprioceptive and sensory data.

And here are the drawbacks: the embodiment of the participants has simple behaviours, i.e. cycling behaviours; there are no non-verbal communication considerations or interactions with the environment; the participants only navigate and communicate with each other using audio.

BrickNet

The BrickNet toolkit provides functionalities geared towards enabling faster and easier creation of networked virtual worlds. It eliminates the need for the developer to learn about low-level graphics, device handling and network programming by providing higher-level support for graphical, behavioural and network modelling of virtual worlds. BrickNet provides the developer with a 'virtual world shell' which is customized by populating it with objects of interest, by modifying its behavioural properties and by specifying the objects' network behaviour. This enables the developer to quickly create networked virtual worlds.

BrickNet introduces an object-sharing strategy which sets it apart from the classic NVE mindset. Instead of all users sharing the same virtual world, in BrickNet each user controls their own virtual world with a set of objects of their choice. They can then expose these objects to the others and share them, or choose to keep them private. The user can request to share other users' objects, providing they are exposed. So, rather than a single shared environment, BrickNet is a set of 'overlapping' user-owned environments that share certain segments as negotiated between the users.

BrickNet does not incorporate any user representation, so the users are bodiless in the virtual environment and their presence is manifested only implicitly through their actions on the objects. The authors of the system do not report on the support for text or audio communication. Facial or gestural communication is not supported.

VISTEL

Ohya et al. (1995) from ATR Research Lab in Japan propose VISTEL, a virtual space teleconferencing system. As its name indicates, the purpose of this system is to extend teleconferencing functionality into a virtual space where the participants can not only talk to each other and see each other, but collaborate in a 3D environment, sharing 3D objects to enhance their collaboration possibilities.

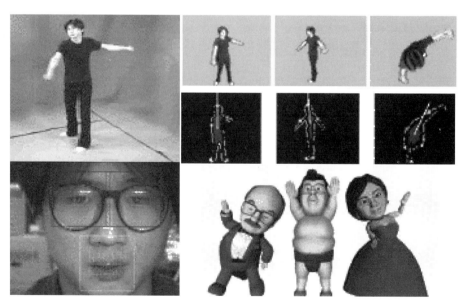

Figure 2-8. Camera tracking to input participant gestures and expressions in VISTEL
(Reproduced by permission of ATR Media Integration and Communications Research Lab)

The current system supports only two users and does not attempt to solve problems of network topology, space structuring or session management, so in a certain sense it is not a complete NVE system. However, it offers some interest for us because most attention is concentrated on reproduction of human motion and facial expressions as means of natural communication in the virtual world.

The human body motion is extracted using a set of magnetic sensors placed on the user's body. Thus the limb movements can be captured and transmitted to the receiving end, where they are visualized using an articulated 3D body representation.

The facial expressions are captured by tracking facial feature points in the video signal obtained from a camera (Figure 2-8). The algorithm of Ohya et al. requires coloured markers to be placed on the user's face (Figure 2-9) to facilitate feature tracking. The movement of facial features is transmitted to the receiving end, where the features of a 3D face model are moved in correspondence.

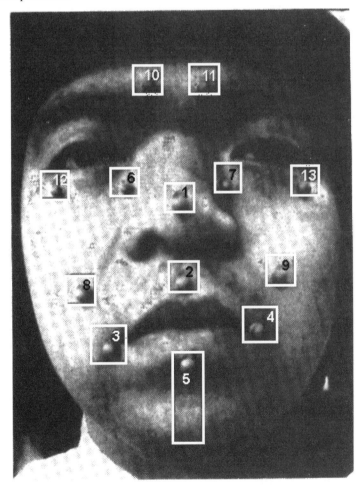

Figure 2-9. Markers taped on user's face for feature tracking (Reproduced by permission of ATR Media Integration and Communications Research Lab)

2.2.2   Data and Task Distribution Scheme

Each virtual object and each participant embodiment within the NVE affects the performance of the different parts of the simulation: network, CPU, graphics. These overheads easily become significant with increasing number of participants and complexity of environments. The main solution to this problem is to let each participant's host computer process only the part of the environment it is interested in. Many researchers propose methods for dividing and sharing the VE data and processing at each host computer. Distribution may depend on the application, client architecture, network topology and other design decisions. Generally, the data distribution is not transparent; the application developer, designer of the applications, and the participants should be aware of the data distribution, so it is neither possible nor necessary to make the distribution fully transparent. In this section and the following sections, we survey the various methods for *sharing* and *distributing* a virtual world over multiple participants, i.e. their host computers.

2.2.2.1   Sharing of the Virtual World

In order to achieve utmost performance, it is inevitable that a subset of data is shared by hosts. That is, the VE's geometry data will be duplicated at each host computer. This means that models can be updated by sending only object updates, such as transformation matrices, which significantly decreases the network overhead. Sharing of the virtual world can be performed in different ways. Perhaps the host computer of each participant stores that part of the virtual world which it can see or interact with. Perhaps the computation task is distributed for executing behaviours; that is, the hosts not only have a local version of the geometry of objects, but also the definition of their behaviours in terms of a script or a program that describes the action, motion and change in the state of the object at each time.

BrickNet: Distributing Behaviour Computation

BrickNet extends the sharing of objects to include dynamic object behaviours (Singh et al. 1995). Representing behaviours is a difficult task and many techniques have been proposed for behavioural simulation. Hence BrickNet provides different types of behaviours. The behaviours are implemented in the Starship interpretive, frame-based language.

- *Simple behaviours* include repetitive, unconstrained changes. They are implemented without the need for synchronization, i.e. once an object is transferred, there is no further communication between the sender and the receiver.
- *Environment-dependent behaviours* take into account the clients' run-time environment: machine configuration, time of execution, etc.
- *Reactive behaviours* implement reaction to events generated by the user or other objects in the virtual environment.
- *Capability-based behaviours* are behaviours that need preconditions for execution. An example is the possession of a key to open a door.

Synchronization is an important issue for sharing behaviours. In BrickNet this is handled by using a *sync* message that is sent by the client to the other clients through a server, and the receiving clients sending a *sync acknowledgement* message back to the server.

BrickNet decreases the network communication in the simulation phase at the cost of increasing the initialization and downloading part of the session. However, there is still a need to reliably synchronize behaviour, and it has not been specified whether this method will decrease the overall network requirements. Another disadvantage is that the behaviours need to be implemented in the special Starship language, limiting generality of the system.

2.2.2.2 Partitioning of the Virtual World

Distribution of the data is necessary to decrease the CPU, network and graphics overheads of the simulation. Additional advantages of distribution are minimized communication between network tail links, and localized reliability problems caused when a host or link goes down (Macedonia et al. 1994). Macedonia et al. (1995) also suggest that there are three possible approaches for partitioning the scene:

- *Spatial partitioning*: This is based on partitioning the scene into areas which can be processed in parallel and independently. Therefore, the participants existing within the same part of the virtual world can interact with each other, i.e. message exchange occurs with only a subset of remote participants.
- *Temporal partitioning*: Some entities might not require the real-time update of all entities every frame, while other entities might require updates every frame. For example, the system management entity needs updates every few minutes in order to have an overall view of the NVE.
- *Functional partitioning*: Entities may belong to a functional class in which an entity may communicate with a subset of entities. For example, a radio communication message can only be sent to the entities having radio receivers. Other types of functional class could be system management or services such as time.

Various research groups have proposed methods for spatial NVE partitioning. In the next section, we will discuss the characteristic solutions to the VE partitioning problem.

2.2.2.3 Space Structuring

In a simple virtual environment consisting of a single room or similar simple space, space structuring is not an issue. However, it becomes an important issue if one tries to model large-scale environments like cities or battlefields inhabited by large numbers of users. It is simply impossible to keep such large structures monolithic; this is due to problems with memory and download time. The multitudes of users that will inhabit these complex environments must be managed efficiently in order to avoid network congestion. Space structuring is closely tied to *area-of-interest management* (AOIM) or *filtering*, which is a strategy to reduce the total network traffic by sending messages to hosts on an as-needed basis. AOIM decides which hosts need to receive which messages, and prunes the unnecessary messages. Therefore we will discuss AOIM alongside space structuring.

Another problem that occurs with large-scale environments is coordinate inaccuracy. As the environment grows larger, the precision with which coordinates can be represented drops because of the inherent imprecision of large floating-point numbers. For example, a 32-bit floating point number with order of magnitude 10^6 has a precision of 0.06. This means that an object positioned in a virtual environment at 1000 km from the origin can be placed with only 6 cm precision (Barrus et al. 1996).

In the next sections, we present four strategies for space structuring:

- Separate servers
- Uniform geometrical structure
- Free geometrical structure
- User-centred dynamic structure

2.2.2.4   Separate Servers

This is the simplest concept of space structuring and resembles the organization of the pages of the World Wide Web. Each world is independent from the rest, but can have links to other worlds just like a Web page has links to other pages (Figure 2-10).

The filtering strategy in this configuration is implicit: the worlds are completely separate and no messages are passed between them.

The advantages of this approach are the relative simplicity of implementation and limitless scalability. Also, the problem of inaccuracy of large coordinate systems is solved by having a separate (and smaller) coordinate system for each world.

However, there are disadvantages. Links between the worlds are only on discrete points—it is impossible to have a continuous boundary. They are unidirectional, so there is no possibility to go back through the same link unless there is a link in the other direction too. Just as with Web pages, complex sets are difficult to maintain. Although it is not a real NVE system, VRML (1997) is an example of this strategy.

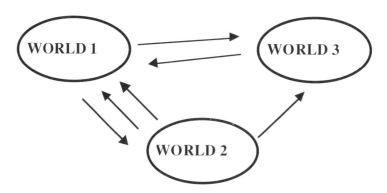

Figure 2-10. Space structuring with separate servers

2.2.2.5 Uniform Geometrical Structure

In this approach the world is partitioned into cells of uniform size and shape (Figure 2-11). An example of this approach is NPSNET (Macedonia et al. 1994) using hexagonal cells. NPSNET exploits an area of interest (AOI) manager that partitions the VE into a set of workable, static, small-scale environments. These small-scale environments are of appropriately sized hexagonal cells, with each cell associated with a multicast group (Macedonia et al. 1995). Then the AOI of an entity is defined as the region surrounding the entity. It listens to the multicast groups associated with each cell within its AOI. Figure 2-12 demonstrates the AOI of a vehicle, consisting of 19 cells.

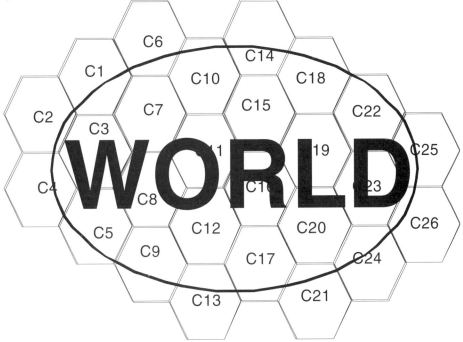

Figure 2-11. Uniform geometrical space structure

The authors' reason for choosing hexagons is because hexagons have a regular shape, uniform orientation and uniform adjacency. As the entity moves from one cell to another, it uniformly adds and deletes the same number of cells, hence multicast groups. In addition, the AOI is defined by a radius, which would be inappropriate in a square partitioning. This gives a decrease in the number of multicast groups.

This approach is most advantageous in large-scale applications with relatively uniform density, such as battlefield simulation; the content of the virtual world is known in advance and created based on a *central mechanism*. Therefore, the mapping of data to each cell and the neighbourhood information of the partitions of the virtual world, both of them are known at the scene creation time. This is also the limiting factor of the API approach for general-purpose applications.

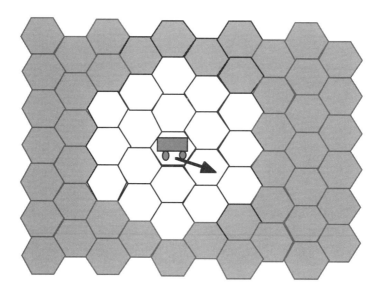

Figure 2-12. Area of interest for vehicle mapped to a subset of multicast groups in NPSNET

2.2.2.6   Free Geometrical Structure

Barrus et al. (1996) introduced the concept of *locales*, and this idea combines good characteristics of the first two approaches. Rather than partitioning the world into uniform cells, the world is composed of subworlds called locales (Figure 2-13). Unlike the first approach with independent worlds, communication between locales is allowed on a neighbourhood basis. Much more flexibility is provided than in the uniform cell approach: the shape and size of each locale are arbitrary, neighbourhood information is user-defined as well as the transformations between neighbouring locales, which are defined by transformation matrices. Each locale has its own coordinate system, solving the problem of inaccuracy in large worlds. For operations that span more than one locale, transformation matrices between locales are used.

2.2.2.7   Cell-to-Cell   Visibility   (RING)

RING supports interaction among large numbers of users in VEs with dense occlusion (e.g. buildings and cities). Again, state changes are sent only to the hosts containing entities that can possibly perceive the change. The influenced region of a state change is computed by object-space visibility algorithms (Funkhouser 1995).

Prior to the multi-user simulation, the shared virtual environment is partitioned into a spatial subdivision of cells whose boundaries are comprised of the static, axis-aligned polygons of the virtual environment. Then the visibility precomputation algorithm processes each cell and finds the set of cells potentially visible to the cell by tracing rays of possible sight-lines through transparent cell boundaries. During the multi-user session, servers keep track of which cells contain which entities, and entity state updates are sent only to those entities in the cell which can potentially see the updated entity (Figure 2-14).

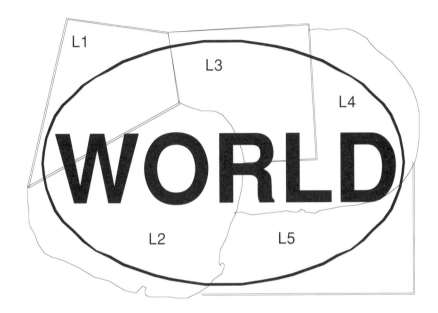

Figure 2-13. Free geometrical space structure

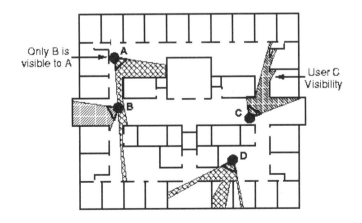

Figure 2-14. Visibility preprocessing within RING

2.2.2.8   User-Centred Dynamic Structure

Fahlen et al. (1993) and Benford et al. (1995) introduce the notions of *aura, focus* and *nimbus* (Figure 2-15). These concepts allow for a fine-grained dynamic management of space structure and users' (or objects') awareness of each other. This approach does not replace the three approaches mentioned so far, but it can be implemented together with any of them.

Using aura, focus and nimbus is somewhat more complex than using the space-structuring approaches introduced up to now, so we will break it down into several subsections.

Space and Objects

The most fundamental concept in this approach is *space* itself. Space is inhabited by *objects* which might represent people, information or other computer artifacts. Any interaction between objects occurs through some *medium*. A medium might represent a typical communication medium (e.g. audio, vision or text) or perhaps some other kind of object-specific interface. Each object might be capable of interfacing through a combination of media and interfaces, and objects may negotiate compatible media whenever they meet in space.

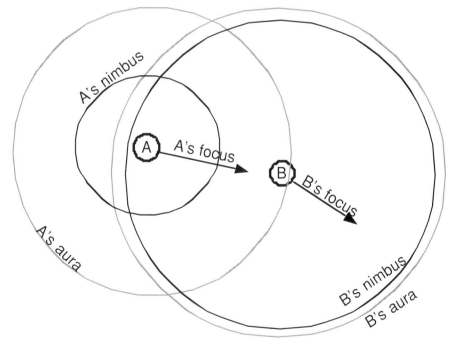

Figure 2-15. User-centred dynamic space structure — aura, focus and nimbus

Aura

The first problem in any large-scale environment is determining which objects are capable of interacting with which others at any given time. Aura is defined to be a subspace which effectively bounds the presence of an object within a given medium and which acts as an enabler of potential interaction (Fahlen et al. 1993). Objects carry their auras with them when they move through space; and when two auras collide, interaction between the objects in the medium becomes a possibility. It is the surrounding environment that monitors for aura collisions between objects. When such collisions occur, the environment takes the necessary steps to put objects in contact with one another (e.g. exchange of object IDs, addresses, references or establishment of associations or connections). Thus, aura acts as a fundamental technological enabler of interaction and is the most elementary way of identifying a subspace associated with an object. An aura can have any shape and size, and it need not be around the object it belongs to. Nor need it be contiguous in space. Also, each object will typically possess different auras for different media (e.g. different sizes and shapes). Thus, as I approach you across a space, you may be able to see me before you can hear me because my visual aura is larger than my audio aura.

Focus, Nimbus and Awareness

Once aura has been used to determine the potential for object interactions, the objects themselves are subsequently responsible for controlling these interactions. This is achieved on the basis of quantifiable levels of awareness between them. The measure of awareness between two objects need not be mutually symmetrical. A's awareness of B need not equal B's awareness of A. As with aura, awareness levels are medium-specific. Awareness between objects in a given medium is manipulated via *focus* and *nimbus,* further subspaces within which an object chooses to direct either its presence or its attention. More specifically, if you are an object in space:

- The more an object is within your focus, the more aware you are of it.
- The more an object is within your nimbus, the more aware it is of you.

The notion of spatial focus as a way of directing attention and hence filtering information is intuitively familiar from our everyday experience (e.g. the concept of visual focus). The notion of nimbus requires a little more explanation. In general terms, a nimbus is a subspace in which an object makes some aspect of itself available to others. This could be its presence, identity, activity or some combination of these. Nimbus allows objects to try to influence others (i.e. to project themselves or their activity to try to be heard or seen).

Objects negotiate levels of awareness by using their foci and nimbi in order to try to make others more aware of them or to make themselves more aware of others. Awareness levels are calculated from a combination of nimbus and focus. More specifically, given that interaction has first been enabled through aura collision:

The level of awareness that object A has of object B in medium M is a function of A's focus in M and B's nimbus in M.

Adapters and Boundaries

Next Benford et al. (1995) consider how aura, focus and nimbus, and hence awareness, are manipulated by objects in order to manage interactions. They envisage four primary means of manipulation:

- Aura, focus and nimbus may most often be *implicitly* manipulated through spatial actions such as movement and orientation. Thus, as I move, my aura, focus and nimbus might automatically follow me.

- They may on occasion be *explicitly* manipulated through a few key parameters. For example, I might deliberately focus in or out (i.e. change focal length) by simply moving a mouse or joystick.

- They may be manipulated through various *adapter* objects which modify them in some way and which might be represented in terms of natural metaphors such as picking up a tool. Adapters support interaction styles beyond basic mingling. In essence, an adapter is an object which, when picked up, amplifies or attenuates aura, focus and nimbus. For example, a user might conceive of picking up a 'microphone'. In terms of spatial model, a microphone adapter would then amplify their audio aura and nimbus. As second example, the user might sit at a virtual table. This adapter object would fold their aura, foci and nimbi for several media into a common space with other people already seated at the table, thus allowing a semi-private discussion with a shared space. In effect, the introduction of adapter objects provides for a more extensible model.

- Finally, aura, focus and nimbus may be manipulated through *boundaries* in space. Boundaries divide space into different areas and regions and provide mechanisms for marking territory, controlling movement and for influencing the interactional properties of space. More specifically, boundaries can be thought of as having four kinds of effects: effects on aura, effects on focus, effects on nimbus and effects on traversal (i.e. movement). Furthermore, these effects can be of four sorts: obstructive, non-obstructive, conditionally obstructive and transforming (Bowers 1992). These effects are also defined on a per medium basis and different boundaries may mix these effects in different ways. For example, a virtual door might conditionally obstruct traversal, aura, focus and nimbus (the condition being the possession of a key) whereas a virtual window might obstruct traversal but not obstruct aura, focus and nimbus. Of course, there may also be types of boundary which do not have any real-world counterpart, e.g. one-way mirrors you can walk through.

For partitioning of the world, MASSIVE-2 exploits the dynamic spatial model of interaction, based on aura, focus and nimbus. Therefore, MASSIVE-2 provides a finer grain of interaction than NPSNET and SPLINE, as the communication is further divided into auras (Greenhalgh 1996).

MASSIVE interfaces are driven by the spatial model described above. Thus, an object cannot be seen until graphics aurae collide and cannot be heard until audio aurae collide. The effects of focus and nimbus are most pronounced in the audio and text interfaces. Audio awareness levels are mapped to the volume with the net effect that audio interaction is sensitive to both the relative distances and orientations of objects involved. Text messages are also displayed according to the mutual level of awareness. In the current implementation, users may explicitly manipulate awareness by choosing between three settings for focus and nimbus: normal (general conversation), narrow (private conversation) and wide (intended for browsing). Two adapter objects are also provided: a podium that extends the aura and nimbus of its user (making them more noticeable) and a conference table that replaces the normal aurae, foci and nimbi with the new set that spans the table (invoking a private conversation around the table).

The MASSIVE-2 solution makes use of the following key techniques:

- Recursively embodying multicast groups, depending on the space-based interactions among objects.
- Flexibly but automatically defining and controlling the scopes of multicast groups, in which subgroups manage their own membership and form hierarchical structures where appropriate.
- Using multicast groups as a basis for abstraction and representation of group activity.

Thus, MASSIVE-2 provides a more dynamical and general association of multicast groups with volumes of space than other systems which use multicast. This approach also admits multilevel structuring of multicast groups.

Loosely Coupled Worlds through Portals

The partitioning of virtual worlds into loosely coupled spaces is a common metaphor in NVEs. For example, multi-user dungeons (MUDs) have exploited this idea to associate *rooms* with various independent environments or discussion groups. These environments are generally independent, loosely coupled VEs with no relationship among them except the links among them, similar to the *WWWinline* links in VRML models. These links were named *portals* in the DIVE and MASSIVE systems.

2.2.3 Network Topology

Figure 2-16 schematically represents a session of an NVE with several participating hosts. If an event occurs at host 1, it is generally necessary for a message about that event to reach all other hosts. How this message is transferred is a question of network topology, i.e. the inside of the cloud in Figure 2-16.

Section 2.1.2 discussed several possible network characteristics: unicast, multicast, broadcast. This section looks at possible network topologies for connecting the clients in the NVE. We consider how the choice of network topology depends on the network characteristics and applications, among other preconditions.

We divide the main network topologies into two categories: *peer-to-peer* and *client–server*. It is also possible to use a combination of these topologies.

Transmitting any event that happens on any host to all other hosts requires a lot of network traffic, growing with $O(N^2)$ where N is the number of users. Fortunately, not all events are essential for all hosts. For example, if two users are very far from each other in the virtual world and cannot see each other, they do not need to know about each other's movements until they are close enough to see each other; therefore their respective hosts do not need to exchange messages. In this section, we only discuss AOIM (Section 2.2.2.3) within the network topologies that we present.

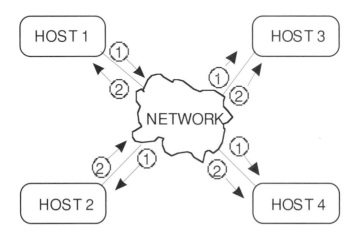

Figure 2-16. Simplified view of networking for collaborative virtual environments

When discussing different network topologies for collaborative virtual environments, another important issue is *session management*. This includes the procedures for a new user to join and leave a session, as well as a strategy for maintaining persistent virtual worlds when no users are present.

2.2.3.1 Peer-to-Peer Topologies

In peer-to-peer design, the system is arranged with a set of workstations that communicate with each other over a network, where every host can send messages directly to any other host. That is, there is no dedicated host responsible for serving other hosts' requests.

A peer-to-peer topology can be implemented using unicast messages, by connecting each node to every other, as shown in Figure 2-17(a). Therefore, when a participant changes the state of an entity (e.g. moves an object), a message is sent to every other participant. Finally, assuming that N hosts exist within the NVE, $O(N^2)$ connections are necessary. VEOS (Bricken and Coco 1993) and MR Toolkit (Shaw and Green 1993) are peer-to-peer systems that use unicast messages. This is obviously the most primitive and least practical strategy. Session management is complicated because a new user needs to connect to all hosts already participating in the session, and it is unclear where the new user can get an up-to-date version of the virtual world. Unless a special service process runs somewhere, the world will not persist when there are no more users in a session. AOIM can be implemented on each host but this also poses problems. The problems arise because the AOIM algorithm itself needs up-to-date information about users' positions; and if this information is filtered out too much, the whole AOIM scheme might collapse.

If a network supporting multicast messages is available, hosts can send their message to a subset of hosts at once (Funkhouser 1996). This decreases the complexity of distributing a single state's update messages from $O(N)$ to $O(1)$. Figure 2-17(b) demonstrates such a topology. NPSNET (Macedonia et al. 1995) and DIVE (Carlsson and Hagsand 1993) are peer-to-peer systems that use multicast. SIMNET (Pope and Schaffer 1991) uses peer-to-peer, broadcast communication. In this configuration, AOIM is done implicitly by joining and leaving multicast groups. This is particularly convenient for geometry-based AOIM strategies, i.e. where groups of users that communicate with each other are determined according to their presence in a certain geometrical space. However, for more complex AOIM strategies this approach might lack flexibility. The session management has the same inconveniences as the peer-to-peer approach. And session management is practical only on networks that allow multicasting, which might require some configuration work.

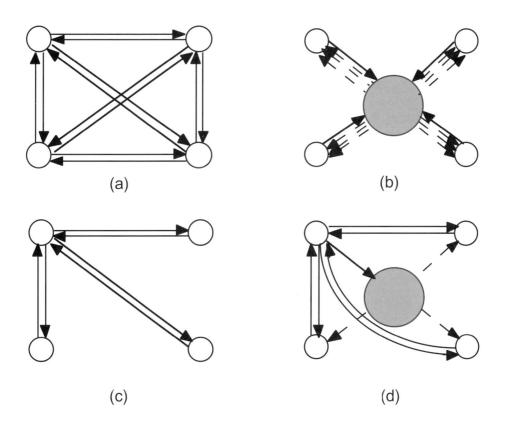

Figure 2-17. Various network topologies: (a) peer-to-peer topology with unicast network, (b) peer-to-peer topology with multicast network, (c) client–server topology with unicast network, (d) client–server topology with multicast and unicast network

2.2.3.2 Client–Server Topologies

In this category, communication between *client* computers is managed by *server* hosts. Clients do not send messages directly to other clients; instead they send them to servers which forward them to other clients and servers participating in the same distributed simulation. Using servers has additional advantages: servers can process messages before propagating them to other clients, culling, augmenting or altering the messages (Funkhouser 1995). For example, a server may determine that a particular update message is relevant only to a small subset of clients and then propagate the message only to those clients. These systems have potential to scale well to many simultaneous users with intelligent server message processing. The processing technique will depend on the nature of interaction among the entities in the virtual world. Any AOIM strategy can be implemented in the server, since it holds all relevant information and controls all network traffic. The inconvenience is that all traffic passes through a single server which will necessarily become congested when the number of users grows.

Message processing could also be done in peer-to-peer systems at each host, but the subsequent mapping of interactions to multicast addresses or a list of receiving hosts is not easy and may be computationally intensive. The client–server protocol easily solves this problem by moving the processing load of messages from each host to a high-end server, leaving the host resources for other NVE tasks.

In this topology, clients generally connect to the servers through a bidirectional unicast link. Similar to the peer-to-peer systems, the distribution of the state updates from the server to clients can be done using unicast or multicast messages.

2.2.3.3 Hybrid Topologies

Peer-to-peer and client–server protocols can be combined in hybrid topologies to pool their advantages. RING uses a topology where clients connect to servers using unicast networks; the servers pass the data to other servers through multicast messaging, as shown in Figure 2-18 (Funkhouser 1995). NetEffect also uses multiple servers connected to each other through a multicast network (Das et al. 1997).

There are two principal approaches for multiple servers:

- *Virtual world subdivision* partitions the virtual world into subspaces and assigns a server to each subspace. When a client passes from one subspace to another, it disconnects from its server and connects to the server responsible for the new subspace. Thus, the server handles a variable number of clients during the simulation, as any client can go from one subspace to another. See Waters et al. (1997) for the solution in SPLINE.
- *Participant subdivision* duplicates the virtual world at each server and assigns the participants to servers. When the participant connects to the virtual world at the beginning of the session, it selects the physically nearest or the most idle server, and this server handles all the message communication. This approach is advantageous when the servers are connected to each other through a fast multicast network. Compared to virtual world subdivision, the server handles a more static set of clients.

Normally the set of participants each server handles should be constant while they are in the virtual world, but maybe more advanced techniques can involve migrating participants from one server to another for load balancing. See Das et al. (1997) for the solution in NetEffect.

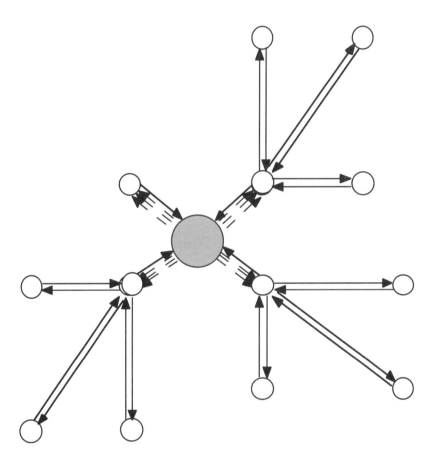

Figure 2-18. Hybrid topologies with multiple servers communicating through multicast network

Hybrid topologies provide the following additional advantages: the systems can support a simple unicast communication model at client sites, eliminating the need to build multicast connections in participants' computers. Secondly, implementation of networking is simplified in the client side, leaving the computer resources for other NVE computations.

The multiple-server approach retains the advantages of the simple client–server approach, but by sharing the network traffic burden between the multiple servers as shown in Figure 2-18 allows more users to connect to the same world. However, it might introduce extra latency due to the longer path of the messages. Also, session management and AOIM become more complex.

BrickNet applies this multiple-server network topology. A BrickNet server acts as an object request broker and communication server for its clients. Servers, distributed over the network, communicate with one another to provide a service to the client without its explicit knowledge of multiple servers or interserver communication. The clients are unaware of the locale of the servers serving the client requests. Clients run asynchronously without having to wait for the data to arrive from the server.

2.2.4   Avatar Representation

As we discussed in the previous chapter, the participant is an important element in the integrated NVE system, so the embodiment should be represented realistically and efficiently. The embodiment has functions for self-representation and for representation to other participants in the same world. Here are some functions for self-representation:

- The visual embodiment of the user
- The means of interaction with the world
- The means of feeling various attributes of the world using the senses

The functions for representing oneself to others, and for visualizing the others, are:

- Perception (to see if anyone is around)
- Localization (to see where the other person is)
- Identification (to recognize the person)
- Representation and visualization of others' interest focus (to see where the person's attention is directed)
- Representation and visualization of others' actions (to see what the other person is doing and what they mean through gestures)
- Social representation of self through decoration of the avatar (to know the task or status of other participants).

The following subsections describe some examples of virtual human embodiments in NVEs.

2.2.4.1   Embodiments in MASSIVE

The user representation in MASSIVE is very simple, involving block-like characters shown in Figure 2-19. Each user may specify their own graphics embodiment via a configuration file. In addition, some default embodiments are provided that are intended to convey the capabilities of the user.

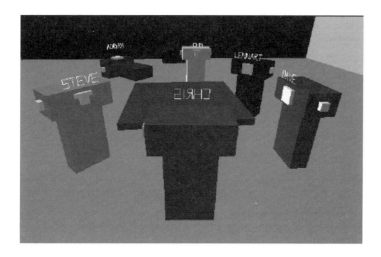

Figure 2-19. User representation in MASSIVE (Benford et al. 1995)

Given MASSIVE's heterogeneity, a major goal of the embodiments is to convey users' capabilities. Thus, considering the graphics interface, an audio-capable user has ears, a desktop graphics user (monoscopic) has a single eye, an immersed stereoscopic user has two eyes, and a text user has a letter T embossed on their head. In the text interface, users are embodied by a single character (usually the first character of their name) that shows position and may help identify the user in a limited way. An additional line (single character) points in the direction the user is currently facing. Thus, using only two characters, MASSIVE attempts to convey presence, location, orientation and identity. Finally, the MASSIVE bodies convey availability by using a sleep gesture if the participant is not at the computer for the moment. Although it has good support for text and audio communication, MASSIVE does not support facial or gestural communication. Figure 2-19 shows a typical view of a graphics user, with several other users in sight.

2.2.4.2 Embodiments in DIVE

For the user representation, DIVE offers several techniques. First, simple 'blockies' are composed from a few basic graphics objects (e.g. cubes). Blockies convey presence and location, and the use of a line extending from the body to the point of manipulation in space represents the action point. In terms of identity, simple static cartoon-like facial features suggest that a blockie represents a human, and the ability of users to tailor their own body images supports some differentiation between individuals (the specification of each individual is stored in a data file and the creation and subsequent management of these embodiments is the responsibility of the DIVE visualizer).

Figure 2-20. A DIVE session (Reproduced by permission of the Swedish Institute of Computer Science)

A more advanced DIVE body for immersive use texture-maps a static photograph onto the face of the body, thus providing greater support for identity. The body itself is a simple articulated structure composed of rigid pieces for limbs and other body parts. Figure 2-20 shows one participant's view of a DIVE conference. The body animations can be defined by a TCL/Tk interface, but the default body has quite simple animation mechanisms.

DIVE has very basic support for gestural communication by choosing predefined gestures to be reproduced on DIVE's body representation. Facial communication is partly supported through the possibility of streaming video into the scene on a 'virtual video monitor'. However, the video is not in any way attached to the user, it is just presented on the virtual monitor. Text and audio communication is supported.

2.2.4.3 Embodiments in dVS

The default body in dVS is a telepointer; however, it is possible to use a body with a hierarchy of surfaces for arms and the body. This embodiment allows viewpoints and actionpoints through head and hand tracking, but gestural communication is limited to the tracked hand. The body representation in dVS 3.0 allows a hierarchy of surfaces connected to each other to form the visual body, and a set of inverse kinematics connections to achieve connectivity. Figure 2-21 shows an example.

Figure 2-21. A dVS environment and actor

2.2.4.4 Figure Embodiments in VISTEL

The VISTEL system contains realistic embodiment of participants. The applications are oriented towards teleconferencing, and they automatically capture and reproduce facial expressions and gestures. The system has the goal of realistically representing bodies of participants (Figure 2-22).

Each user wears a single dataglove, and the system captures only the right hand and the head; however, the designers of the system worked on full-body capture using a camera.

2.2.4.5 Embodiments in NPSNET

The NPSNET system has investigated integrating the virtual human figures in the DIS-compliant environment. The main application goal is a battlefield simulation, hence the designers considered levels of detail for representation, body-tracking technology and a set of postures; hierarchical networks have been proposed for embodiments (Pratt et al. 1997).

The NPSNET provides four levels of detail (LOD) for embodiments:

* High LOD: 478 polygons, 50 degrees of freedom
* Medium LOD: 50 polygons, 19 degrees of freedom
* Medium-far LOD: 30 polygons, 12 degrees of freedom
* Far LOD: 3 polygons, 0 degrees of freedom

Figure 2-22. A VISTEL session (Reproduced by permission of ATR Media Integration and Communications Research Lab)

The appropriate level of detail is selected depending on whether the embodiment is within the view volume or in a viewing range, as well as the maximum distance of interest.

The animation type is selected depending on the level of detail selected. The upper body is animated by using a tracker attached to each hand, and another on the head. The Jack model, by Norman Badler's group at the University of Pennsylvania, has been used for this purpose (Badler et al. 1993), although the new version of NPSNET is based on a model by BDI Systems. The lower body animation is based on a set of predefined postures: upright, kneeling, prone, crawling. The posture state of the body is sent through standard DIS protocol data units, and procedurally computed at receiving hosts, and the upper body joints are sent using the unused fields in the standard DIS PDUs. Figure 2-23 shows an example.

Figure 2-23. A participant in an NPSNET environment (Courtesy of Michael J. Zyda)

Additionally, the NPSNET system can represent groups of humans by animating the group leader and letting the others follow. In this way, the group state is managed as a single PDU instead of multiple. Further improvements are achieved through sharing the embodiments of different virtual humans, for tasks like military troops walking.

NPSNET succeeded to insert virtual humans into large-scale NVEs; however, the multi-layer networking solution is limiting, although it does comply with the DIS standard. Additionally, the general issues are missing, e.g. identification and social representation.

2.2.4.6 Embodiments in SPLINE

SPLINE, and the representing application Diamond Park, use virtual humans riding bicycles in the NVE. This is to incorporate whole-body interaction with the virtual world. The supported actions are those that can be done while riding a bicycle. The bicycle-riding animation is performed using simulated cyclists designed at Georgia Tech (Hodgins et al. 1995). The system also supports procedurally animated pedestrians that can walk, jog and run. These motions give an appropriate interface for navigating in the NVE, and using different bodies they provide identification; however, the use of a virtual body for interpersonal communication is not studied in the system. Figure 2-24 shows an example.

2.2.5 Protocol

Developers of NVE systems should consider all the factors described up to now, in order to define the architecture of the system, the topology for communication, avatar representation, and the classification of entities in the VE. Once the NVE system designer makes these decisions, the system should implement a protocol to be able to communicate efficiently. This mainly depends on how the participants and virtual objects are represented, as well as the preconditions and design decisions of the NVE system. The protocol will ideally contain session management, state and event information, and interaction among objects.

Until now there has been a lack of efficient standard protocols for managing NVE systems. The Distributed Interactive Simulation (DIS) system provides a special-purpose protocol for military applications. On the other hand, a general-purpose reliable multicast protocol is used to synchronize distributed versions of the NVE world data. We describe these solutions in the following subsections. There is also a new standardization effort within the ISO SC29 MPEG-4 body to standardize bitstream syntax and semantics for computer graphics applications, and we are active in the specification of face and body animation within MPEG-4; see Chapter 7.

Figure 2-24. User representation in SPLINE (Reproduced by permission of MERL, Mitsubishi Electric Research Lab)

2.2.5.1 The DIS Standard

NPSNET conveys simulation state and event information in 27 protocol data units (PDUs), defined by the IEEE 1278 DIS standard. Only four of the PDUs are used for actual entity interaction, the remaining PDUs for transmitting information for actions, simulation control, etc. The entity state PDU is a list of fields as in Table 2-3.

As seen in Table 2-3, DIS heavily depends on the application that has motivated its creation: battlefield simulation. Therefore, it fails to include efficient human representation and fails to replicate human-to-human interactions and conversations efficiently in the natural form. Nor does it support flexible sharing, creating and modifying of new objects and user interactions, for highly interactive applications.

Table 2-3. DIS entity state PDU fields

Field size (bytes)	Entity state PDU field	Description
12	PDU header	Protocol version PDU type Padding Time stamp Length in bytes
6	Entity ID	Site Application Entity
1	Force ID	
1	Number of articulation parameters	N
8	Entity type	Entity kind Domain Country Category Subcategory Specific Extra
8	Alternative entity type	Same as above
12	Linear velocity	X,Y,Z (32-bit components)
24	Location	X,Y,Z (64-bit components)
12	Orientation	H,P,R (32-bit components)
4	Appearance	
40	Dead-reckoning parameters	Algorithm Other parameters Entity linear acceleration Entity angular velocity
12	Entity markings	
4	Capabilities	32 Boolean fields
$N \times 16$	Articulation parameters	Change ID Parameter type Parameter value

2.2.5.2 Scalable Reliable Multicast Protocol

Another approach is to guarantee having approximate copies of the same environment, through a general-purpose reliable multicast protocol. This approach views the problem as a database synchronization, and it guarantees eventual delivery of certain kinds of messages, therefore the systems using this protocol can eliminate keep-alive messages, and build upon robust transfer of data and deletion of objects. Additionally, the messages can contain differential data, instead of full definition of object states, which is the case for DIS.

Hagsand (1996) discusses the use of reliable multicast in NVEs. He discusses how the reliable multicast is implemented in the transport layer of the network, and does not necessarily use network-layer multicast capability. There are two solutions for reliable multicast: based on positive acknowledgement and based on negative acknowledgement. The positive acknowledgement solution easily overflows the network by positive acknowledgement messages sent from receivers to senders. The negative acknowledgement would decrease this number of messages, but it is an ongoing research problem.

2.2.6 Further Improvements of NVE Fidelities

Chapter 1 discussed different fidelities that improve the qualities of different elements in the NVE system. These fidelities can be further improved by introducing the following additional features in the virtual environment:

- *Default parameters for different worlds*: The NVE system can provide default behaviours of objects in order to minimize the world design complexity. For example, the gravity property can be part of the world classification, and the application designer of the virtual world does not need to specify gravity behaviour for each entity.
- *Collisions*: Collisions significantly improve the quality of the virtual world simulation.
- *Access rights*: Virtual environments with large numbers of participants create the problem of accessing different objects and parts of the virtual world. This can be moderated by introducing access rights that participants need to be given to enter parts of the world, similar to access rights for files in operating systems.
- *Picking resolution*: By default, most of the current NVEs provide a coarse resolution to compute intersection tests for picking. This can be improved by introducing fine object manipulation techniques (Boulic et al. 1996).
- *Force feedback*: Haptics is an important factor that increases the natural interaction within the virtual environment.

Furthermore, the NVE system developers can exploit various techniques to decrease the communication and computation overhead for tasks connected with participant-to-participant communication; and there are other techniques to increase the quality and response rate of the simulation. Here are some of them. We will analyse these techniques for virtual human representation in the next chapters.

- *Level of detail*: for representing the geometrical data in different resolutions, and selecting the appropriate amount during the session.
- *Motion level of detail*: for sending the state update messages to remote hosts in different rates, depending on their distance.
- *Filtering messages*: so that only interested hosts receive the state changes of an entity.
- *Dead reckoning*: a technique to decrease the network requirements, based on extrapolation of future states of entities.
- *Compression of messages*: sending messages with a loss of information, for using less bandwidth.
- *Techniques for synchronization*: so that each host machine has similar states of the same virtual world.

2.3   Summary of Existing NVE Systems

Table 2-4 presents an overview of the analysed systems concentrating on issues concerning user representation and human communication. The table shows that most of the systems use a body representation consisting of rigid segments, and some use more primitive representations. It is even more evident that gestural, and in particular facial communication are poorly supported in most current NVE systems.

Table 2-4. Comparison of current NVE systems

	User representation	Audio comm.	Text comm.	Gestural comm.	Facial comm.	Network topology	Space structure	Origin
NPSNET	Articulated rigid-segment body	Yes	Yes	Predefined gestures/ behaviours	No	Multicast	Uniform	Naval Postgraduate School, Monterey CA, USA
DIVE	Articulated rigid-segment body	Yes	Yes	Predefined gestures	No	Multicast	Dynamic	Swedish Institute of Computer Science, Stockholm, Sweden
BrickNet	None	N/A	N/A	No	No	Multiple servers	Separate servers	National University of Singapore
MASSIVE	Simple block-like structure	Yes	Yes	No	No	Multicast	Dynamic	University of Nottingham, UK
SPLINE	Articulated rigid-segment body	Yes	N/A	No	No	Multicast	Free	Mitsubishi Electric Research Labs, Cambridge MA, USA
VLNET	Fully virtual humans (avatars and autonomous)	Yes	Yes	Yes	Yes	Client–server (multiple servers developed)	Portals	MIRALab, U. of Geneva, and EPFL Computer Graphics Lab, Switzerland
VISTEL	Articulated rigid-segment body	Yes	No	User wears magnetic trackers	User wears markers on the face	Peer to peer	None	ATR Research Labs, Kyoto, Japan

N/A = data not available

3 The VLNET System

This chapter covers the goals and design decisions of the VLNET (Virtual Life Network) system developed at Computer Graphics Lab, EPFL and MIRALab, University of Geneva. Several publications describe in detail various aspects of the system (Capin et al. 1998, 1997a, 1997b, 1995; Pandzic et al. 1997a, 1997b, 1996a; Thalmann et al. 1997, 1995; Noser et al. 1996). In VLNET we tried to integrate artificial life techniques with virtual reality techniques in order to create truly virtual environments shared by real people, and with autonomous living virtual humans with their own behaviour, who can perceive the environment and interact with participants. The VLNET system supports a networked shared virtual environment that allows multiple users to interact with each other and their surrounding in real time. The participants are represented by 3D virtual human actors, who serve as means to interact with the environment and other participants. The virtual humans have appearance and behaviours similar to the real humans, a prerequisite for giving users a sense of presence in the environment. In addition to user-guided virtual humans, the environment is also extended to include fully autonomous virtual humans. Virtual humans can also be controlled at the task level, in order to represent the currently unavailable partners, allowing asynchronous cooperation between distant partners. The modularity of the system allows for fairly easy extensions and integration with new techniques, making it an interesting test bed for various domains from 'classic' VR to psychological experiments.

The environment incorporates different media (Figure 3-1): sound, 3D models, gestural and facial interaction among the users, images represented by textures mapped on 3D objects, textual interaction and real-time movies.

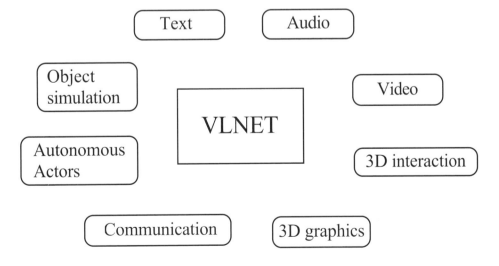

Figure 3-1. VLNET incorporates different media in a single 3D environment

Instead of having different windows or applications for each medium, the environment integrates all tasks in a single 3D surrounding, therefore it provides a natural interface similar to the actual world. Interaction within the environment is an important aspect of NVEs. We classify objects in the environment into two groups: fixed (e.g. walls) or free (e.g. a chair). Only the free objects can be picked, moved and edited. This allows faster computations in database traversal for picking. Once a user picks an object, he or she can edit the object. Each type of object has a user-customized program corresponding to the type of object, and this program is spawned if the user picks and requests to edit the object. Figure 3-2 shows examples.

Figure 3-2. Overview of the VLNET system

This chapter includes the presentation and analysis of the VLNET system through the perspective presented in the previous chapter: we discuss the general design decisions, preconditions, parameters and further architecture efficiency considerations. However, this chapter only looks at the architecture of the system, i.e. how different components are integrated. In the next chapters, we discuss the representation and control of the virtual humans and their integration with the system from an application viewpoint.

3.1 Overview and Preconditions

VLNET has six main goals:

- Rapid development of applications with NVEs that involve virtual human embodiments and autonomous virtual humans.
- Integration of previously developed applications for simulation and virtual human animation within one open architecture.
- Supporting multiple media types.
- Considering participant embodiments as the main element of the virtual world.
- Investigation of different approaches for virtual human communication as a test bed for future applications.
- Considering efficiency as the main goal, without compromising generality.

We postulate that content creation will be an important factor to determine the success in virtual reality application development. The content creators are users; they exploit the appropriate tools, developed earlier, to create virtual worlds akin to the popular systems today (WWW, IRC, etc.).

We see the NVE as a large number of separated virtual meeting places created by users of the system, contrary to a single large-scale world consisting of organized subspaces, such as in NPSNET (Macedonia et al. 1995) and SPLINE (Waters et al. 1997).

3.1.1   Precondition 1: Target Applications

Our target applications are multiple-participant, same-time same-place activities for collaboration and leisure activities. We postulate that the creators of the virtual world content will be application developers, and they will want to integrate their programs in an easy way. Additionally, world designers without sufficient programming background will select their drivers from a set of preprogrammed drivers. We expect that the applications will emerge or change during the simulation, therefore rapid development and integration of new applications is an important factor. We aim to plug in existing simulation and human animation programs to the virtual environment easily. Typically, there will be multiple virtual environments, each created by a separate user; and each virtual environment will integrate multiple simulation programs at the same or different sites controlling different objects.

3.1.2 Precondition 2: Underlying Network

We provide a solution that can work independently of the underlying network, with a slight performance penalty. We do not optimize the efficiency of the solution to specific technologies. For example, ATM requires 48 bytes for data at each transmission unit, called a cell. The NVE system protocol can be optimized for ATM to conform to the message length of an integer multiple of 48 bytes. We have adopted the solution to send fixed-length messages independent of the network, with the penalty of sending multiple cells for each packet. In addition, we use a general unreliable connection method, and we do not assume the existence of a multicast network.

For portability, we use communication based on sockets utilizing UDP/IP protocol. UDP/IP provides a fast, low-overhead method for transferring data. Contrary to the TCP/IP protocol, UDP provides connectionless datagram services, where data delivery is not guaranteed. In TCP/IP protocol, the receiver sends back the sender an acknowledgment of the received messages transparently to the application developer, therefore the latency and bandwidth penalty provided by UDP is significantly lower than for TCP/IP. We compare the TCP/IP and UDP/IP sockets in Table 3-1.

Table 3-1 illustrates how, compared with TCP/IP, the UDP/IP protocol provides faster mechanisms to transfer packets, with the extra cost of implementing a more complicated protocol and losing packets. Therefore, we have chosen to implement the protocol that works on connectionless datagram services, where delivery is not guaranteed.

Table 3-1. Comparison of TCP/IP and UDP/IP sockets

Property	TCP/IP socket	UDP/IP socket
Delivery of data	Guaranteed, in order	Not guaranteed. Packets may be lost, duplicated or arrive out of order
Bandwidth requirements for a single packet	Lower than UDP	Higher, as each packet should contain the destination and source addresses
Bandwidth requirements for the protocol	Higher as protocol requires receiver to send ack messages	Lower, because the protocol does not require any further transmission
Latency	High, because the protocol handles transmission errors	Lower, because the protocol does little error control
Application	The applications let the protocol take care of the error control, data packet ordering, guaranteed data delivery. Therefore, the applications can send incremental data that depends on the previously sent messages	The applications need either to take care of the error control in the application level, or build on messages that do not depend on previously sent data

3.1.3 Precondition 3: Projected Number of Connecting Hosts

We postulate that, usually in activities involving humans, there is generally a limit on the number of persons with which we can communicate in full duplex and continuously. Most of the informal and formal meetings in real life are limited by interaction with at most tens of participants. Having more people in the same space indirectly implies there is one performer that makes a presentation; the other participants are passive viewers and they can be granted the right to speak by turn-taking. The number of people exceeding this number either decreases the effect of participants' actions, or allows the world to be visualized as independent subspaces. Kollock and Smith (1996) discuss the following ideas for collaborative real-life and net-based online communities.

One of the most common and accepted tenets in the literature on cooperation is that 'the larger the group, the less it will further its common interests' (Olson 1965). Researchers have identified a number of reasons why cooperation may be more difficult as group size increases. First, as the group becomes larger, the costs of an individual's decision to free-ride[1] are spread over a greater number of people (Dawes 1980). If an individual's action does not appreciably affect others, the temptation to free-ride increases. More generally, the larger the group, the more difficult it may be to affect others' outcomes by one's own actions. Thus, an individual may be discouraged from cooperating if their actions do not affect others in a noticeable way. Second, it is often the case that as group size increases, anonymity becomes increasingly possible and an individual can free-ride without others noticing their actions. Third, the costs of organizing are likely to increase (Olson 1965), i.e. it becomes more difficult to communicate with others and coordinate the activities of members in order to provide collective goods and discourage free-riding.

The previous paragraph discusses general group sizes formed for collaborative purposes. Furthermore, in NVEs, additional complexity arises due to the display, computational and networking complexity with a large number of detailed embodiments. Therefore, for our target applications, the solution to have independent rooms where there is no limit on participant embodiments provides more effective solutions than the solution with a large number of simple embodiments.

However, we do not ignore the significance of systems with a large number of participants. Our view of the system is similar to the IRC (Internet Relay Chat) approach, where a web of channels create boundaries separating interparticipant communications. According to Ostrom (1990), one of the most important features of successful communities is that they have clearly defined boundaries. Separating the virtual world into rooms clearly defines boundaries between groups. Ideally, however, participants should be given utilities to be aware of channels outside the times when they are active.

---

[1]Kollock defines free-riding as not being cooperative within the community, and behaving selfishly.

3.1.4 Input Devices and Rendering Systems

We wanted to support as many input devices as possible, including extendibility for future devices. The integration of input devices can be done by a well-defined, efficient and simple interface based on the tasks in NVEs. We define a set of tasks that the user can perform: navigation, manipulation of objects, viewing the virtual world, non-verbal communication. Navigation is defined as moving around the environment using appropriate mechanisms. Object manipulation is achieved by picking an object first and then moving it or editing it. Typically, the action point is attached to the right hand centre; however, a driver can be implemented that can move it to another body part, e.g. the left hand centre. Currently, we limit the number of action points to one, as we do not handle two-handed manipulation within the kernel level (although the application developers can implement a two-handed manipulation driver, outside the VLNET kernel). The viewpoint is typically attached to the embodiment's eye position, but can also be independent from the body or moving with the body. A multiplicity of viewpoints can be defined for stereo viewing. Figure 3-3 shows the coordinate systems.

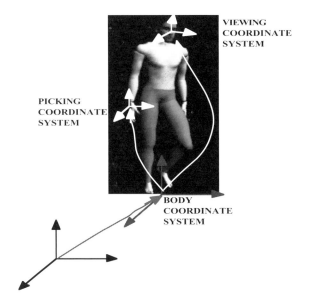

Figure 3-3. The main coordinate systems and their relationships

Various input devices can be used for each task. The driver for the input device has to be programmed using the main convention used in all VLNET drivers. Once this is performed, the same driver can be used for different objects and virtual worlds, allowing the reuse of previously developed tools for new applications. We have implemented drivers for the commonly used devices such as 2D mouse, SpaceBall from SpaceBall Technologies, Flock of Birds from Ascension Technology.

For defining the display devices, we provide a configuration file that lists the properties of the output device. The configuration file contains the number of channels, the viewing frustum parameters, and viewport parameters for each channel. By replacing the configuration file, the user of the system can integrate new display devices.

As we have stated earlier, we have not considered haptic devices. Furthermore, for auditory channel, we realize audio communication by a public domain audioconferencing program, VAT.

The next section explains our choice for the client architecture then Section 3.3 discusses the other design decisions:

1. Partitioning the virtual worlds based on rooms connected by portals (Section 3.3.1)
2. Data distribution scheme: sharing of data (Section 3.3.2)
3. Network topology: client–server (Section 3.3.3)
4. Participant embodiments as realistic virtual humans (Section 3.3.4 and Chapter 4)
5. VLNET session management and communication protocol (Section 3.3.5)

3.2 Client Architecture: Multiprocess Integration

As we have discussed above, the virtual environment simulation systems are typically complex software systems, so a modular design is indicated. It is appropriate to design the run-time system as a collection of cooperating processes, each of which is responsible for its particular task. This also allows easier portability and better performance of the overall system through the decoupling of different tasks and their execution over a network of workstations or different processors on a multiprocessor machine. In VLNET we use this multiprocess approach.

We distinguish between two types of processes: internal VLNET processes and external application processes. The first type constitutes the VLNET core and is precompiled. External applications are programs developed for special applications, input/output devices, etc., which are implemented by the application developer using the VLNET system. This type of separation offloads the normal NVE tasks such as communication and rendering from the application developer, then hides the implementation details for these tasks so that applications are developed in the higher level. We can draw an analogy between these processes and operating systems. The VLNET core is similar to a UNIX kernel and the associated protocols such as the Network File System (NFS) protocol: VLNET core consists of a set of programs, each performing a different service. The application programs are similar to the application layer of the operating system, where the programmers have to conform to the defined API for each service. In VLNET we call the kernel processes *core VLNET processes*, and we call the application programs *drivers.* The communication between VLNET core processes and drivers takes place through *external interfaces* which are shared memory segments visible to both sides. There exists a set of libraries to be linked by application programs which attach to the shared memory, as well as read/write structured data from this memory.

Figure 3-4 summarizes the role of VLNET as a layer between application programs and lower-level network and VE task layers, and it shows the position of external interfaces. We discuss each component of the system, and in Chapter 4 we concentrate on embodiment aspects of the system and the application programs to control this embodiment.

3.2.1   Overview of Heterogeneous Parallelism in VLNET

Among the different modules of VLNET, we do not use a synchronous approach; instead we use asynchronous parallelism: different functional parts of the NVE client proceed independently, and communication between the parts block neither the sender nor the receiver component. Using asynchronous parallelism has the following advantages:

- The system processes and displays the most recent updates that are received; this property decreases the *latency*. The updates can originate from the other users through the network, external applications simulating parts of the system, or programs reading user input.
- The NVE software can execute components on multiprocessor computers in parallel, speeding up the computations required for one frame.
- The architecture offloads the display and networking details from the application as much as possible, simplifying application development, hence increasing rapid prototyping of applications.
- As the communication process carries out the network tasks independently from CPU-intensive tasks, it can receive more data with UDP communication. This decreases the packet loss rate.
- The solution avoids the overhead of synchronization and processor idle time for processes waiting for synchronization.

The communication among different processes is based on shared memory. Shared memory is a segment of memory that can be accessed and updated asynchronously by more than one process. Shared memory has the following advantages:

- It is easy to use.
- When the number of entities using shared memory is not excessive (e.g. less than 10), it provides an efficient mechanism for interprocess communication.
- It allows both asynchronous and non-blocking communication mechanisms. In asynchronous communication, when a process sends a message to another, the sending process continues with the next operation even if the receiver is not ready to receive the message. In non-blocking communication, an entity can check for incoming messages without waiting indefinitely for a message to arrive. This allows other operations to be implemented in the receiver process while the network is idle.

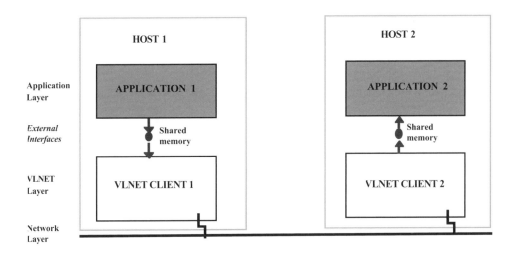

Figure 3-4. VLNET system is a layer between the applications and the lower-level network and rendering layers

We use the System V shared memory functions (SVR4 shared memory library) in VLNET. Each shared memory segment is associated with an external integer identification number, and more than one process can use this identifier to attach to the shared memory segment.

Drivers typically run on the same machine where their associated VLNET clients run; but they can also exist on machines other than their clients. The remote drivers require a mechanism to share data between processes running on different machines. However, System V shared memory utilities require that two processes exist on the same host. Therefore, we have implemented a pair of lightweight *daemons* which are responsible for passing the data back and forth from the application to the drivers. The sender daemon process continuously reads local application updates from the shared memory, and sends these updates in the form of well-defined packets to the receiver daemon process through a UDP socket. The receiver daemon process continuously receives packets from the sender daemon process, and places the updates in the interface on the client host. Figure 3-5 shows the principles.

In our scheme, we consider that the external application has been developed independently, and we assume that the code consists of a loop that inputs data from VLNET, its internal simulations or physical world; computes the simulation; and outputs updates to the VLNET shared world in terms of new object properties, participant actions, etc. This is visualized by the VLNET system as *busy–waiting* instead of using other synchronous interprocess communication techniques such as semaphores. This choice depends on the assumption that the applications, whether they are participant-sensing programs or simulation programs, normally run independently from the VLNET core; therefore introducing semaphores or other *synchronous* communication mechanisms to signal the drivers, places constraints on how the applications are developed. We do not want these constraints on application programs. We now discuss each component of the system in more detail.

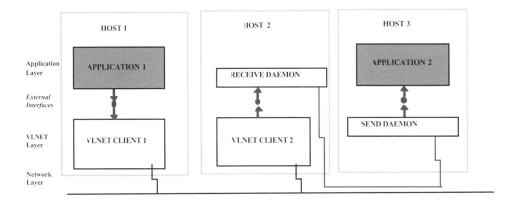

Figure 3-5. Remote drivers connect through two daemon processes. Here VLNET client 1 is on host 1 with a local driver, and VLNET client 2 is on host 2 with a driver on host 3.

3.2.2   VLNET Client Architecture

The modular design consists of splitting the functionalities into a number of processes. We separate the two types of processes: the *core* VLNET processes and external *driver* processes. The VLNET core is a set of processes, interconnected through shared memory, that perform basic VLNET functions. The main process performs higher-level tasks, like object manipulation, navigation, body representation, while the other processes provide services for networking (communication process), database loading and maintenance (dbase process) and rendering (cull process and draw process). The driver processes are typically application programs that need to be inserted within the VLNET virtual environment. Note that many applications can exist within the same world, connected to various clients, as well as connected to the same client. Furthermore, driver processes can run on the same host as the client they are attached to, or they can run on a remote host. The core processes are an integral part of the VLNET system; they are not programmed by application developers. The application developer sees the core processes as daemons running in addition to the application, which is responsible for main VE tasks. VLNET has an open architecture, with a set of interfaces allowing a user with some programming knowledge to access the system core and extend the system by plugging custom-made modules into the VLNET interfaces. In the next subsections we explain in some detail the VLNET core with its various processes, as well as the interfaces and the possibilities for system extension they offer. Figure 3-6 shows the architecture of a VLNET client.

Communication between drivers and core processes is through VLNET external interfaces. This is implemented using a lightweight library that contains functions for manipulating various properties of the objects. This open architecture allows an application developer to easily integrate their application, with transparent access to the VE tasks.

The main process consists of seven logical entities, called *engines*, covering different aspects of VLNET. It also initializes the session and spawns all other internal and external processes. Each engine is equipped with an interface for the connection of external processes. An engine is a part of client code that is responsible for processing different requests of drivers. There exists an engine for each media in the virtual environment.

The *object behaviour engine* takes care of the predefined object behaviours, like rotation or falling, and has an interface enabling the external processes to control object behaviours.

The *navigation and object manipulation engine* takes care of the basic user input: navigation, picking and displacement of objects. Three coordinate systems are defined: BODY matrix defines the global positioning of the body in the virtual environment. PICK matrix is used for defining a pointer where the participant can interact with objects. VIEW matrix defines the viewpoint of the participant, typically located on the eyes of the virtual body. If no navigation driver is activated, standard mouse navigation exists internally. Navigation drivers also exist for the SpaceBall and FOB/Cyberglove combination, although new drivers can easily be programmed for any device.

The *body representation engine* is responsible for reading animation information for the articulated body. In any given body posture (defined by a set of joint angles) this engine will provide a deformed body ready to be rendered. The body representation is based on the HUMANOID body model (Boulic et al. 1995), adapted for real-time operation (Thalmann et al. 1996). This engine provides the interface for changing the body posture in terms of animation parameters. A standard body posture driver is provided; it also connects to the navigation interface to get the navigation information, then uses the walking motor and the arm motor (Boulic et al. 1990; Capin et al. 1997a) to generate the natural body movement based on the navigation.

The *facial representation engine* provides the synthetic faces with the possibility of changing expressions or their facial texture. The facial expression interface is used for this purpose. A set of parameters exists within the interface for defining the facial expression. These parameters are listed in Table 5.1. The facial representation is a polygon mesh model with free-form deformations simulating muscle actions (Kalra et al. 1992). Each animation parameter is interpreted as a free-form deformation of a particular region of the facial polygon mesh. This level of representation for expressions and animation is very general because the set of parameters is based on a study of muscle actions, hence the parameters are sufficient to express any facial expression. At the same time, with 63 parameters the representation is compact, which is important for communication in a networked environment.

For changing or animating the facial texture, the video engine is used to receive and decompress the texture images, and the facial representation engine maps the texture on the face.

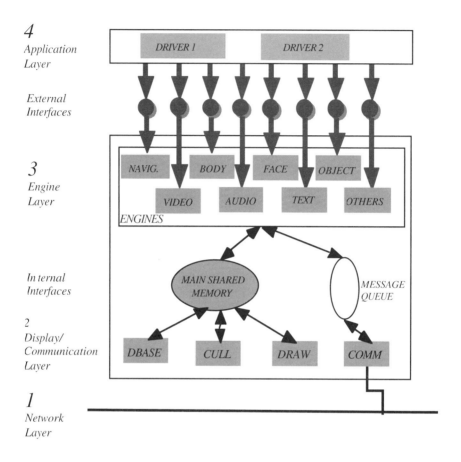

Figure 3-6. Architecture of the VLNET client

The *video engine* manages the streaming of dynamic textures to the objects in the environment and their correct mapping. Its interface provides the possibility of streaming video textures on any objects in the environment. The engine compresses the outgoing video images and decompresses the incoming images, then maps the images on the objects in the environment. In the special case of mapping the texture on a face, the images are passed to the facial representation engine as already explained. The SGI compression library is used for compression and decompression.

The *information engine* provides output of the VLNET to the drivers, i.e. drivers can obtain dynamic information about the scene through this interface. Therefore, this interface provides a unique interface for all drivers. The relevant information includes number of participants, number of objects and their location in the 3D world.

The *text engine* provides the textual communication between clients, from external drivers. It may be used to provide a chat facility between participants and to provide textual information about objects.

All the engines in VLNET are connected to the main shared memory and to the incoming and outgoing message queues. The engines process updates within the interfaces, and pass them to the main shared memory and outgoing message queue. They also receive updates from remote clients through incoming messages and other core processes; and they process these updates and modify the associated external interfaces.

The main, cull, draw and dbase processes make use of the IRIS Performer library (Rohlf and Helman 1994). IRIS Performer employs a coarse-grained, pipelined, multiprocessing scheme, where a relatively small number of processes concurrently work on different stages of the rendering pipeline. Thus, processes concurrently handle different frames. The partitioning of work into multiple processes is based on *processing stages*. A processing stage is a discrete section of a processing pipeline and it encompasses a specific type of work. The processing stages in Performer correspond to various traversals of the scene graph within one frame: application (APP), intersect (ISECT), cull (CULL) and draw (DRAW). The APP process consists of the application code as well as the database, viewpoint, and system modifications using the toolkit routines. The ISECT traversal processes intersection requests for collision detection and following terrain. The CULL traversal rejects the objects outside the viewing frustum, computes level-of-detail switches, and sorts geometry by rendering mode. The DRAW process sends geometry and graphics commands to the graphics subsystem.

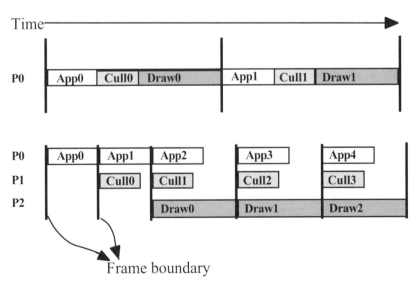

Figure 3-7. Multiprocess partitioning and timing diagram for APP, CULL and DRAW processes

Figure 3-7 illustrates timing diagrams for the application, cull and draw processes of the VLNET core, using one processor and using three processors. Boxes represent the execution time of a stage, and each row of boxes corresponds to a single process. Therefore, multiple rows of timing boxes demonstrate the parallel execution of pipeline stages. Note that the overall time between frame boundaries, hence the time required for a frame, decreases with three processors. The IRIS Performer library also allows the frame rate to be locked to a user-specified rate, e.g. 20 Hz. However, we selected a *run to completion* frame control mechanism instead of fixing a frame rate, in order to process all the remote entities in the VE.

The main VLNET process corresponds to the APP stage of the pipeline, and this process comprises engines for communicating with drivers. Therefore, we use extra multiprocessing in addition to Performer stages for the communication module and drivers; this is the mechanism that we use for implementing other processes in the VLNET core. Therefore, the processor utilization of various programs is similar to Figure 3-8. Note that drivers can run on the same processor as any of the VLNET core processes. Scheduling of drivers to run on a particular processor is normally performed at the operating system level, depending on each processor's load; this optimizes processor utilization to achieve higher frame rates. Running two programs on the same processor independently is called *pseudoparallelism.*

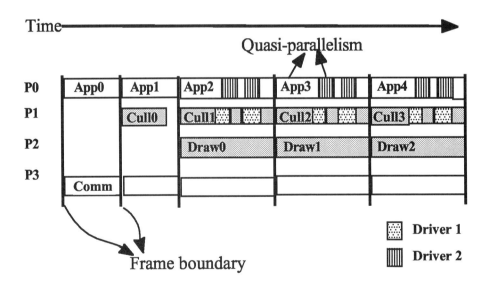

Figure 3-8. Multiprocess partitioning and timing diagram for APP, CULL and DRAW processes, together with communication and driver processes

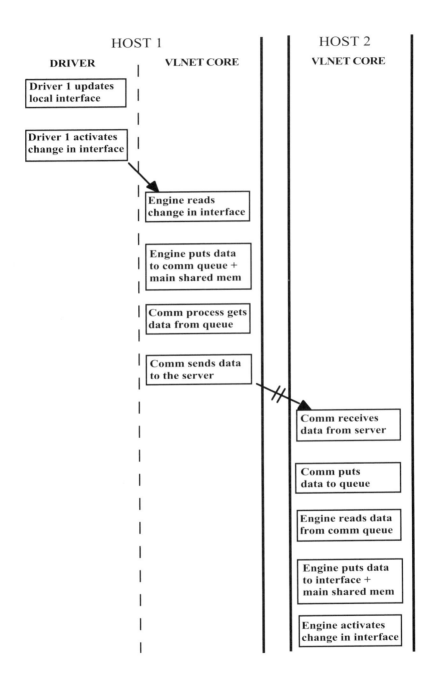

Figure 3-9. Steps for propagating driver change to other clients

We consider the NVE simulation as an iterative process. Each iteration corresponds to one frame of the simulation. A frame consists of the following steps. Figure 3-9 shows how driver's changes are propagated to other clients.

1. Driver simulation computations
2. Driver update to the external interfaces
3. Engine detection of update in external interfaces
4. Engine internal computations
5. Engine update of the internal shared memory and VLNET output queue
6. Communication computations to convert data into VLNET packets for sending
7. Communication process receipt of VLNET messages from other clients
8. Communication process update of messages to VLNET input queue
9. Engine reading of related messages from VLNET input queue
10. Engine update of internal shared memory
11. Cull computations to reject invisible geometry
12. Display computations to send visible geometry to display engine

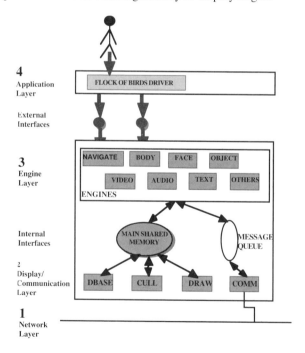

Figure 3-10. Flock of Birds driver connects to the body interface

3.2.3 Driver Simulation Computations

Various default sets of drivers exists for each functionality such as mouse navigation or walking motion. The participant can select one of the default drivers. This allows previously developed code to be conveniently reused, and it provides an extensible system for developing drivers based on existing ones such as Flock of Birds (Figure 3-10) or SpaceBall (Figure 3-11).

Some of the drivers are mandatory, some are optional. The default navigation method is the 2D mouse; the default body animation behaviour is walking while navigating, manipulating objects with the right hand, and viewing the environment through head movements. Figure 3-12 shows a driver controlling two clients.

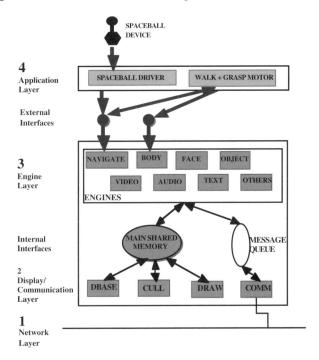

Figure 3-11. SpaceBall driver connects to the navigation interface, walking motor connects to the navigation and body interface

Drivers run asynchronously and independently from the VLNET core processes. We assume that drivers typically execute a loop, which consists of performing simulations for each frame. This is the approach that most of the graphics and simulation libraries have, therefore our view of the application program is not a limiting one. Each driver loop iteration typically consists of the stages shown in Figure 3-13.

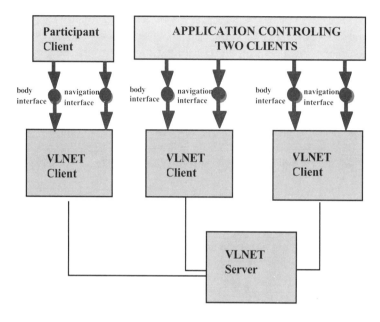

Figure 3-12. A driver controlling two clients through two interfaces, and its connection to a third client

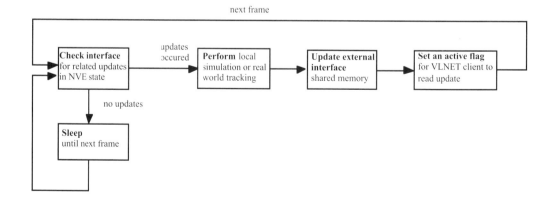

Figure 3-13. Program structure of the driver process

The first stage is to check whether any updates the driver is listening for have occurred. The external interfaces are used for this purpose. If no update has occurred and the driver has no additional tasks, it waits until the next frame boundary. If any update has occurred, the driver performs its simulation depending on this update. Once it has finished its simulation, it places its updates on the external interfaces, and sets a flag to inform the engines for the external interfaces it has connected to.

Note that the first stage, detection of updates in the NVE, is optional. Consider a driver that animates an automatic door when a user approaches it; this needs to check at each frame for the position of other users, so it needs to have the detection stage. However, a driver interpreting magnetic trackers attached to a participant's body may not need to check for updates within the other parts of the NVE, so it will not have the detection stage.

3.2.4   Driver Update to the External Interfaces

VLNET interfaces provide the simple and flexible means to access and control all the functionalities of VLNET internal processes. Each engine in VLNET provides a simple interface to its particular functions (for description of engines see Section 3.2.2), and it is possible to connect one or more external processes to all needed interfaces, depending on the desired functions.

The interfaces are implemented as shared memory segments, each with a simple API (see Section 3.2.2) allowing access to all functions of the engine. A transparent network connection is automatically installed by VLNET if an external process connects to VLNET interfaces from a remote host. This allows distributed computing within a single VLNET client. The contents of the shared memory depend on the type of interface it represents. Below we present the interface shared memory contents specifically for participant embodiments: navigation and body interfaces.

3.2.4.1   Interface Types

The *facial expression interface* is used to control expressions of the user's face. The expressions are defined using minimal perceptible actions (MPAs) (Kalra et al. 1992). The MPAs provide a complete set of basic facial actions, and using them it is possible to define any facial expression. A list of MPAs is provided in Table 5.1. The API of the facial expression interface allows the MPAs to be set and the expression to be activated.

The *body posture interface* controls the motion of the user's body. The postures are defined using a set of joint angles corresponding to 72 degrees of freedom of the skeleton model used in VLNET. An obvious example of using this interface is direct motion control using magnetic trackers (Molet et al. 1996). A more complex body posture driver is connected to the interface to control body motion in a general case when trackers are not used. This driver connects also to the navigation interface and uses the navigation trajectory to generate the walking motion and arm motion. It also imposes constraints on navigation, e.g. not allowing the hand to move further than the arm's length or to take an unnatural posture. The API for the body posture interface allows the joint angles of the body to be set followed by deformation of the body into the given posture.

The *navigation interface* is used for navigation, hand movement, head movement, basic object manipulation and basic system control. The basic manipulation includes picking up objects, carrying them and letting them go, as well as grouping and ungrouping of objects. The system control provides access to some system functions that are usually accessed by keystrokes, e.g. changing drawing modes, toggling texturing, displaying statistics. Typical examples of using this interface are a SpaceBall driver, tracker + glove driver, extended mouse driver (with GUI console). There is also an experimental facial navigation driver, letting the user navigate using their head movements and facial expressions tracked by a camera (Pandzic et al. 1994). If no navigation driver is connected to the navigation interface, internal mouse navigation is activated within the navigation engine. The API for the navigation interface makes it possible to change the global position, viewpoint and hand position matrices, as well as making it possible to request picking up or letting go of objects and to activate keystroke commands.

The *object behaviour interface* is used for controlling the behaviour of objects. Currently it is limited to controlling motion and scaling. Examples include the control of a ball in a tennis game and the control of graphical representation of stock values in a virtual stock exchange. The API for the object behaviour interface makes it possible to set and get transformation matrices of objects in the environment.

The *video interface* is used to stream video texture (but possibly also static textures) onto any object in the environment. Alpha channel can be used for blending and to achieve mixing of real and virtual objects and persons. This interface can also be used to stream facial video onto the user's face representation for facial communication (Pandzic et al. 1996a). This will be presented in more detail in Chapter 5.

The API for the video interface makes it possible to set images to be mapped onto any object in the environment. The images are passed as simple RGB format pictures in shared memory and the object on which to map the image is designated by an object ID. Changing images in time produces the video effect.

The *text interface* is used to send and receive text messages to and from other users. An inquiry can be made through the text interface to check whether there are any messages, and the messages can be read. The interface gives the ID of the sender for each received message. A message sent through the text interface is passed to all other users in a VLNET session. The API for the text interface makes it possible to set a message to be sent, check if there are any incoming messages, read them and find out who is the sender.

The *information interface* is used by external applications to gather information about the environment from VLNET. Because of its particular importance for implementation of autonomous actors and other complex external applications, we will present this interface in somewhat more detail. It provides high-level information while isolating the external application from the VLNET implementation details. It offers two ways of obtaining information, namely the request-and-reply mechanism and the event mechanism.

In the request-and-reply mechanism, a request is described and submitted to the VLNET system. Then, the request will be processed by the information interface engine in the VLNET system and a reply will be generated.

In the event mechanism, an event registration is described and submitted to the VLNET system. The event registration will be processed by the information interface engine and be stored in an event register. At each rendering frame, the VLNET system will process the event register and generate events accordingly. These event registrations will remain registered and be processed in each rendering frame until a removal from the event register is requested.

Figure 3-14 illustrates the information flow between the program controlling the autonomous actors and the VLNET system.

There are two message queues linking the program and the VLNET system. One message queue is used to submit requests, event registrations and event removals to the VLNET system. The other message queue is used to obtain replies and events from the VLNET system.

Within the VLNET system, the information engine is responsible for processing the requests, event registrations and event removals. The event registrations and event removals are sent to the event register, so it can be updated accordingly. After processing the requests by the information interface engine, replies and events are generated and placed in the outgoing message queue from the VLNET system.

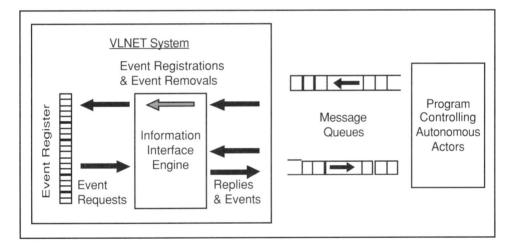

Figure 3-14. Data flow through the information interface

The following information can be requested from VLNET through the information interface API. Figure 3-15 shows the contents of external body and navigation interfaces.

- Description (name) of an object in the virtual world, given the object ID
- List of objects (object IDs and corresponding descriptions) whose description contains the given keywords
- List of users (user IDs and corresponding descriptions) whose description contains the given keywords
- Transformation matrix of an object in world coordinates, given the object ID
- Transformation matrix of a user in world coordinates, given the user ID

- Number of objects in the virtual world that are picked up by a user, given the user ID
- Number of users in the virtual world
- Collisions between users and between objects

```
typedef struct {

        /* The state that is displayed and deformed within VLNET client */
        int active;
        float joint_values[NB_USERS][NB_JOINTS];
        float joint_lhand_values[NB_USERS][NB_HAND_JOINTS];
        float joint_rhand_values[NB_USERS][NB_HAND_JOINTS];

        /* The temporary driver updates */
        int no_local_drivers;
        float temp_driver_joints[NB_DRIVERS][NB_JOINTS];
        int temp_driver_active[NB_DRIVERS];
        int priority [NB_DRIVERS][NB_JOINTS];

        /* Downloadable driver contents */
        int download_local_drivers;
        float download_driver_joints[NB_DRIVERS][NB_JOINTS];
        int download_driver_active[NB_DRIVERS];
        int download_priority [NB_DRIVERS][NB_JOINTS];
} BODY_SHARED_MEMORY;

typedef struct {
        /* Booleans and variables to pass data between driver and engine */
        int active;
        int corrected;
        int pick_info,
        int unpick_info;
        int free_move;
        int key_action;
        /* Three functional coordinate systems related to navigation,viewing,
                picking */
        float body_matrix[4][4],
                view_matrix[4][4],
                pick_matrix[4][4];

        /* Corrected coordinate systems based on navigation constraints */
        float corrected_body_matrix[4][4],
                corrected_view_matrix[4][4],
                corrected_pick_matrix[4][4];

} NAVIGATE_SHARED_MEMORY;
```

Figure 3-15. Contents of external body and navigation interfaces

Note that synchronization between the driver and the engine is achieved through an active flag. This flag is set by the driver to tell the engine that an update has occurred, therefore the engine can process it. This helps to decrease the computations done at the engine side: engines make computations only if there is a change in the interface. Another consequence is that the engines read complete data; this avoids processing updates that are currently written by the driver.

There is the possibility that before the engine reads the driver update belonging to the current frame, the driver can update the shared memory once more. Therefore, the engine can skip one frame in driver updates. Furthermore, while the driver is writing the updates for the next frame, the engine may read the update for the previous frame, therefore it could perhaps read partial data, with two halves corresponding to different frames. The length of the memory portion in the shared memory is small (e.g. 4×4 matrices, 64 bytes), therefore it is not very likely that this will happen. Even if it does, assuming that the updates for consecutive frames are with a small change, we have not observed a problem in terms of simulation and rendering. This problem can be solved by replacing shared memory by semaphores; however, semaphores introduce an overhead in accessing shared contents. Thus, we have chosen the shared memory approach.

For passing data from the VLNET engines to the driver in the reverse direction, there exists two mechanisms:

- *Asynchronous input*: This is typically the data that has to be read by the driver at each frame or continuously. This can be done in two ways: the engines post data changed by the other clients or the system to the different areas in the same interface that they are responsible for. The other possibility is a special *information interface* that responds to general requests, in a question–answer manner.
- *Event-driven input*: This is input that occurs rarely, only a few times within the session. A typical example is changing worlds. In this case the engine sends the driver a user-defined signal.

3.2.4.2 APIs for External Processes

For each type of interface there is an API that lets the external process connect to VLNET. These APIs are very simple. All of them include function calls to open and close the shared memory interface, to update the data (e.g. a position matrix for the navigation driver, a facial expression parameter set for the face driver) and to activate the data, i.e. to give the signal to VLNET that the data is updated and action needed. Only the information interface API is a little more complex, as explained in the previous subsection, due to the need for a more general data exchange.

Figure 3-16 shows an example of a valid facial expression driver that connects to the facial expression interface and rhythmically opens and closes the mouth.

3.2.4.3 Configuring the Application Layer

A simple, yet complete command line convention makes it possible to specify any configuration of drivers and applications running on local or remote hosts. The external process to be spawned is defined by giving the name of the executable, and the interfaces to which it should be connected, indicated by the option letter: F for face, B for body, N for navigation and O for object behaviours, V for video, T for text, I for information interface. The external process can be spawned on a remote host by specifying the executable in the form `executable@host`.

```
#include "vlnet_face.h"
void main(int argc, char *argv[])
  {
        float exp[MAX_MPAS];
        int shmKey = atoi(argv[2])  /* Get the shared memory key from the arguments */
        vrf_init(shmKey);                           /* Connect to the interface */
        while(1)
          {
                if(exp[MPA_OPEN_JAW] >= 1.0)       /* Control the mouth opening */
                  exp[MPA_OPEN_JAW] = 0.0;
                else
                  exp[MPA_OPEN_JAW] += 0.05;
                vrf_set_expression(exp);                    /* Set the expression */
                vrf_active();                                /* Activate */
          }
  }
```

Figure 3-16. Facial expression driver

Here is a command line example:

```
% vlnet ... -F faced -N spaceballd
```

*spawns the 'faced' driver for the face
control and 'spaceballd' driver for navigation*

When spawning an external process, VLNET creates the shared memory interfaces and passes the shared memory keys to the process. The process will receive as arguments the shared memory key for each engine interface it has to connect to. So, the 'faced' driver in the first example would receive the arguments –F <shmkey>, -F meaning it has to connect to the facial expression interface and <shmkey> being the shared memory key to use for that connection.

3.2.5   Engine Detection of Update in External Interfaces

The computations that the engines need to perform are divided into four steps: *synchronization, preframe, frame, postframe*. The *synchronization* step allows the frames to be synchronized in the frame boundaries, and it makes use of the IRIS Performer synchronization mechanism. The *frame* step corresponds to the preparation of display lists to pass to the cull process, and it too is an IRIS Performer utility.

The *preframe* and *postframe* steps are the parts where engines perform computations from local driver updates and remote client updates. At the preframe step, the engines process the local drivers' updates, by reading new data from their interface, if any, and pass this data to the output queue of the communication process. The preframe computations need to be minimal to decrease the frame latency time. At each postframe step, the engines read data containing other clients' changes from the communication process through the input queue, and make the changes in the main shared memory.

Thus, engines check for updates in their interfaces in their preframe step, testing the active flag in the shared memory. If the active flag is set, the engines continue with processing of the update. If this flag is not set, the engines return.

3.2.6 Engine Internal Computations

If an engine detects that a driver has set the active flag for its associated interface, it continues with internal computations. These computations involve setting internal variables, modifying the scene hierarchy (Figure 3-17) and the transformations, applying global constraints, deforming bodies and faces, etc. Here we discuss the two engines, navigation and body engines.

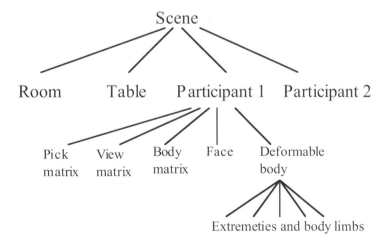

Figure 3-17. Participants as part of the virtual environment hierarchy

The engines communicate with the external drivers, and reflect the updates in the local scene hierarchy. The navigation engine has the preframe pseudocode shown in Figure 3-18.

The function *applyGlobalConstraints* performs correction of the body matrix input from the driver, and performs global constraints, such as inclination, aligning with the object under the body. The techniques for applying global constraints to the body are described in Chapter 4. The function *updateLocalScene* updates the matrix values in the scene hierarchy.

The body representation engine performs the preframe computations that are shown in Figure 3-19. The preframe computations for the human engine include checking the external interface for updates from all the external body drivers, and merging their effect by considering their priorities and values in the body representation. We will discuss the merging technique in the next chapter.

Note that the preframe computation required for the engines is only for the local representation, hence it is relatively small in order to minimize latency for drawing the scene.

```
if (vrn_check_active( NAVIGATE_INTERFACE, BODY_MATRIX)) {
        vrn_get_bodymat( NAVIGATE_INTERFACE,body_matrix);
        body_matrix = applyGlobalConstraints( body_matrix);
        updateLocalScene( body_matrix);
        placetoOutputQueue( body_matrix);
        vrn_set_corrected_bodymat(NAVIGATE_INTERFACE,body_matrix);
        vrn_set_corrected( NAVIGATE_INTERFACE);
}
if (vrn_check_active( NAVIGATE_INTERFACE,VIEW_MATRIX)) {
        vrn_get_corr_viewmat( NAVIGATE_INTERFACE,view_matrix);
        updateLocalScene( view_matrix);
        placetoOutputQueue( view_matrix);
}
if (vrn_check_active( NAVIGATE_INTERFACE,PICK_MATRIX)) {
        vrn_get_corr_viewmat( NAVIGATE_INTERFACE,pick_matrix);
        updateLocalScene( pick_matrix);
        placetoOutputQueue( pick_matrix);
}
```

Figure 3-18. Preframe processing for navigation engine

3.2.7   Engine Update of the VLNET Output Queue

This stage corresponds to the *placeOutputQueue* functions as shown in Figure 3-18 and Figure 3-19. The engines pack the new state of navigation matrices, body and object properties into a packet, and pass this packet in the outgoing queue of the communication process (Figure 3-20). Note that this is an asynchronous operation, and the engine continues without waiting for the communication process to send it to the server.

```
if (vrh_check_active( BODY_INTERFACE)) {

    /* Body joint angles */
    for (i=1 to NO_LOCAL_DRIVERS) do {
      vrh_get_joints_int( BODY_INTERFACE, driver_joints[]);
      vrh_get_priorities_int( BODY_INTERFACE, driver_priorities[]);
    }

    mergeDriverJoints(BODY_PTR,driver_joints[],driver_priorities[],body_joints[]);
    vrh_set_joints_int( BODY_INTERFACE, body_joints[]);
    placetoOutputQueue( body_joints[]);

    /* Left hand joint angles */
    vrh_get_hand_joints_int( BODY_INTERFACE, LEFT_HAND,driver_lhand_joints[]);
    vrh_set_hand_joints_int( BODY_INTERFACE, LEFT_HAND,driver_lhand_joints[]);
    placetoOutputQueue( driver_lhand_joints[]);

    /* Right hand joint angles */
    vrh_get_hand_joints_int(BODY_INTERFACE,RIGHT_HAND,driver_rhand_joints[]);
    vrh_set_hand_joints_int(BODY_INTERFACE,RIGHT_HAND,driver_rhand_joints[]);
    placetoOutputQueue( driver_rhand_joints[]);

}
```

Figure 3-19. Preframe computations for body engine

ENGINES

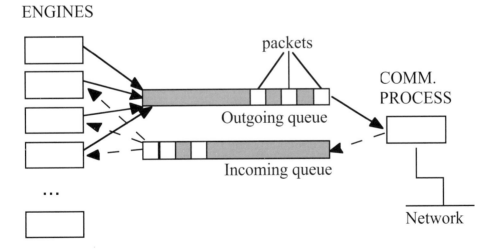

Figure 3-20. Engines and communication process communicate through queues

3.2.8 Communication Computations to Send VLNET Messages

The communication process helps to decouple communication tasks from the application and simulation. Its task is to hide the networking details from the other components of the system. It reads from the input queue and sends the contents of the packet to the server through the UDP socket.

3.2.9 Communication Receipt of VLNET Messages

The communication process receives any messages from the network and puts them into the incoming message queue. All the engines read from the queue and react to messages that concern them (e.g. the navigation engine would react to a move message, but ignore a facial expression message, which would be handled by the facial representation engine). All messages in VLNET use the standard message packet. The packet has a standard header determining the sender and the message type, and the message body. The message body content depends on the message type but is always of the same size (80 bytes), satisfying all message types in VLNET.

Note that receiving updates from remote clients can be excessive compared to sending local embodiment data. Typically, the amount of information received is linearly proportional to the number of participants in the same virtual environment. For certain types of messages (positions, body postures) a dead-reckoning algorithm is implemented within the communication process (Capin et al. 1997a); see Chapter 6 for more details.

3.2.10 Communication Update of Messages to VLNET Input Queue

Similar to step 5, the communication process takes the updates it receives from the server and stores them in the incoming message queue. For simplicity, the incoming and outgoing message queues are independent queues, in reverse directions.

3.2.11 Engine Reading of Related Messages from VLNET Input Queue

The engines read the relevant packets from the incoming queue. The selection of the VLNET messages is through checking the tags of the messages in sequence until a message with a related message tag is found.

3.2.12 Engine Update of Internal Shared Memory

If an engine cannot detect any related message in the incoming message queue, it returns immediately. If it detects a message, it updates the main shared memory, in the same manner as step 4.

As a result, engines perform potentially many more computations in the postframe phase than in the preframe phase. The preframe phase is approximately constant, as it involves processing only for the local user. The amount of postframe phase computations is proportional to the number of participants in the virtual environment.

3.2.13 Cull and Display Processes

The main process and the dbase, cull and draw processes make use of the Performer library. The main computations are based on the pipeline approach. At frame i, the engine reads input from the connected driver. At frame $i + 1$, it passes a list of triangles as a display list to the cull process; the cull process eliminates the geometry that is not within the viewing frustum, and passes to the display process. At frame $i + 2$, the display process renders this display list. The dbase process handles asynchronous loading of new users and objects. They need to be synchronized at the beginning of each frame (Rohlf and Helman 1994).

3.2.14 Dbase Process

The dbase process is an IRIS Performer mechanism to asynchronously load scene data while continuing the simulation. We have modified this mechanism to load and remove participants dynamically.

Note that it is not known before the start of the session who will connect to the environment, therefore participants will be loaded dynamically. Downloading of a new participant's embodiment, which typically consists of a set of large files through HTTP protocol, might take a significant amount of time. And there is an extra overhead in saving the downloaded files into memory and initializing the participant's representation. If the client program has to block other computations during this process and prevent the participant from moving, the client will spend most of the time being blocked, especially with increasing number of participants. Therefore, we implemented these tasks in the dbase process (Figure 3-21). The next chapters look at computations in the dbase process for new participants.

3.2.15 Complexity of Phases within a Frame

We consider the NVE simulation as an iterative process. Each iteration corresponds to one frame of the simulation. As discussed in Section 3.2.2, each frame comprises the 12 phases. Each phase contributes to the total execution time of the frame. The total execution time changes if a uniprocessor machine or a multiprocessor machine is used. Assuming that only one driver exists, the total time to update local VLNET client variables from a driver's change is

$$t^i_{local} = t^i_1 + t^i_2 + t^i_3 + t^i_4 + t^i_5 + t^i_6 + t_{latency\_local}$$

where

t_j^i = time required to execute step j at frame i.

$t_{latency\_local}$ = a random latency value that represents the time difference between the time when the result of one step is ready, and the time when the next step reads this result.

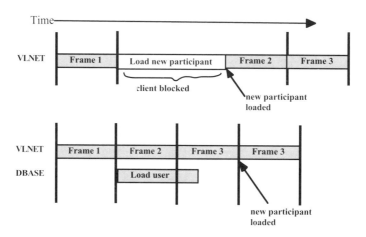

Figure 3-21. Dbase process prevents blocking VLNET client, while loading a new participant.

The time to update simulation based on an update message from a remote VLNET client is

$$t_{remote}^i = t_7^i + t_8^i + t_9^i + t_{10}^i + t_{latency\_remote}$$

Similarly, the time to cull and render frame i at the VLNET client is

$$t_{render}^i = t_{11}^i + t_{12}^i + t_{latency\_render}$$

Computations involved in an individual frame should be investigated while considering a proper interface between successive frames. Strong computational and data dependencies exist between successive phases such that each phase requires the computational results of the previous phase in the iteration. Therefore, each process should be implemented considering these dependencies between successive phases. Furthermore, there exist data dependencies among components at each phase. We analyse each phase with a detailed description of the structure for the used data.

Thus, the total time required by frame i on a single processor host is

$$t^i_{frame} = t^i_{local} + Nt^i_{remote} + t^i_{render}$$

where N is the average number of updates from remote clients per frame

Ideally, t_{frame} needs to be less than 100 ms in order to meet the minimal 10 frames per second interaction speed.

On a multiple-processor host, the total time required by one frame is decreased, as multiple steps of different frames can be processed in parallel, in the driver, engine, communication and display levels. Figure 3-22 shows the execution of the steps for multiple processes.

Then the computational complexity for frame i on a multiple-processor host is

$$t_{frame} = \max(t^i_1 + t^i_2, t^i_3 + t^i_4 + t^i_5, t^i_6 + N(t^i_7 + t^i_8), N(t^i_9 + t^i_{10}), t^i_{11} + t^i_{12})$$

This equation demonstrates that, in the multiprocess version of the client, the performance depends on the results of various components of the system.

$t^i_1 + t^i_2$	= time required for driver to compute one frame; this depends on the nature of the driver, and what it computes.
$t^i_3 + t^i_4 + t^i_5$	= time required for engine to read the changes of the driver, and update internal shared memory and outgoing message queues; this value is close to constant as it involves computations for local representation.
$t^i_6 + N(t^i_7 + t^i_8)$	= time required by communication process to send local participant's updates, receive remote clients' updates and place them in the incoming queue; this value depends on the number of remote participants who create updates in one frame in the scene.
$N(t^i_9 + t^i_{10})$	= time required by the engine to compute the state of local copy scene for remote clients' updates; this depends on the number of remote participants who move in one frame in the scene, and the type of computations required for each update
$t^i_{11} + t^i_{12}$	= time required to render the local scene; this value depends on the geometrical complexity of the participants in the scene, and the objects in the scene.

Thus, there are different conditions that can affect the performance of the system: local driver computations, the number of participants who create updates in one frame, the number

of computations required to modify local scene copy based on the received updates, and the
geometrical complexity of the scene.

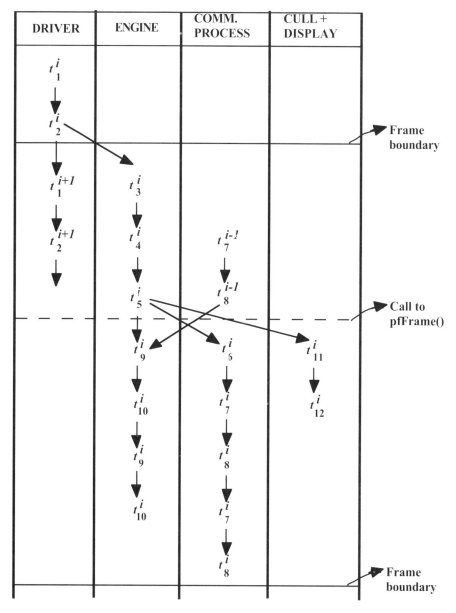

Figure 3-22. Execution of different steps within one frame

3.2.16 Dependencies among Components

There exist different data dependencies between the external face and body process and other components of the environment simulation system. Autonomous virtual humans are able to have a behaviour, which means they must have a manner of coding and using the environment's effects on the virtual body. The virtual human should be equipped with visual, tactile and auditory sensors. These sensors are used as a basis for implementing everyday human behaviour such as visually directed locomotion, handling objects, and responding to sounds and utterances. Similarly, we want the virtual human to be able to act on the environment; for example, the participant can grasp and reposition an object. In the next section, we discuss different human figure motion control methods for creating complex motion. This requires the sharing of information between the object and navigation engines, and external human processes using their external interfaces.

The second type of dependency relates to the representation of the participant by virtual human figures. This representation introduces constraints sourced by the joint limits and viewing positions. When the participant uses non-immersive input techniques, these constraints become especially crucial. For example, when the participant moves their pick point attached to their right hand in the scene using a mouse, this pick point should not move further than the maximum reach point of the body. This problem is solved as follows: besides the functions that activate change in the interface, there are additional functions to correct them. When a change occurs in the navigation driver, it activates the change in the navigation interface. The human driver attaches to the same interface, and when a change is activated in the interface, it receives the data and performs action computations (e.g. right arm movement for picking). Depending on the local posture, the human driver corrects the contents of the navigation interface. Finally, the VLNET engines react to the corrected data, instead of their activation. Note that this solution is a convention for general cases, and does not always have to be adopted (for example, the user might want to see themselves instead of the view through their eyes). The behaviour can be overwritten by modifying drivers and it has been implemented.

The third type of dependency among all the components of the VLNET client and the driver is related to their frame rate. Typically, the driver frame rate needs to match the frame rate of the client's display frame. Otherwise, the intermediate updates made to the external interface while the client is busy with the previous frame, will not be updated. Therefore, allowing the driver to sleep for some predefined period of time will avoid performing unnecessary work on the driver, and will permit other work to be done by other drivers or VLNET core processes. On the other hand, a driver may need to have higher frame rates than the VLNET client. For example, a dynamics animation driver may need to have higher frame rates in order to have more correct behaviour. For this purpose, it is left to the creator of the driver to adjust the frame rate.

3.3 Other Design Decisions

3.3.1 Partitioning of the Virtual World: Rooms Connected by Portals

For the data partitioning scheme, we have selected loosely coupled worlds connected through portals. Therefore, we visualize each application as a separate room created by one of the many users. Therefore, the users are free to select the neighbouring rooms to link from their rooms, as in the design of HTML pages. This gives an uncentralized means for connecting different worlds created by different people, and for connecting various applications without any central placement mechanism.

3.3.2 Data Distribution Scheme: Sharing of Data

The data comprising each room is stored at all clients connected to that room. Therefore, the information exchange is not the description of the whole scene, but only the updates to objects, such as transformations. The clients use the protocol, as discussed below, containing messages to send updates.

3.3.3 Network Topology: Client–Server, Future Work on Multiple Servers

VLNET is based on a client–server topology, therefore clients cannot send messages to each other directly. This introduces an extra overhead for sending the message to the server and then to the remote client; however, the server performs intelligent filtering operations to decrease the network requirements at each client.

The same server can also serve on multiple interfaces, allowing internetworking in the network layer. In this case there will be multiple ports per world server, and the server will distribute the message that it receives from one interface to all clients connected to each port. Currently, the server connects to one interface, and the internetworking is performed in the network layer. We achieve this by building a route in the network layer, through the IRIX *route add* command, that forwards the traffic between two interfaces.

3.3.3.1 Connection of Several Clients to the Same Server

The same server can be responsible for multiple worlds, allowing an additional level of filtering in the world level on the same server host. A VLNET server site consists of an HTTP server and a VLNET Connection Server. They can serve several worlds, which can be either VLNET world description files or VRML files. A VLNET world description file is a metafile containing pointers to files describing graphical objects which can be in various formats (VRML, Inventor, Alias/Wavefront, 3D Studio, etc.). The VLNET file manages a scene hierarchy tree consisting of these graphical objects. Behaviours, sounds, light-emitting properties or links to other worlds can be attached to objects (Figure 3-23).

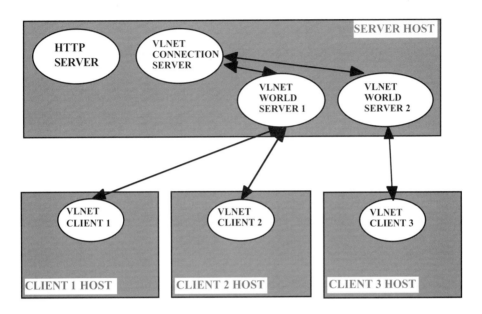

Figure 3-23. Connection of several clients in different worlds to the same server

Each world is differentiated by its URL, therefore clients connecting to a world specify the URL of the world they want to connect to. For each world, a world server is spawned as necessary, i.e. when a client requests a connection to that particular world. The life of a world server ends when all clients are disconnected.

Figure 3-23 schematically depicts a VLNET server site with several connected clients. A VLNET session is initiated by a client connecting to a particular world designated by a URL. The client first fetches the world database from the HTTP server using the URL. After that it extracts the host name from the URL and connects to the VLNET connection server on the same host. The connection server spawns the world server for the requested world if one is not already running and sends to the client the port address of the world server. Once the connection is established, all communication between the clients in a particular world passes through the world server. The user provides their personal data by distributing a URL from which all participants can fetch the data.

In order to reduce the total network load, the world server performs the filtering of messages (AOIM) by checking the users' viewing frusta in the virtual world and distributing messages only on an as-needed basis.

During a session, the world server keeps the world data up to date with any changes happening in the world, so new users can get the up-to-date version of the world. It can save the state of the world in a file at the end of the session, keeping the world persistent in between sessions.

The connection to the world server takes the steps shown in Figure 3-24.

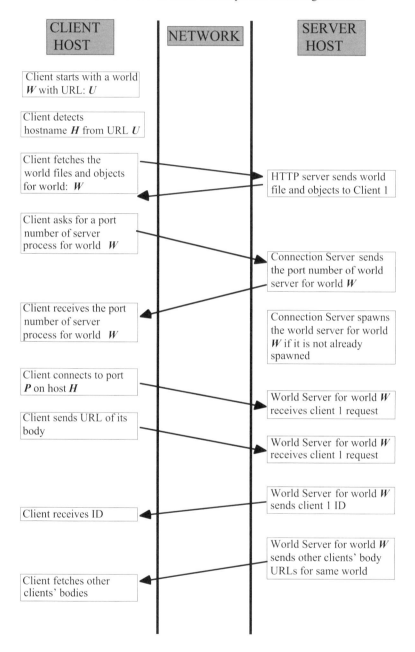

Figure 3-24. Steps for connection of VLNET client and world server

3.3.3.2 Computations at the World Server

The world server is responsible for receiving messages from clients and propagating them to the other clients in the same world. We take advantage of using a server, by processing messages before distributing them on the server host. The server culls, augments and alters messages for scaling with increasing number of participants. The world server sends a message from client i to client j only if client j can see client i.

3.3.4 Participant Embodiments as Realistic Virtual Humans

We believe that VLNET is the NVE that offers the best virtual humans in terms of realism, animation and behaviour. For this reason, we will discuss the virtual human representation, control and communication issues in more detail in the next chapters.

3.3.5 VLNET Session Management and Communication Protocol

The protocol in VLNET consists of session management, state and event information, and interaction among objects. We use fixed-length messages to communicate different information between the server and the clients.

Session management messages are typically used when establishing connection with the server, and negotiating between the client and the server. Here are some of them:

- *Error*: mentioning that an error has occurred
- *End*: client is ending the session
- *Busy*: client is busy
- *Ready*: client is ready to receive messages
- *Get_Body*: client requests URL for the new user
- *Send_Body*: client sends URL of its body
- *Port*: connection server sends the port number of the world server
- *Send_uid*: connection server sends the client's ID in the virtual world
- *Set_name*: client sets its name
- *New_user*: world server sends the URL of the new user's body

State messages are the properties of the objects and participants in the scene. There exist different types of state messages:

- *Move* contains a transformation matrix for the object or the participant's position, pick or view matrices.
- *Joints* contains the joints in the body.
- *Hand joints (optional)* contains the hand joints of the body.
- *Face_expression* contains the facial expression value.

Using special messages for participant embodiments allows the compression of data, therefore virtual human figure representations can be efficiently managed. Event messages are for things that happen only occasionally:

- *Pick* contains the event that the participant picked an object.
- *Unpick* contains the event that the participant released an object.
- *Group* contains the event that the participant grouped objects.
- *Ungroup* contains the event that the participant ungrouped objects.

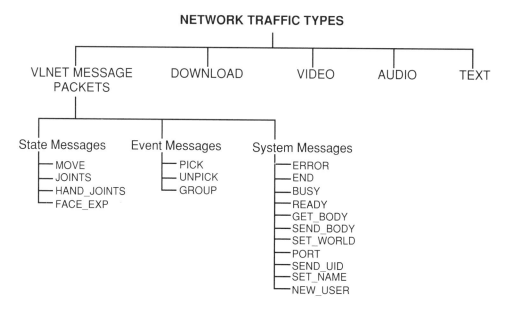

Figure 3-25. Network traffic types

In addition to the virtual stream containing VLNET traffic, there are extra virtual channels for MPEG-1 compressed video, audio and textual communication traffic. The streams are not multiplexed, i.e. they use different socket communication (Figure 3-25). For VLNET state messages, we use a stateless protocol. That is, the data contained in these messages does not depend on the previous packets, hence the latest message overrides the previous messages. This allows data loss to be tolerated, along with performance differences among machines, latency and time delay. Therefore, we can use UDP communication between clients and the server. The structure of VLNET messages is shown in Figure 3-26.

Note that there are special messages for participant embodiments. Making use of the skeleton structure allows us to send postures efficiently. We propose different ways of communication for sending embodiment state, depending on the accuracy requirements of the application, the network, and the host site capacities, as discussed in later chapters.

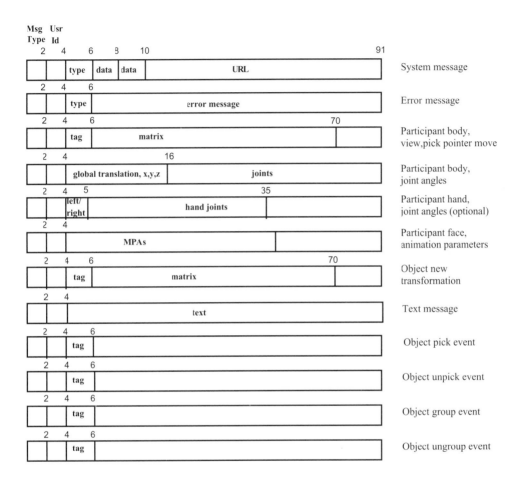

Figure 3-26. VLNET packet types: the messages have constant size

4 Representation of Virtual Humans

4.1 Virtual Humans

Virtual humans is a research domain concerned with the simulation of human beings on computers. It involves representation, movement and behaviour. There is a wide range of applications: film and TV productions, ergonomic and usability studies in various industries (aerospace, automobile, machinery, furniture, etc.), production line simulations for efficiency studies, clothing industry, games, telecommunications (clones for human representation), medicine, etc. These applications have various needs. A medical application might require an exact simulation of certain internal organs; the film industry requires the highest aesthetic standards, natural movements and facial expressions; ergonomic studies require faithful body proportions for a particular population segment and realistic locomotion with constraints.

The sheer complexity of the simulated subject, i.e. the human body, combined with the multitude of applications and requirements, make virtual humans a vast research domain comprising numerous research topics:

- *Anatomy and geometry*, dealing with creation of human shape in 3D graphics, with methods ranging from point-to-point digitizing from clay models (Blum 1979; Smith 1983) through various software tools for geometry deformation and modelling (Barr 1984; Sederberg and Parry 1986; Allan et al. 1989; Magnenat Thalmann et al. 1989) to laser 3D scanners.
- *Hair and skin representation and rendering* (Pearce et al. 1986, Watanabe and Suenaga 1989; Daldegan et al. 1993; Kurihara et al. 1993; Leblanc et al. 1991)
- *Skeleton animation*, or animation of joint angles of the skeleton structure (Badler and Smoliar 1979) defining the articulated body and consisting of segments (representing limbs) and joints (representing degrees of freedom). Main methods of skeleton animation are parametric keyframe animation (Lee and Kunii 1989; Brotman and Netravali 1988), direct and inverse kinematics (possibly with constraints) (Badler et al. 1986, Girard and Maciejewski 1985; Girard 1987; Forsey and Wilhelms 1988), direct and inverse dynamics (Arnaldi et al. 1989; Armstrong et al. 1987; Wilhelms 1987).
- *Body surface animation and deformation*, trying to simulate natural-looking movement and deformation of visible body surface with respect to the movement of the underlying skeleton structure (Magnenat Thalmann and Thalmann 1987; Chadwick et al. 1989; Komatsu 1988; Thalmann et al. 1996).

- *Hand animation and deformation* (Badler and Morris 1982; Magnenat Thalmann et al. 1988; Gourret et al. 1989; Moccozet and Magnenat Thalmann 1997; Moccozet et al. 1997).
- *Facial animation*, playing an essential role for human communication. There are two mainstream ares of facial animation research: parameterized models (Parke 1982) and muscle models (Waters 1987; Magnenat Thalmann et al. 1989; Waters and Terzopoulos 1991; Kalra et al. 1992).
- *Clothes simulation* (Lafleur et al. 1991; Carignan et al. 1992; Volino et al. 1995).
- *Walking*, i.e. generating natural-looking walking motion based on a given trajectory and velocity (Calvert and Chapman 1978; Zeltzer 1982; Magnenat Thalmann and Thalmann 1987; Boulic et al. 1990).
- *Obstacle avoidance*, finding the optimal trajectory for walking while avoiding obstacles (Schroeder and Zeltzer 1988; Breen 1989; Renault et al. 1990; Bandi and Thalmann 1998).
- *Grasping*, i.e. producing appropriate arm and hand motion to reach for and grab an object (Korein and Badler 1982; Mas and Thalmann 1994; Huang et al. 1995; Moccozet et al. 1997).
- *Behavioural animation*, striving to give more character and personality to the animation, thus making it look more natural than mechanics-based animations (Cohen 1989; Reynolds 1987; Badler et al. 1993; Magnenat Thalmann and Thalmann 1993; Blumberg and Galyean 1995; Noser and Thalmann 1996).

4.2 Why Virtual Humans in NVE?

The participant representation in an NVE system has several functions:

- Perception
- Localization
- Identification
- Visualization of interest focus
- Visualization of actions
- Communication

Perception and localization are the very basic functions of participant representation in NVEs. They allow us to perceive the presence of others in the environment and see where they are. Even a crude embodiment can fulfil these tasks.

Identification is an important function because we usually want to know who is in front of us. Means of identification can range from simple ones, like displaying the first letter of one's name (Benford et al. 1995) to complex body and face models resembling a particular person.

Visualization of interest focus can be achieved by any embodiment that somehow represents the direction of gaze—usually this means a graphical model that has eyes or symbols representing eyes, so we can see in which direction it is looking.

Visualization of actions requires the embodiment to have some end-effectors that perform actions. In a low-end implementation this might be a simple line reaching to the manipulated object, or it might be a virtual hand grasping the object.

Communication in real life is in many ways tied to our body—gestures and facial expressions (including lip movement that improves speech understanding) are a natural part of our daily communication. If this communication is to be supported in NVEs, the participant representation needs to be fairly sophisticated.

Although many of these functions can be fulfilled with very simple embodiments, it is obvious that most can be fulfilled better using more sophisticated virtual humans, and some functions cannot be fulfilled without them.

Virtual humans can fulfil these functions in an intuitive, natural way resembling the way we achieve these tasks in real life. Even with limited sensor information, a virtual human frame can be constructed in the virtual world, reflecting the activities of the real user. Slater and Usoh (1994) indicate that such a body, even if crude, already increases the sense of presence that the participants feel. Therefore it is expected that a better and more realistic embodiment will have a further positive effect on the sense of presence and mutual presence (Section 1.6).

4.3   Architecture for Virtual Humans in NVEs

Introducing virtual humans in the distributed virtual environment is a complex task combining several fields of expertise (Pandzic et al. 1997a):

- *Virtual human simulation*, involving real-time animation/deformation of bodies and faces, and some of the other challenges outlined in Section 4.1.
- *Virtual environment simulation*, involving visual database management and rendering techniques with real-time optimizations.
- *Networking*, involving communication of various types of data with varying requirements in terms of bit rate, error resilience and latency.
- *Interaction*, involving support of different devices and paradigms.
- *Artificial intelligence* (in case autonomous virtual humans are involved), involving decision-making processes and autonomous behaviours.

Each of the components involved represents a whole area of research and most of them are very complex. When combining them together, it is essential to consider the interaction between components and their impact on each other. For example, using virtual humans sets new requirements on interaction. It has to allow not only simple interaction with the environment, but also the visualization of actions through the body and face representing the user; the need to communicate data through the network forces more compact representation of face and body animation data.

Considering the total complexity of these components, a divide-and-conquer approach is a logical choice. By splitting the complex task into modules, each with a precise function and with well-defined interfaces between them, several advantages are achieved:

- High flexibility
- Easier software management, especially in a teamwork environment
- Higher performance
- Leveraging the power of multiprocessor hardware or distributed environments when available

Flexibility is particularly important, because of the multitude of emerging hardware and software technologies that can potentially be linked with NVE systems (various input devices and techniques, AI algorithms, real-time data sources driving multi-user applications). This is especially interesting in a research environment where an NVE system can be used as a test bed for research in fields such as AI, psychology, medical information systems. In general, a good NVE system must allow implementation of different applications while transparently performing its basic tasks (networking, user representation, interaction, rendering, etc.) and letting the application programmer concentrate on the application-specific problems.

From the software management point of view, a monolithic system of this complexity would be extremely difficult to manage, in particular by a team of programmers.

By carefully assigning tasks to processes and synchronizing them intelligently, higher performance can be achieved (Rohlf and Helman 1994).

Finally, a multiprocess system will naturally harness the power of multiprocessor hardware if it is available. It is also possible to distribute modules on several hosts.

Once it is decided to split the system into modules, roughly corresponding to the above listed components, it is necessary to define in detail the task of each module and the means of communication between them.

4.4   Design Choices for Representation

4.4.1   Articulated Structure for Virtual Human Modelling

We have selected virtual human representation of participants for embodiments. Typically, an articulated structure corresponding to the human skeleton is needed for the control of the body posture. Structures representing the body shape have to be attached to the skeleton, and clothes may be wrapped around the body shape. We use the HUMANOID articulated human body model with 75 degrees of freedom without the hands, and an extra 30 degrees of freedom for each hand (Boulic et al. 1995). The skeleton, shown in Figure 4-1, is represented by a 3D articulated hierarchy of joints, each with realistic maximum and minimum limits. The skeleton is encapsulated with geometrical, topological and inertial characteristics of different body limbs. The body structure has a fixed topology template of joints, and different body instances are created by specifying five scaling parameters: global scaling, frontal scaling, high and low lateral scaling, and the spine origin ratio between the lower and upper body.

The default posture is the figure standing up, with palms looking inward. All the joint angles have value 0 in this default posture.

Note that the body posture is represented by an array of 75 floating-point values, each representing the value of another degree of freedom in the body (with an extra 30 degrees of freedom for bodies with hands). Therefore, we exploit this array representation within the body representation interface.

There are different parameter sets for defining virtual human postures.

Global Positioning Domain Parameters
These are the global position and orientation values of particular observable points on the body, in the body coordinate system. The points are top of head, back of neck, mid-clavicle, shoulders, elbow, wrist, hip, knee, ankle, bottom of mid-toe.

Joint Angle Domain Parameters
These parameters comprise the joint angles defined above, connecting different body parts.

Hand and Finger Parameters
The hand is capable of performing complicated motions and there are at least 15 joints in the hand, not counting the carpal part. As using hand joints almost doubles the total number of degrees of freedom, we separate the hand parameters from those for other body parts.

The distribution of total degrees of freedom into body parts is shown in Table 4-1.

Table 4-1. List of degrees of freedom for each body joint group

Body section	Total degrees of freedom
Vertebrae	10
Shoulder/clavicle/scapula	2*7
Elbow	2*2
Wrist	2*2
Pelvis	3+2*3
Hip	2*3
Knee	2*2
Ankle/toe/midfoot	2*4
Hands	2*30
Total (no hands)	75
Total (with hands)	135

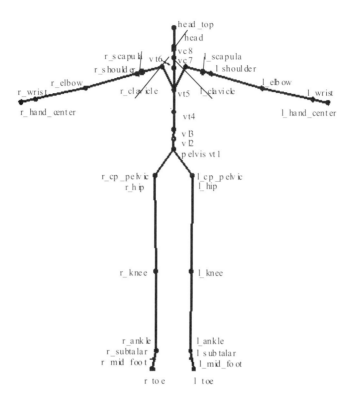

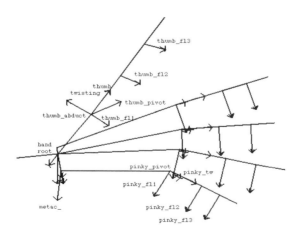

Figure 4-1. Virtual human representation: the body model has 75 degrees of freedom, with an extra 30 degrees of freedom for each hand (Boulic et al. 1995)

Attached to the skeleton, is a second layer that consists of blobs (metaballs) to represent muscle and skin (Thalmann et al. 1996). The method's main advantage lies in permitting us to cover the entire human body with only a small number of blobs. The method is based on deformations of the body based on cross-sections, and is summarized as follows. The body is divided into 17 parts: head, neck, upper torso, lower torso, hip, left and right upper arm, lower arm, hand, upper leg, lower leg, and foot. Because of their complexity, head, hands and feet are not represented by blobs, but instead with triangle meshes. For the other parts a cross-sectional table is used for deformation. This cross-sectional table is created only once for each body by dividing each body part into a number of cross-sections and computing the outermost intersection points with the blobs. These points represent the skin contour and are stored in the body description file. During run-time the skin contour is attached to the skeleton, and at each step is interpolated around the link depending on the joint angles. From this interpolated skin contour the deformation component creates the new body triangle mesh. Thus, the body information in one frame can be represented as the rotational joint angle values. See Thalmann (1996) for details on the method. However, the body deformation is optional: the body can also be defined by solid body parts attached to the skeleton.

Thus, we define the state space of all possible configurations of the articulated body by a vector space. The set of independent parameters defining the orientations and positions of all body parts, forms the basis of the state space. We define that the body in a configuration is described by a state vector

$$\vartheta = (\vartheta_1, \vartheta_2, \vartheta_3, \dots, \vartheta_N)$$

where $\vartheta_1, \vartheta_2, \vartheta_3, \dots, \vartheta_N$ are the individual degrees of freedom in the body and the dimension of the vector is equal to the total degrees of freedom. The dimension of our model is 135 with complex hands, and 75 without hand mobilities.

4.4.2 Scalability for Virtual Human Representation

As we have discussed above, there is a need to represent embodiments in multiple levels of complexity. This scalability problem has different dimensions:

- *Processing scalability* refers to the local overhead of a virtual human figure on the host computer. This type of scalability is divided into different subtypes:

  - *Computational scalability*: the computational overhead that is needed in order to update the posture of the body from a set of body animation parameters. This overhead is proportional to the animation parameter type, and the number of manipulated degrees of freedom.
  - *Graphics scalability*: the amount of graphics power that is needed to display a body in real time.

- *Networking scalability* refers to the networking overhead of a virtual human figure. This type of scalability is divided into three elements:

  - *Loading scalability*: the amount of computational and network overhead needed to download a body model and load it in the memory, during the initialization phase of the new participant.
  - *Bandwidth scalability*: the amount of traffic (in terms of bits per second) needed to communicate the body state in real time,
  - *Coding scalability*: the number of computations needed to encode and decode the transferred messages to a list of body animation parameters ready to animate the remote copy of the representation, at a remote client.

In this section, we discuss processing scalability, while networking scalability will be detailed in Chapter 6. Notice that these scalability types are not orthogonal although they put demands on different parts of the problem.

4.4.3 Computational Scalability

Computational complexity defines the computational overhead in order to update the posture of the virtual body from a set of animation parameters. If the animation is defined that directly updates individual degrees of freedom, this complexity decreases to traversal of the body hierarchy and updating the transformation of each joint. The computational complexity of the traversal is proportional to the number of nodes to be traversed.

Table 4-2 shows some experimental results to update body posture from a set of body joints. Various possibilities exist:

- Full body with hand mobilities (75 DOFs)
- Full body without hand mobilities (135 DOFs)
- Upper body update only (total 41 DOFs)
- Lower body update only (total 17 DOFs)
- A subset of joints with higher visual influence on the overall posture: thigh (3*2 DOFs), knee (2*2 DOFs), shoulder (3*2 DOFs), elbow (2*2 DOFs), flexion (fl1 and fl2 flexion) values of hands as shown in Figure 4-1 (10*2 DOFs) total = 20 or 40 DOFs

Note that the complexity to update the skeleton is independent of the geometrical complexity of the attached skin layers (e.g. number of polygons), but changes with number of traversed nodes.

Table 4-2. Computational complexity of body posture update rates from body animation parameters

CPU	Full body with hand mobilities	Full body without hand mobilities	Upper body update only	Lower body update only	A subset of mobilities
100 MHz	67 frames/s	119 frames/s	225 frames/s	324 frames/s	155 frames/s
150 MHz	128 frames/s	234 frames/s	435 frames/s	665 frames/s	322 frames/s
200 MHz	180 frames/s	324 frames/s	571 frames/s	901 frames/s	439 frames/s
250 MHz	233 frames/s	400 frames/s	905 frames/s	1000 frames/s	655 frames/s

4.4.4 Graphics Scalability

The graphical level of detail concept has been used in several 3D rendering packages and languages such as IRIS Performer and VRML. For each virtual human figure, we use four levels of detail (although this number is not necessarily constant, we have selected this number for optimizing the requirements of various parts of the system: memory, CPU, networking overhead for downloading). The four levels of detail have the same overall view silhouette, in order to maximize the similarity between different levels of detail.

Table 4-3. Levels of detail for the default body representation and their complexity and range characteristics

	Very high resolution	High resolution	Medium resolution	Low resolution
Body	13518	2086	1322	634
Head/hands/feet	10000	10000	500	500
Total	23518	12086	1822	1134
Range	0 to 1.5 feet	1.5 to 4 feet	4 to 10 feet	> 10 feet

The automatic switching of the level of detail takes place within the deformation library, depending on the distance to the viewpoint, with the selected range for each level of detail. A crucial choice is to select these ranges of each degree of freedom. The range is normally highly dependent on the display *or window* characteristics, the lighting in the scene, the complexity of the VE, etc. One solution would be to use the distances proportional to the degree of intimacy in interpersonal communication—the intimate space (Section 5.7.1), the personal space, the social-consultive space, and the public space beyond (Weitz 1974). Another solution is to ignore the extra parameters and use a full-screen window to take the user trial measurements. Figure 4-2 shows the different levels of detail for the bodies that we use, and Table 4-3 illustrates the number of polygons and range for each level of detail. Note that the differences between levels of detail get more unrecognizable with further distances.

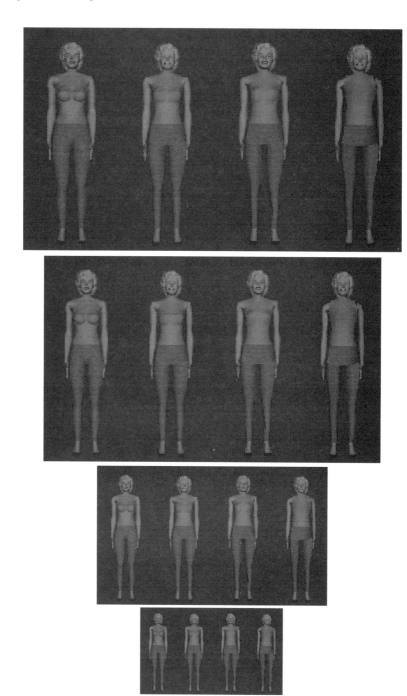

Figure 4-2. Levels of detail, and visual results seen from four distances

4.5   Design Choices for Control

In this section, we describe the techniques for controlling virtual human figures in VLNET. We want to combine participants with immersive and desktop equipment within the same virtual world. Additionally, we want to allow autonomous actors without any user intervention to integrate with the system as participants. We can describe the main tasks for virtual human control as *perceptual tasks*, e.g. identification of environment, *cognitive tasks*, e.g. information processing and decision making, *communicative tasks*, e.g. gestures and other media, and *motor tasks* such as walking, grasping.

4.5.1   Types of Virtual Human Control

The participant should animate their virtual human representation in real time; however, the human control is not straightforward: the complexity of virtual human representation needs a large number of degrees of freedom to be tracked. In addition, interaction with the environment increases this difficulty even more. Therefore, the human control should use higher-level mechanisms to be able to animate the representation with maximal facility and minimal input. We divide the virtual human control methods into three classes (Thalmann et al. 1995):

- *Directly controlled virtual humans*: the state vector of the virtual human is modified directly (e.g. using sensors attached to the body) by providing the new DOF values directly (e.g. by sensors attached to the body).
- *User-guided virtual humans*: the external driver *guides* the virtual human by defining tasks to perform, and the virtual human uses its motor skills to perform this action by coordinated joint movements (e.g. walk, sit).
- *Autonomous virtual humans*: the virtual human is assumed to have an internal state which is built by its goals and sensor information from the environment, and the participant modifies this state by defining high-level motivations, and state changes (e.g. turning on vision behaviour).

The control methods are not independent, higher-level controls require lower-level capabilities. Autonomous behaviour assumes motor skills to accomplish control, and motor skills modify individual DOFs (Figure 4-3).

4.5.1.1   Directly Controlled Virtual Humans

The virtual human is required to have a natural-looking body and be animated with respect to the actual body. This corresponds to a real-time form of traditional rotoscopy. Traditional rotoscopy in animation consists of recording the motion by a specific device for each frame and using this information to generate the image by computer. Using the terminology introduced by Thalmann (1993), we call the real-time rotoscopy method a method consisting of recording input data from a VR device in real time allowing us to apply the same data to a graphics object on the screen. For example, when the animator opens the fingers 3 cm, the hand in the virtual scene does exactly the same. In addition, playing previously recorded keyframes requires real-time input of body posture geometry. The input geometry can be given as global positioning parameters, or joint angle parameters.

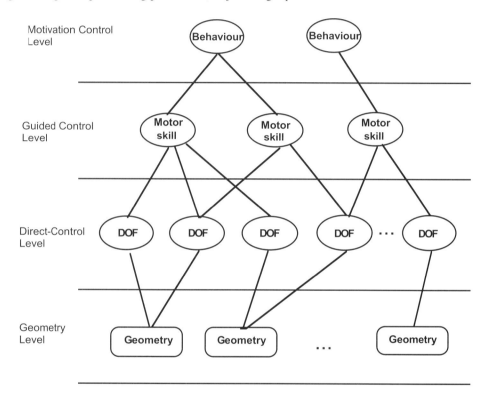

Figure 4-3. Multilevel control of virtual humans

A complete representation of the participant's virtual body should have the same movements as the real participant body for more immersive interaction. This can be best achieved by using a large number of sensors to track every degree of freedom in the real body. Molet et al. (1996) discuss how a minimum of 14 sensors are required to manage a biomechanically correct posture, and Semwal et al. (1996) present a closed-form algorithm to approximate the body using up to 10 sensors. However, many of the current VE systems use only head and hand tracking. Therefore, the limited tracking information should be connected with human model information and different motion generators in order to 'extrapolate' the joints of the body which are not tracked. This is more than a simple inverse kinematics problem, because there are generally multiple solutions for the joint angles to reach the same position, and the most realistic posture should be selected. In addition, the joint constraints should be considered for setting the joint angles.

The main lowest-level approaches to this extrapolation problem are inverse kinematics using constraints (Badler et al. 1993), closed-form solutions (Semwal et al. 1996), and table lookup solutions (Capin et al. 1995). The inverse kinematics approach is based on an iterative algorithm, where an end-effector coordinate frame (e.g. the hand) tries to reach a goal (the reach position) coordinate frame, using a set of joints which control the end-effector. The advantage of this approach is that any number of sensors can be attached to any body part, and multiple constraints can be combined through assigning weights. However, this might slow down the simulation significantly as it requires excessive computation. The closed-form solution solves this problem using 10 sensors attached to the body, and solving for the joint angles analytically. The human skeleton is divided into smaller chains, and each joint angle is computed within the chain it belongs to. For example, the joint angle for the elbow is computed using the sensors attached to the upper arm and lower arm, and computing the angle between the sensor coordinate frames. However, this approach still needs 10 sensors. Table lookup solution uses previously stored experimental data. The right arm chain is an example. Assume that only the 6 degrees of freedom of the right hand are obtained as sensor input, the body driver controlling the arm computes the joint angles within the right arm using this input. The arm motion makes use of experimental data obtained using sensors, and stored in a precomputed table of arm joints. This precomputed table divides the normalized volume around the body into a discrete number of subvolumes, and stores a mapping from subvolumes to joint angles of the right arm. Afterwards, the normal inverse kinematics computations are performed using this posture as the starting state.

Formally, we can define that the new state vector of the virtual body as a function of the previous state vector values, and a set of user input parameters:

$$\vartheta(\vartheta_1^i, \vartheta_2^i, \vartheta_3^i, ..., \vartheta_N^i), I(\vartheta_1, \vartheta_2, ..., \vartheta_N) \rightarrow \vartheta(\vartheta_1^{i+1}, \vartheta_2^{i+1}, ..., \vartheta_N^{i+1})$$

where $I(\vartheta_1, \vartheta_2, ..., \vartheta_N)$ is the input vector that contains angle values for subset of degrees of freedom.

4.5.1.2 Guided Virtual Humans

Guided virtual humans are those which are driven by the user but which do not correspond directly to the user motion. They are based on the concept of real-time direct metaphor, a method consisting of recording input data from a VR device in real time, allowing us to produce effects of different natures but corresponding to the input data. There is no analysis of the real meaning of the input data. To understand the concept, we may take an example of traditional metaphor: the puppet control. A puppet may be defined as a doll with jointed limbs moved by wires or strings. Similarly glove puppets are dolls whose body can be put on the hand like a glove, the arms and head being moved by the fingers of the operator. In both cases, human fingers are used to drive the motion of the puppet.

In VLNET an example of virtual human guidance is guided navigation. The participant uses the input devices to update the transformation of the eye position of the virtual human. This local control is used by computing the incremental change in the eye position, and estimating the rotation and velocity of the body centre. The walking motor uses the instantaneous velocity of motion to compute the walking cycle length and time, from which it computes the joint angles of the whole body. The sensor information or walking can be obtained from various types of input device such as special gesture with DataGlove, or SpaceBall, as well as other input methods.

Formally, we can define that the new state vector of the virtual body is a motor function of the previous state vector values:

$$\vartheta(\vartheta_1^i, \vartheta_2^i, ..., \vartheta_N^i), I(I_1, I_2, ...) \rightarrow MOTOR\ FUNCTION \rightarrow \vartheta(\vartheta_1^{i+1}, \vartheta_2^{i+1}, ..., \vartheta_N^{i+1})$$

where $I(I_1, I_2, ...)$ defines the vector of high-level parameters controlling the motor skills.

4.5.1.3 Autonomous Virtual Humans

An autonomous system is a system that is able to give to itself its proper laws, its conduct, as opposed to a heteronomous system which is driven from the outside. Guided virtual humans as introduced in Section 4.5.1.2 are typically driven from the outside. Including autonomous virtual humans that interact with participants increases the real-time interaction with the environment. Therefore, it is likely to increase the sense of presence of the real participants in the environment. The autonomous virtual humans are connected to the VLNET system in the same way as human participants, and also improve the usage of the environment by providing services such as replacing missing partners and helping in navigation. As these virtual humans are not guided by the users, they should have their own behaviour to act autonomously when accomplishing their tasks. This requires building behaviours for motion, as well as appropriate mechanisms for interaction.

Our autonomous virtual humans (Thalmann 1994; Magnenat Thalmann and Thalmann 1995) are able to have a behaviour, which means they must have a manner of conducting themselves. Formally, we can define that the new state vector of the virtual body is a behavioural control function of the previous state vector values:

$$\vartheta(\vartheta_1^i, \vartheta_2^i, ..., \vartheta_N^i), I(I_1, I_2, ...) \rightarrow BEHAVIOURAL\ CONTROL \rightarrow$$
$$\vartheta(\vartheta_1^{i+1}, \vartheta_2^{i+1}, ..., \vartheta_N^{i+1})$$

where $I(I_1, I_2, ...)$ defines the vector of motivation parameters, such as transformation of object of interest, textual communication in the scene, etc.

4.6 Motion Control Implementation

Basic navigation involves using some input device to control walk-through or fly-through motion. In the context of NVEs, this notion is vastly extended, especially when they involve human-like embodiments for the users (Pandzic et al. 1997a). In this context, navigation involves (at least) the following problems:

- Walking or flying
- Basic object manipulation
- Mapping of actions on embodiments
- General input device support
- Implementing constraints

Walking and flying represent navigation in its basic sense, allowing the user to explore the environment from any point of view.

Basic object manipulation capabilities allow the user to pick up and displace objects in the scene. This may be extended by object behaviours that can make objects react in some other way to being picked up.

Mapping of actions on the embodiment is important for two reasons. First, it allows the local user to see what they are doing, e.g. by seeing their hand grab an object. Second, in a multi-user session it allows users to intuitively understand what the others are doing. Mapping of actions on the embodiment involves generation of walking motion while moving, as well as generation of natural arm motion while manipulating objects.

General device support means that it should be straightforward to connect any device to the system. This implies general solutions that will accommodate different kinds of devices, e.g. *incremental* devices like SpaceBall vs. *absolute* devices like magnetic trackers, devices that generate *events* like a button generating a 'grab' event vs. devices generating *states* like a data glove generating a 'grab' state while the fist is tightened.

Constraints are an extremely important component of any navigation. They avoid the user getting lost, turning upside-down or coming into all sorts of impossible situations. They allow the navigation paradigm to be tailored in a precise manner. We divide them into two groups:

- Global motion constraints
- Body posture constraints

The global motion constraints involve some global knowledge of the virtual world (e.g. up direction) and/or collision detection. They determine whether the user can walk or fly, where it is possible to go, and what are the possible orientations. A typical set of constraints for walking might include an inclination constraint keeping the user upright, a vertical collision constraint keeping them on the floor (as well as making it easy to climb and descend stairs or ramps) and a horizontal collision constraint keeping the user from going through the walls.

Body posture constraints keep the user's embodiment in natural-looking postures, e.g. the head can't wander from its position on the shoulders, the arm can reach only that far.

Drivers controlling virtual humans typically connect to both navigation and body interfaces of their VLNET client. This representation introduces constraints sourced by the joint limits and viewing positions. When the participant uses non-immersive input techniques, these constraints become especially crucial. For example, when the participant moves their pick point attached to their right hand in the scene using a mouse, this pick point should not move further than the maximum reach point of the virtual body. This problem is solved as follows: in addition to functions that place new updates in the VLNET external interface, additional functions exist to correct them. When a change occurs in the navigation driver, it activates the update in the navigation interface. The human driver attaches to the same interface, and it receives this update and performs motion control computations (e.g. right arm movement for picking). Depending on the local posture, the human driver corrects the contents of the navigation interface.

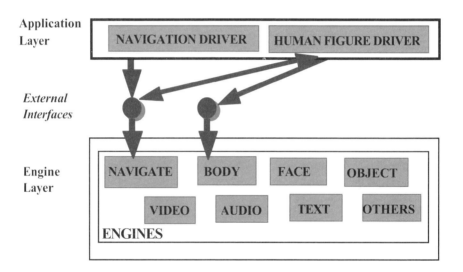

Figure 4-4. Navigation and human drivers are tightly coupled

Finally, the VLNET engines react to the corrected data, instead of their activation. Note that this solution is a convention for general cases, and does not need to be adopted in all cases (for example, the user might want to grasp objects beyond reach).

Thus, the control of the representation takes two steps. In the first step, the navigation driver sets new navigation transformations within the navigation interface. In the second step, these transformations are corrected by the human driver and navigation engine to introduce constraints. Note that navigation and body drivers and engines work in a tightly coupled manner in order to introduce constraints created by the representation (Figure 4-4). Figure 4-5 shows a picking constraint by embodiment. The representation loop is shown in Figure 4-6.

Figure 4-5. The picking constraint introduced by this embodiment allows the action points of users to be visualized clearly

4.6.1 Implementation of Human Animation Drivers

For communication between human drivers and engines, we use two types of function: those that update and read the external interface with new data, and those that correct the contents of the external interface and read these values. The VLNET core processes and the external drivers read the corrected values for processing.

Then the code of drivers and engines takes the form shown in Figure 4-7.

As a result of these steps, the pick and view matrices are set correctly, considering the constraints introduced by virtual human representation. Note that the correction of navigation matrices is optional, and drivers can be developed that omit steps 3 and 5.

4.6.1.1 Implementation of Different Virtual Human Types

We have presented our classification of virtual human control: direct, user-guided, and autonomous. There exists a major difference between directly controlled virtual humans and the other two types. Directly controlled virtual humans modify the degrees of freedom of the body without further knowledge of the animation method (such as keyframe animation, dynamics, etc.). However, the two other types of virtual humans (guided and autonomous) assume an underlying motion control. For example, the walking motor needs to convert the speed value to a step length, and then joint angles. There are basically two approaches for implementing these two types of virtual humans: either build a library of high-level motions inside the VLNET core, or delegate these functionalities into drivers, and let the drivers convert high-level parameters into joint angles. We have selected the second approach as default.

The advantage of delegating high-level control to drivers is that general new high-level motion control techniques can be developed without recompiling VLNET core processes, as only the drivers are developed and integrated during run-time. The disadvantage of this choice is that it may need more bandwidth as joint angles and extra high-level parameters may need to be sent through the network rather than high-level small-size parameters. We solved this problem by introducing the concept of *downloadable drivers*. In this scheme, the motion control program that converts high-level parameter into lower-level parameters is seen as part of the representation of the participant, and this program is downloaded and executed when the new participant connects to the same VE. We discuss this technique in Chapter 6 on networking.

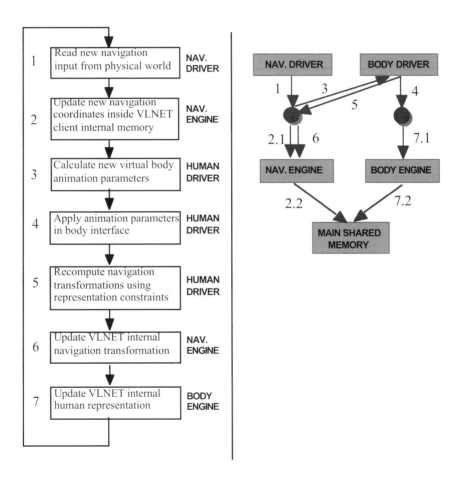

Figure 4-6. Representation loop and configuration of steps

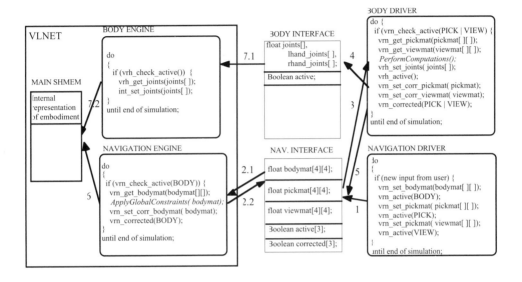

Figure 4-7. Implementation technique for drivers and engines

4.6.1.2 Global Constraints

In the previous section, we have presented the constraints applied on the viewpoint and picking points caused by the virtual human representation. Furthermore, constraints exist caused by the navigation of the participant: the embodiment should be prevented from going through walls, the floor and other objects. The global position of the embodiment should not be inclined more than a predetermined angle from the scene normal. Note that these constraints are by default, and can be turned off by the user if needed.

As these constraints are part of the navigation and should be done within the core considering all the VE scene data, the navigation engine is responsible for performing the computations. At each frame, the navigation engine performs the following computations:

- Global inclination constraint
- Elevation constraint
- Collision constraint

Global Inclination Constraint
This is mainly useful for desktop participants and autonomous virtual humans. It allows the body to be set so that its normal is inclined within a predetermined maximum angle from the scene normal (Figure 4-8).

Figure 4-8. Global inclination constraint inclines the body normal with the scene normal

Elevation Constraint

Elevation constraint is useful for uneven terrain, stairs, etc. (Figure 4-9). It is based on shooting a ray downwards from the body centre, and selecting collisions with the first object, and translating the body down.

Collision Constraint

Collision constraint prevents walking through walls or objects in the scene. It is based on shooting a ray in the direction of walking and detecting the intersection. The source of the ray is the centre of mass of the representation.

4.6.1.3 Direct Control with Flock of Birds

The most direct input corresponding to the participant's physical body is through trackers attached to parts of the body. For this, we use our anatomic converter (Molet et al. 1996). This software permits conversion of the raw tracker transformation matrix data into the state vector containing joint angles. This software is viewed as a body posture driver by the VLNET system, and VLNET communicates with it through the body posture interface. By coupling the Flock of Birds driver with VLNET, we can obtain full gestural communication in a very direct, though intrusive, way. Each frame consists of the stages shown in Figure 4-10.

In Figure 4-10 the first 17 matrices are the transformation values of trackers attached to the body, $\vartheta(\vartheta_1, \vartheta_2, ..., \vartheta_N)$ refers to the state vector of the body, pickmatrix and viewmatrix defined in the navigation interface.

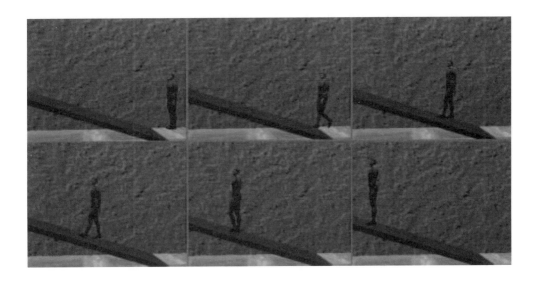

Figure 4-9. Elevation constraint moves the body on the floor

4.6.1.4   Guided Control for Walking

Especially for desktop users and autonomous virtual humans, it is necessary to provide visual tools that demonstrate navigation of the virtual human within the VE. Walking motion gives the action that is visually similar to the physical world, therefore we consider it as the default animation technique for navigation.

For walking, the guided control is achieved as follows. The participant uses the input devices, typically a mouse or a SpaceBall, to update the transformation of the eye position of the virtual actor. This local control is used by computing the incremental change in the body position, and estimating the rotation and velocity of the body centre. The walking motor uses the instantaneous velocity of motion, to compute the walking cycle length and time, by which it computes the necessary joint angles. The motor is based on the HUMANOID walking model, guided by the user interactively or automatically generated by a trajectory. This model can also include kinematical personification depending on the individuality of the user, and it is based on the mathematical parameterization coming from biomechanical experimental data. We refer the reader to Boulic et al. (1990) for detailed description of the walking motor. Figure 4-11 shows an example of walking motion in real time. The model that we are using supports frontal walking and lateral stepping; running, turnaround and backwards stepping are not supported.

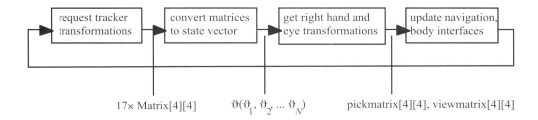

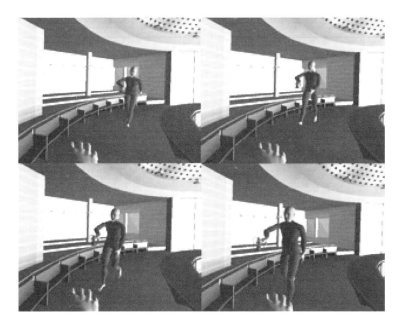

| request tracker transformations | convert matrices to state vector | get right hand and eye transformations | update navigation, body interfaces |

17× Matrix[4][4] $\vartheta(\vartheta_1, \vartheta_2 \dots \vartheta_N)$ pickmatrix[4][4], viewmatrix[4][4]

Figure 4-10. Steps in Flock of Birds driver

Figure 4-11. A real-time walking sequence

The walking motor driver has the structure shown in Figure 4-12. Note that we perform a test to check whether the time elapsed from the last frame is greater than some maximum time, here 0.1 with the assumption of 10 frames per second. This is to smooth out the motion created by using a larger frame rate, which would otherwise produce jerkiness.

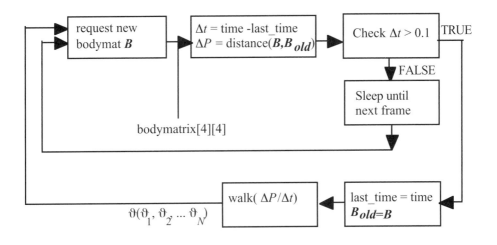

Figure 4-12. Steps in walking motion driver

4.6.1.5 Guided Control for Picking

The arm motion for picking an object is a similar problem to walking: given 6 degrees of freedom (position and orientation) of the sensed right hand with respect to the body coordinate system, the arm motor should compute the joint angles within the right arm. This is more difficult than a simple inverse kinematics problem, because there are generally multiple solutions for the joint angles to reach to the same position, and the most realistic posture should be selected. In addition, the joint constraints should be considered for setting the joint angles. For real-time purposes, we exploit a three-link chain with 7 degrees of freedom within the right arm, with the right shoulder as the root (Figure 4-13). The grasping computations have the structure shown in Figure 4-14.

The step *applyPickLimits* modifies the pick matrix set by the navigation module if it is necessary. This necessity arises if the pick matrix is at a distance greater than the arm length. The algorithm for this step is shown in Figure 4-15.

For the inverse kinematics step, we implemented two solutions: iterative and table lookup solutions. The iterative algorithm is based on the Jacobian matrix. The Jacobian matrix construction is well-defined for articulated structures, and this matrix is used to iteratively solve for joint angles for a given set of end-effectors. The change in joint angle vector is related to change dX by the formula

$$d\vartheta = J^{-1}(dX)$$

This enables us to construct the Jacobian matrix and iterate until the end-effector is reached. See Watt (1992) for details of the solution.

The second approach uses heuristics to obtain approximate arm joint angles, given the position of the right hand. This is done with the help of a precomputed table that divides the normalized volume around the body (Figure 4-16) into a number of discrete subvolumes (e.g. $4 \times 4 \times 4$), and stores a mapping from subvolumes to joint angles in the right arm. This mapping was calculated by experimental observation of a real subject, using a DataGlove and sensors attached to the right arm. The current position of the right hand is used to find the subvolume in which it resides with respect to the body, and the joint values are set using this mapping. Figure 4-17 shows an example using this approach.

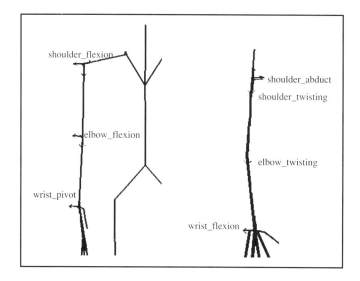

Figure 4-13. Degrees of freedom for the right arm

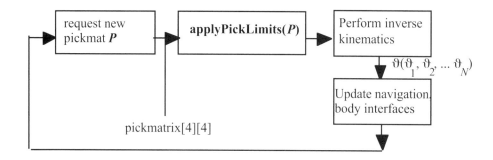

Figure 4-14. Steps for grasping driver

The disadvantages of this method are the extra quantities of subvolume data, which become more difficult to store and more difficult to obtain experimentally with finer discretization of the volume. An extension would be to obtain a more accurate mathematical parameterization of the arm movement, without using the discretization of the space into big subvolumes.

```
if (x<xmin OR x>xmax)
          outside = TRUE;
          if (x<xmin)
                    t = (xmin - xshoulder) / (x - xshoulder)
          else
                    t = (xmax - xshoulder) / (x - xshoulder)
          endif
          tmin = t;
endif
if (y<ymin OR y>ymax)
          outside = TRUE;
          if (y<ymin)
                    t = (ymin - yshoulder) / (y - yshoulder)
          else
                    t = (ymax - yshoulder) / (y - yshoulder)
          endif
          tmin = min(t, tmin);
endif
if (z<zmin OR z>zmax)
          outside = TRUE;
          if (z<zmin)
                    t = (zmin - zshoulder) / (z - zshoulder)
          else
                    t = (zmax - zshoulder) / (z - zshoulder)
          endif
          tmin = min(t, tmin);
endif
if (outside == TRUE)
          x = xshoulder + t * (x - xshoulder);
          y = yshoulder + t * (y - yshoulder);
          z = zshoulder + t * (z - zshoulder);
endif
```

Figure 4-15. Algorithm for applying pick limits

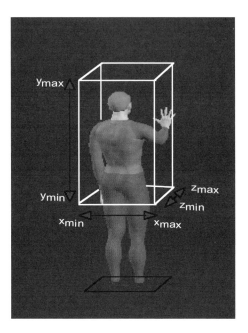

Figure 4-16. Bounding box for pick limits

4.6.1.6 Guided Control for Bending

Using the right arm for manipulating objects has limitations: only objects within reach can be picked up; and it is impossible to reach objects lower down, perhaps on the floor. For moving the hand lower, we have implemented a bending behaviour driver. Bending also uses inverse kinematics as in arm motion, but this is a two-step process. First, the driver checks whether the pick matrix is within the reach of the right arm (i.e. the distance to the shoulder is less than the length of the arm); if this test is false, the spine of the body is adjusted using inverse kinematics so that the shoulder is within an arm's length of the pick matrix. Then, in the second step, the inverse kinematics algorithm is applied in the right arm chain to reach the end-effector, as described above.

4.6.1.7 Guided Control for Breathing

Breathing is a natural behaviour that gives the embodiment its life, removing the robot-like look; therefore we have implemented a breathing behaviour. Although, in physical life, breathing inflates and deforms the outside envelope of the body, we have found a heuristic solution that modifies the upper torso and shoulder angles.

Our breathing behaviour is based on a cyclic linear increase and decrease of particular joint angles. Although using a higher-order function would increase the realism of movements, we realized that the resulting difference is visually negligible, as the joint angle undergoes very small changes within a cycle.

The breathing behaviour generator takes two arguments: breathing cycle length and breathing intensity (Figure 4-18). The algorithm for breathing is shown in Figure 4-19.

Figure 4-17. A real-time grasping sequence created by table lookup solution

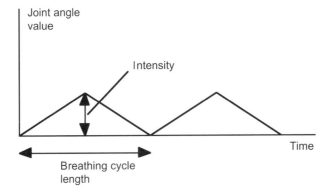

Figure 4-18. Breathing behaviour parameters

```
while (currentTime - prevTime) > cycleLength
        prevTime += cycleLength;
if (currentTime - prevTime) < cycleLength/2
        currentFactor = (currentTime-prevTime)/(cycleLength/2)
else
  currentFactor =
        (prevTime+cycleLength-currentTime)/(cycleLength/2)
endif
joints[VL3] = currentFactor * maxAngle[VL3]
joints[L_CLAV_ABD] = currentFactor*maxAngle[L_CLAV_ABD]
joints[R_CLAV_ABD] = currentFactor*maxAngle[R_CLAV_ABD]
joints[L_SHOU_ABD] = currentFactor*maxAngle[L_SHOU_ABD]
joints[R_SHOU_ABD] = currentFactor*maxAngle[R_SHOU_ABD]
```

Figure 4-19. Breathing algorithm

4.6.2   Combination of Drivers

More than one external driver should normally be able to connect to the human posture interface, and the task of the engine is to resolve conflicts among the external drivers. For example, while the walking motor updates the lower body, the NVE application will control the upper part of the body. The human posture engine should convert these motion effects into a single virtual body posture. This simplifies the development of additional animations consisting of special behaviours.

Motion combination requires that the human posture interface (Figure 4-20) contains parameters for each external driver in addition to body control data. The external driver should be able to define its range within the body parts, and the weight of this driver's output on the final posture for this range.

Our solution to combining motions is transparent to the drivers. The drivers post their values to the shared memory segment associated with them, and the body animation engine combines these values. In addition to joint values, each driver is also associated with a priority, between 1 and 10, and a weight on each joint angle. The default values are 5 for priorities and 1 for weights. The drivers have the right to change their priorities and weights for each joint angle. The algorithm for the drivers is shown in Figure 4-21.

Figure 4-22 shows an example of motion combination, and Figure 4-23 presents the algorithm for reading and combining motions. This algorithm functions as follows. At each frame the client first finds the drivers with highest priority among all drivers. Then it takes a weighted average of joint angles for these drivers. Note that the priority and weight of each joint can change their values at any frame during the course of the session. This gives flexibility for combining motions as actions change.

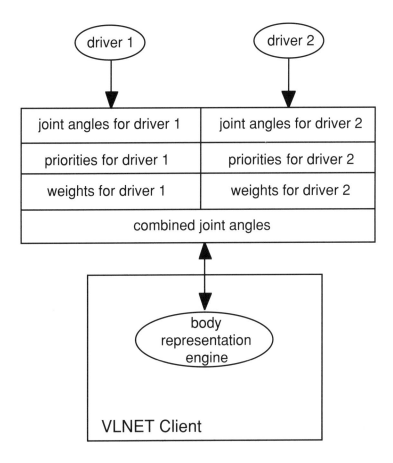

Figure 4-20. Contents of body posture interface for motion combination

```
for each frame {
    Wait for some amount of time to synchronize with client
    Read last joint angles J from body posture interface
    Update local simulation either based on last values of J,
        or independent of last values
    Put joint angles Jmyid to its portion of body interface
}
```

Figure 4-21. Algorithm for body posture driver to update its portion of the body interface

It becomes more complicated to combine different motions if some of the external drivers contain goal-directed motion, as the final posture should satisfy the condition that the goal is reached. For example, when the hand is tracked by an external posture driver while another external driver plays a previously recorded keyframe, the hand position in the posture should be in the tracked position of the actual hand. Therefore, the motion combination should consider correcting the direct-updated posture, so that the difference between the goal position and the effector is minimal. In this book, we have not considered this difficult problem, therefore the position of the virtual hand with respect to the virtual body might not correspond to the position of the real hand with respect to the real body.

Currently, the walking motion and the arm motion are combined in the following way. For the walking motion driver, all the joints belonging to the upper part of the body have the default priority 5. The lower body joints have a higher priority of 6. Therefore, the walking motor's effects are visible on the lower part of the body. Similarly, the arm motion driver has the priority 6 for the right arm joints. The gesture driver has default priorities for the whole body. Therefore, the effects of the gesture driver are added equally with the arm motion and the walking motion for all parts of the body except the walking motor and the right arm.

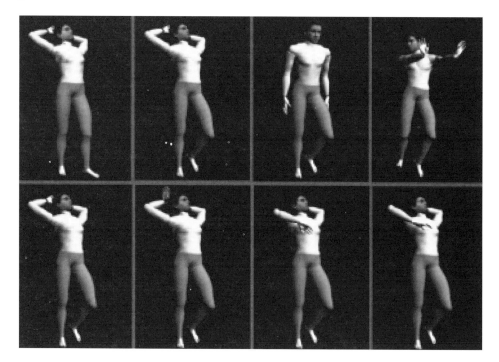

Figure 4-22. A motion combination output; the lower part of the body is animated by the walking driver; the upper body is animated by the non-verbal communication program

This motion combination achieved the initial goal: to provide a solution that is transparent to each driver, i.e. communication is necessary among drivers except for the indirect priorities and weights. In this way, while developing the non-verbal communication application, we did not consider walking and grasping motion implementation. In addition, the solutions generated acceptable results (Figure 4-22). However, problems sometimes appeared while merging the inverse kinematics driver of the right arm and a posture that involved extreme joint angles of the right arm. The solution for these anomalies would be to implement a more complex body posture driver: postures generally use only a portion of the joint angles, and the body posture should detect the joints that are used in the current posture/gesture, increasing the priority for these joints.

```
max_p: array of maximum driver priority value for each joint
total_w: array of maximum driver priority value for each joint
no_max_drivers: array of no of drivers with max priority
final_value: array of final joint value for each joint
for each frame {
        for (i =1 to no_drivers) do
        {
                Read joint angles array for driver i: J_i
                Read joint priorities array for driver i: P_i
                Read joint weights array for driver i: W_i
                for (j=1 to no_joint_angles) do {
                        if (P_ij > max_p_j)
                                max_p_j = P_ij
                                total_w_j = W_ij
                                no_max_drivers_j = 1
                        else if (P_ij = max_p_j)
                                total_w_j = total_w_j + W_ij
                                no_max_drivers_j = no_max_drivers_j + 1
                        endif
                }
        }

        for (j=1 to no_joint_angles) do {
                final_value_j = total_w_j / no_max_drivers_j
        }
}
```

Figure 4-23. Algorithm for VLNET client to combine effects of different drivers

4.7 Autonomous and Interactive Perceptive Actors

4.7.1 Perception and Action

We have seen that autonomous actors are able to have behaviours or a manner of conducting themselves. Behaviour is not only reacting to the environment but should also include the flow of information by which the environment acts on the living creature as well as the way the creature codes and uses this information. If we consider the synthetic environment as made of 3D geometric shapes, one solution to this problem is to give the actor access to the exact position of each object in the complete environment database corresponding to the synthetic world. This solution could work for a very 'small world', but it becomes impracticable when the number of objects increases. Moreover, this approach does not correspond to reality where people do not have knowledge about the complete environment. Another approach has been proposed by Reynolds (1987): the synthetic actor has knowledge about the environment located in a sphere centred on him or her. Moreover, the accuracy of the knowledge about the objects of the environment decreases with the distance. This is of course a more realistic approach, but as mentioned by Reynolds, around an animal or a human there are always areas where sensitivity is more important. Consider the vision of birds; they have a view angle of 300° and a stereoscopic view of only 15°. The sphere model does not correspond to the sensitivity area of bird vision. Reynolds goes one step further and states that if actors can see their environment, they will improve their trajectory planning. This means that the vision is a realistic information flow. Unfortunately, what is realistic for a human being walking in a corridor seems unrealistic for a computer. However, using hardware developments, it is possible to give a geometric description of 3D objects together with the viewpoint and the interest point of a synthetic actor in order to get the vision on the screen. This vision may then be interpreted like the synthetic actor vision. More generally, in order to implement perception, virtual humans should be equipped with *virtual sensors*.

Perception is defined as the awareness of the elements of environment through physical sensation. In order to implement perception, virtual actors should be equipped with visual, tactile and auditory sensors. These sensors should be used as a basis for implementing everyday human behaviour such as visually directed locomotion, handling objects, and responding to sounds and utterances. For synthetic audition, we begin by modelling a sound environment where the synthetic actor can directly access to positional and semantic sound source information of audible sound event. Simulating the haptic system corresponds roughly to a collision detection process. But the most important perceptual subsystem is the vision system. A vision-based approach for virtual humans is a very important perceptual subsystem and is essential for navigation in virtual worlds. It is an ideal approach for modelling a behavioural animation and offers a universal approach to pass the necessary information from the environment to the virtual human in the problems of path searching, obstacle avoidance and internal knowledge representation with learning and forgetting.

Typically, the actor should perceive the objects and the other actors in the environment through virtual sensors: visual, tactile and auditory. Based on the perceived information, the actor's behavioural mechanism will determine the actions they will perform. An actor may simply evolve in their environment or they may interact with this environment or even communicate with other actors. In this latter case, we will consider the actor as an *interactive perceptive actor* (Thalmann 1996).

4.7.2 Virtual Vision

Although the use of vision to give behaviour to synthetic actors seems similar to the use of vision for intelligent mobile robots (Horswill 1993; Tsuji and Li 1993), it is quite different. This is because the vision of the synthetic actor is itself a synthetic vision. Using a synthetic vision allows us to skip all the problems of pattern recognition and distance detection, problems which are still the most difficult aspects of robot vision. However, some interesting work has been done on the topic of intelligent mobile robots, especially for action–perception coordination problems. Crowley (1987), working with surveillance robots, states that 'most low level perception and navigation tasks are algorithmic in nature; at the highest levels, decisions regarding which actions to perform are based on knowledge relevant to each situation'. This remark gives us the hypothesis on which our vision-based model of behavioural animation is built.

We first introduced (Renault et al. 1990) the concept of synthetic vision as a main information channel between the environment and the virtual actor. Reynolds (1993) more recently described an evolved, vision-based behavioural model of coordinated group motion; he also showed (Reynolds 1994) how obstacle avoidance behaviour can emerge from evolution under selection pressure from an appropriate measure using a simple computational model of visual perception and locomotion. Tu and Terzopoulos (1994) use a kind of synthetic vision for artificial fishes.

In Renault et al. (1990) each pixel of the vision input has the semantic information giving the object projected on this pixel, and numerical information giving the distance to this object. So it is easy to know, for example, that there is a table just in front at 3 m. With this information, we can directly deal with the problematic question, What do I do with such information in a navigation system? The synthetic actor perceives their environment from a small window of typically 30×30 pixels in which the environment is rendered from their point of view. As they can access z buffer values of the pixels, the colour of the pixels and their own position, they can locate visible objects in their 3D environment. This information is sufficient for some local navigation.

We can model a certain type of virtual world representation where the actor maintains a low-level fast synthetic vision system but where they can access some important information directly from the environment without having to extract it from the vision image. In vision-based grasping, for example, an actor can recognize in the image the object to grasp. From the environment they can get the exact position, type and size of the object; this allows them to walk to the correct position, where they can start the grasping procedure of the object based on geometrical data of the object representation in the world. This mix of vision-based recognition and world representation access will make the actor fast enough to react in real time. The role of synthetic vision can even be reduced to a visibility test and the semantic information recognition in the image can be done by simple colour coding and non-shading rendering techniques. Thus, position and semantic information of an object can be obtained directly from the environment world after being filtered.

4.7.3 Virtual Audition

In real life the behaviour of persons or animals is very often influenced by sounds. For this reason, we developed a framework for modelling a 3D acoustic environment with sound sources and microphones. Now our virtual actors are able to hear (Noser and Thalmann 1995). Any sound source (synthetic or real) should be converted to the AIFF format and processed by the sound renderer. The sound renderer takes into account the real-time constraints. So it can render each time increment for each microphone in 'real time' by taking into account the final propagation speed of sound and the moving sound sources and microphones. So the Doppler effect is audible, for example.

4.7.4 Virtual Haptic

One of our aims is to build a behavioural model based on tactile sensory input received at the level of skin from the environment. This sensory information can be used in tasks such as touching objects, pressing buttons or kicking objects For example, at the basic level, humans should sense physical objects if any part of the body touches them, and they should gather sensory information. This sensory information is employed in tasks such as reaching out for an object and navigation. For example, if a human is standing, the feet are in constant contact with the supporting floor. But during walking motion each foot alternately experiences the loss of this contact. Traditionally these motions are simulated using dynamic and kinematic constraints on human joints. But there are cases where information from the external environment is needed. For example, when a human descends a staircase, the motion should change from walk to descent, based on achieving contact with the steps of the stairway. Thus the environment imposes constraints on the human locomotion. We propose to encapsulate these constraints using tactile sensors to guide the human figure in various complex situations besides normal walking.

As already mentioned, simulating the haptic system corresponds roughly to a collision detection process. In order to simulate sensorial tactile events, a module has been designed to define a set of solid objects and a set of sensor points attached to an actor. The sensor points can move around in space and collide with the solid objects. Collisions are not detected if they occur with objects that do not belong to this set. The only objective of collision detection is to inform the actor that there is a contact detected with an object and which object it is. Standard collision detection tests rely on bounding boxes or bounding spheres for efficient simulation of object interactions. A very important but special case is the contact between the hands and objects during the grasping process. Our approach (Huang et al. 1995) is based on multi-sensors. These sensors are considered as a group of objects attached to the articulated figure. A sensor is activated for any collision with other objects or sensors. Here we select sphere sensors for their efficiency in collision detection. The sphere multi-sensors have both tactile and length sensor properties. Each sphere sensor is fitted to its associated joint shape with different radii. This configuration is important in our method because when a sensor is activated in a finger, only the articulations above it stop moving, whereas others can still move. By doing it this way, all the fingers are finally positioned naturally around the object.

Based on virtual sensors, typically vision sensors, the actor decides which object to grasp. The actor may have to walk in order to be near to the object.

Based on a grasp taxonomy (Mas and Thalmann 1994), an automatic system decides the way the actor grasps the object. For example, the system decides to use a pinch when the object is too small to be grasped by more than two fingers or to use two hands when the object is large. Inverse kinematics is used to find the final arm posture. Using multi-sensors, the fingers are adjusted in order to have an accurate grasp (see Figure 4-24).

Figure 4-24. Grasping different objects

4.7.5 Interactive Perceptive Actors

We define an interactive perceptive synthetic actor (Thalmann 1996) as an actor aware of other actors and real people. Such an actor is also assumed to be autonomous. Moreover, they are able to communicate interactively with the other actors, whatever their type, and the real people.

4.7.6 Intercommunication between Synthetic Actors

Behaviours may also depend on the emotional state of the actor. We have also developed a model of non-verbal communication (Bécheiraz and Thalmann 1996). The believability of virtual actors is improved by their capability to interpret and use a non-verbal language. A non-verbal communication is concerned with postures and their indications of what people are feeling. Postures are a means to communicate and are defined by a specific position of the arms and legs and the angles of the body. Usually, people don't consciously use non-verbal communication, but they instinctively understand it to a considerable extent and they respond to it without any explicit reasoning. This non-verbal communication is essential to drive the interaction between people (Figures 4-25 and 4-26).

Figure 4-25. Non-verbal communication

4.7.7 Sensing the Real World for a Synthetic Actor

The real people are of course easily aware of the actions of the virtual humans through VR tools like head-mounted displays, but one major problem to solve is to make the virtual humans conscious of the behaviour of the real people. Virtual humans should sense the participants through their virtual sensors. Such a perceptive actor would be independent of each VR representation and, in the same manner, they could communicate with participants and other perceptive actors. Perceptive actors and participants may easily be exchanged, as demonstrated in Section 8.2 on virtual tennis. For virtual audition, the real-time constraints in VR demand fast reaction to sound signals and fast recognition of the semantic it carries. Concerning the tactile sensor, we may consider the following example. The participant places an object into the virtual space using a CyberGlove and the autonomous virtual actor will try to grasp it and put it on a virtual table. The actor interacts with the environment by grasping the object and moving it.

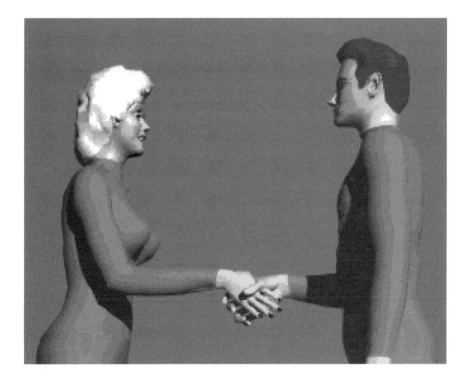

Figure 4-26. Interaction between two actors

As an example, we have produced a fight between a real person and an autonomous actor. The motion of the real person is captured using a Flock of Birds. The gestures are recognized by the system (Emering et al. 1997) and the information is transmitted to the virtual actor, who is able to react to the gestures and decide which attitude to assume. Figure 4-27 shows an example.

Figure 4-27. Fight between a participant and an interactive perceptive actor

4.7.8 Towards 'Intelligent' Actors

A high-level behaviour generally uses sensorial input and specialist knowledge. A way of modelling behaviours is to use automata. Each actor has an internal state which can change at each time step according to the currently active automata and the actor's sensorial input. In the following we use 'behaviour' and 'automata' as synonyms. To control the global behaviour of an actor, we use a stack of automata. At the beginning of the animation, the user provides a sequence of behaviours (the script) and pushes them on the actor's stack. When the current behaviour ends, the animation system pops the next behaviour from the stack and executes it. This process is repeated until the actor's behaviour stack is empty. Some of the behaviours use this stack too, in order to reach subgoals by pushing themselves with the current state on the stack and switching to the new behaviour, allowing them to reach the subgoal. When this new behaviour has finished the automata pop the old interrupted behaviour and continue. This behaviour control using a stack allows an actor to become more autonomous and to create their own subgoals while executing the original script.

Introducing seemingly autonomous virtual beings into virtual environments to cohabit and collaborate with us is a continuous challenge and source of interest. The latest proof of human excitement for virtual life is the current worldwide craze for electronic pets that must be fed and cared for lest they develop a bad character or die. Even more interesting is the inclusion of autonomous actors in NVEs. They provide a meeting place for people from different geographical locations and virtual beings. In NVEs we do not see our correspondents, only their graphical representations in the virtual world; the same goes for the virtual beings. Therefore the communication with virtual beings can come naturally. These computer-controlled, seemingly autonomous creatures would inhabit the virtual worlds, make them more interesting, and help users to find their way or perform a particular task. For example, a virtual shop might have an autonomous virtual shopkeeper to help the customer find whatever they want to buy; complex virtual environments might have guides to lead visitors and answer questions; in a game, an opponent or a referee might be an autonomous virtual actor.

4.7.9   Interfacing Autonomous Virtual Humans with the NVE

The behaviour of the autonomous virtual human is typically affected by the VE. The autonomous actor program needs to receive the state of the VE from the NVE system. The input can be through synthetic sensors, such as the transformation of objects in the VE, but it can also be a natural language text interface.

The NVE system should be open, allowing the developer of the autonomous actor program to choose whichever animation technique they want: the developer should have minimum concern about the other details of the NVE, and the autonomous virtual human program should not depend on a specific approach. The behaviours should be easily extensible, not limited to predefined behaviours.

As NVE systems are already very complex themselves, our approach to autonomous behaviours (AB) in NVEs is interfacing the two systems externally rather than trying to integrate them completely in a single large system. Such an approach also facilitates the development of various AB systems to be used with a single NVE system, making it a test bed for various algorithms.

This interfacing leads to a kind of symbiosis between an NVE system and an AB system, where the AB system provides the brains and the NVE system provides the body to move around, be seen and act upon objects, but also to see, hear and get the external information to the brain (Figure 4-28). In order to implement this strategy, the NVE system must provide an external interface to which AB systems can be hooked. This interface should be as simple as possible to allow easy connection of various autonomous behaviours. At the same time it should satisfy the basic requirements for a successful symbiosis of an NVE system and an AB system: allow the AB system to control its embodiment and act upon the environment, as well as gathering information from the environment upon which to act.

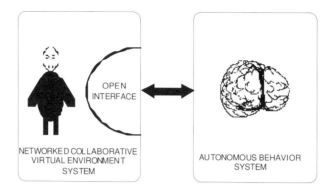

Figure 4-28. Symbiosis between the AB and NVE systems

We study the functionalities that the NVE system must provide to the AB system through the open interface. We have identified the following important functionalities that must be provided for a successful symbiosis:

- Embodiment
- Locomotion
- Capacity to act upon objects
- Feedback from the environment
- Verbal communication
- Facial communication
- Gestural communication

Embodiment, or a graphical representation, is a fundamental requirement to allow the presence of the virtual actor in the environment. Though this can be a very simple graphical representation (e.g. a textured cube), some of the more advanced functionalities (e.g. facial and gestural communication) require a more human-like structure as support.

Locomotion is necessary for getting from one place to another, and might involve generation of walking motion or simple sliding around. Essentially, the AB system must be able to control the position of the embodiment in the environment.

Capacity to act upon objects in the environment is important because it allows the AB system to interact with the environment. The interface should provide at least the possibility to grab and move objects.

Without some feedback from the environment, our virtual actors might be autonomous but blind and deaf. It is essential for them to be able to gather information from the environment about objects and other users.

If the AB system is to simulate virtual humans, it is necessary for real humans to be able to communicate with them through our most common communication channel, i.e. verbal communication. Because the audio signal might in most cases be meaningless to the AB system, ASCII text seems to be the most convenient way to interface verbal communication to and from the AB system. This does not exclude the possibility of a speech recognition/synthesis interface on the human end, allowing us to actually talk to the virtual actors.

Finally, it is desirable for a virtual actor to have the capacity of facial and gestural communication and therefore the ability to have a more natural behaviour by showing emotions on the face or passing messages through gestures.

5 Facial and Gestural Communication

5.1 Introduction

Facial expressions play an important role in human communication. They can express the speaker's emotions and subtly change the meaning of what was said. At the same time, lip movement is an important aid to the understanding of speech, especially if the audio conditions are not perfect or in the case of a hearing-impaired listener. Also gestural communication may be essential, especially in the case of non-verbal communication. In Section 1.4, we have already stressed the importance of facial and gestural communication in NVEs. Here we outline the technical challenges involved in supporting them, concentrating more on facial communication.

The problem of communication in an NVE can be split into three parts: data acquisition, transmission and reproduction. To illustrate this using a simple example, in a telephone conversation the data acquisition is done by a microphone—audio signal is transmitted through the network and reproduced by a loudspeaker in the handset on the other side.

For both facial and gestural communication in an NVE system the reproduction is done by means of a virtual human model, where body and face can interpret postures, gestures and facial expressions. The transmission involves expressing gestures and expressions in a form that can be transmitted digitally.

The hardest problem is in fact data acquisition: How does the user input gestures and expressions? Ideally, this would be done by performing them in the natural way without any constraints. The problem is how to capture the movement. The 'obvious' solution is to use one or more cameras to capture the user and analyse the video frames to extract the movement. However, this is quite a difficult computer vision task, especially for the tracking of body postures. The results can be greatly improved by using coloured markers on the body and face. However, this method cannot be classified as non-intrusive. It is unrealistic to expect the users to paint their faces in order to use an NVE system.

For the acquisition of gestures, it is quite common to use magnetic trackers placed on the body. They can track body motion in real time. However, current tracker models are connected by wires and are cumbersome to put on and wear.

A simple solution for data acquisition is letting the user choose from a set of predefined gestures, postures and facial expressions. This approach matches well with explicit behaviour transmission, although the movements can also be generated locally and transmitted.

When talking about facial and gestural communication in a networked setting, it is difficult to avoid comparison with common videoconferencing systems. Obviously, as people can see each other, facial expressions and gestures are perceived naturally. However, videoconferencing lacks the capabilities of the NVE systems to simulate a 3D environment and allow users to interact with 3D objects as well as with each other. Also, if more than two users participate in a videoconferencing session, each user sees a number of windows on their screen, each window showing one participant, making the spatial relationship between participants confusing. On the other hand, video does provide a very good solution for acquisition, transmission and reproduction of facial expressions. Therefore, in situations where the additional bandwidth required for video can be afforded, it is worth considering a hybrid approach. The hybrid approach might transmit the facial expressions in the form of video and integrate the video in the 3D environment instead of showing it simply in a window. In this approach the video may be placed in a logical place in the virtual environment (i.e. on the face of the virtual human representation), keeping the spatial relationship between the users.

In the next section, we explain the role of minimum perceptible actions in facial animation. Then, in the following sections, we discuss four methods of integrating facial expressions in an NVE: video texturing of the face, model-based coding of facial expressions, lip movement synthesis from speech and predefined expressions or animations. The methods vary in computational and bandwidth requirements, quality of the reproduced facial expressions and means of data acquisition. Therefore they are suitable for different situations an applications. We discuss merits, drawbacks and potential applications of each method.

5.2 Facial Animation Using MPAs

Facial animation, as any other animation, typically involves execution of a sequence of a set of basic facial actions. We use what we call a minimum perceptible action (MPA) as a basic facial motion parameter. Each MPA has a corresponding set of visible movements of different parts of the face resulting from muscle contraction. Muscular activity is simulated using rational free-form deformations (Kalra et al. 1992). MPAs also include actions like head turning and nodding. An MPA can be considered as an atomic action unit similar to AU (action unit) of FACS (Facial Action Coding System) (Ekman and Friesen 1967), execution of which results in a visible and perceptible change in a face. We can aggregate a set of MPAs and define expressions and phonemes. Furthermore they can be used for defining emotion and sentences for speech. Animation at the lowest level, however, is specified as a sequence of MPAs with their respective intensities and time of occurrence. The discrete action units defined in terms of MPAs can be used as fundamental building blocks or reference units for the development of a parametric facial process. Development of the basic motion actions is non-specific to a facial topology and provides a general approach for the modelling and animation of the primary facial expressions. In our facial model the skin surface of the face is considered as a polygonal mesh. Hence the model considered has sufficient complexity and irregularity to represent a virtual face, and is not merely represented as a crude mask as considered in many other systems.

For the real-time performance-driven facial animation, the input parameters to the facial animation are the MPAs. These MPAs have normalized intensities between 0 and 1 or −1 and 1. The analysis of the recognition module is mapped appropriately to these MPAs. In most cases the mapping is straightforward. Due to the speed constraint, we have concentrated on only a few parameters for the motion. This reduces the degrees of freedom for the animation. However, we believe that a complete range of facial motion is in practice not present in any particular sequence of animation. It is possible to mimic the motion of a real performance using only a set of parameters . Table 5-1 shows the complete list of MPAs.

With the input from real performance, as described in Section 5.3, we are able to reproduce individual features on the synthetic actor's face in real time (e.g. raising the eyebrows and opening the mouth). However, reproducing these features together might not

Table 5-1. Minimal perceptible actions

MPA name	MPA description	Bidirectional (B) or unidirectional (U)	Direction of movement for positive intensities [a]
move_h_l_eyeball	Horizontal movement of the left eyeball	B	Right
move_h_r_eyeball	Horizontal movement of the right eyeball	B	Right
move_h_eyeballs	Horizontal movement of both eyeballs	B	Right
move_v_l_eyeball	Vertical movement of the left eyeball	B	Downward
move_v_r_eyeball	Vertical movement of the right eyeball	B	Downward
move_v_eyeballs	Vertical movement of both eyeballs	B	Downward
close_upper_l_eyelid	Vertical movement of the upper left eyelid	B	Downward
close_upper_r_eyelid	Vertical movement of the upper right eyelid	B	Downward
close_upper_eyelids	Vertical movement of both upper eyelids	B	Downward
close_lower_l_eyelid	Vertical movement of the lower left eyelid	B	Upward
close_lower_r_eyelid	Vertical movement of the lower right eyelid	B	Upward
close_lower_eyelids	Vertical movement of both lower eyelids	B	Upward
raise_l_eyebrow	Vertical movement of the left eyebrow	B	Upward
raise_r_eyebrow	Vertical movement of the right eyebrow	B	Upward
raise_eyebrows	Vertical movement of both eyebrows	B	Upward
raise_l_eyebrow_l	Vertical movement of left part of left eyebrow	B	Upward
raise_r_eyebrow_l	Vertical movement of left part of right eyebrow	B	Upward
raise_eyebrows_l	Vertical movement of left part of both eyebrows	B	Upward
raise_l_eyebrow_m	Vertical movement of middle part of left eyebrow	B	Upward
raise_r_eyebrow_m	Vert. movement of middle part of right eyebrow	B	Upward
raise_eyebrows_m	Vert. movement of middle part of both eyebrows	B	Upward
raise_l_eyebrow_r	Vertical movement of right part of left eyebrow	B	Upward
raise_r_eyebrow_r	Vertical movement of right part of right eyebrow	B	Upward
raise_eyebrows_r	Vertical movement of right part of both eyebrows	B	Upward
squeeze_l_eyebrow	Horizontal movement of the left eyebrow	U	Toward face centre
squeeze_r_eyebrow	Horizontal movement of the right eyebrow	U	Left

Table 5-1. *Continued*

squeeze_eyebrows	Horizontal movement of both eyebrows	U	Right
move_o_l_eyeball	Outside/inside movement of the left eyeball	B	Forward
move_o_r_eyeball	Outside/inside movement of the right eyeball	B	Forward
move_o_eyeballs	Outside/inside movement of both eyeballs	B	Forward
open_jaw	Vertical movement of the jaw	U	Downward
move_hori_jaw	Horizontal movement of the jaw	B	Right
depress_chin	Upward and compressing movement of the chin (like in sadness)	U	Upward
raise_l_cornerlip	Vertical movement of the left corner of the lips	U	Upward
raise_r_cornerlip	Vertical movement the right corner of the lips	U	Upward
raise_cornerlips	Vertical movement the corners of the lips	U	Upward
puff_l_cheek	Puffing movement of the left cheek	B	Left
puff_r_cheek	Puffing movement of the right cheek	B	Right
puff_cheeks	Puffing movement of both cheeks	B	Towards face edges
lift_l_cheek	Lifting movement of the left cheek	U	Upward
lift_r_cheek	Lifting movement of the right cheek	U	Upward
lift_cheeks	Lifting movement of both cheeks	U	Upward
lower_l_cornerlip	Vertical movement of the left corner of the lips	U	Downward
lower_r_cornerlip	Vertical movement of the right corner of the lips	U	Downward
lower_cornerlips	Vertical movement of the corners of the lips	U	Downward
raise_upperlip	Vertical movement of the upper lip	U	Upward
lower_lowerlip	Vertical movement of the lower lip	U	Downward
raise_u_midlip	Vertical movement of middle part of the upper lip	U	Upward
raise_l_midlip	Vertical movement of middle part of the lower lip	U	Upward
raise_midlips	Vertical movement of the middle part of the lips	U	Upward
pull_midlips	Protruding movement of the mouth (like when producing 'ou' sound)	U	Forward
stretch_cornerlips	Stretch the corners of the lips	U	Toward face edges
stretch_l_cornerlip	Stretch the left corner of the lips	U	Left
stretch_r_cornerlip	Stretch the right corner of the lips	U	Right
suck_lips	Inward movement of the lips (like when producing the 'm' sound)	U	Backward
squeeze_cornerlips	Squeeze the corners of the lips	U	Toward face centre
squeeze_l_cornerlip	Squeeze the left corner of the lips	U	Right
squeeze_r_cornerlip	Squeeze the right corner of the lips	U	Left
stretch_nose	Stretch/squeeze movement of the nose	B	Toward face edges
raise_nose	Vertical movement of the nose	U	Upward
turn_head	Turning movement of the head	B	Right
nod_head	Nodding movement of the head	B	Down
roll_head	Rolling movement of the head	B	Clockwise

[a]The directions are expressed with respect to the gaze direction of the face.

faithfully reproduce the overall facial emotion (smile, surprise, etc.). In order to achieve this, a better interpreting or analysing layer between recognition and simulation may be included. A real performance to animate a synthetic face is one kind of input accessory used for our multimodal animation system. The system can capture the initial template of animation from a real performance with accurate temporal characteristics. This motion template can then be modified, enhanced and complemented as required by other accessories in order to produce the final animation.

5.3   Video Texturing of the Face

In this approach, the video sequence of the user's face is continuously texture-mapped onto the face of the virtual human. The user must be in front of the camera in such a position that the camera captures their head and shoulders. A simple and fast image analysis algorithm is used to find the bounding box of the user's face within the image. The algorithm requires that the head-and-shoulder view is provided and that the background is static (though not necessarily uniform). Thus the algorithm primarily consists of comparing each image with the original image of the background. Since the background is static, any change in the image is caused by the presence of the user, so it is fairly easy to detect their position. This allows the user a reasonably free movement in front of the camera without the facial image being lost.

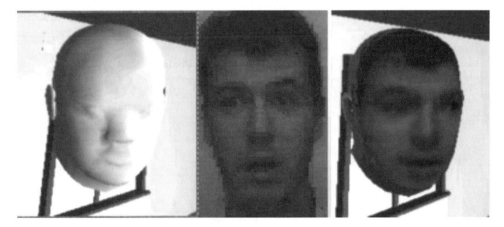

Figure 5-1. Texture mapping of the face

The VLNET video interface is used to pass textures to VLNET, and the video engines (Section 3.2.3) of all VLNET clients in the session receive the texture and map it onto the face of the user's embodiment. The texture mapping is illustrated in Figure 5-1, which shows the face model without the texture, the image used as texture and the final texture-mapped result. We use a simple frontal projection for texture mapping. A simplified head model with attenuated features is used. This allows for less precise texture mapping: if the head model with all the facial features is used, any misalignment of the topological features in the 3D model and the features in the texture produces quite unnatural artifacts.

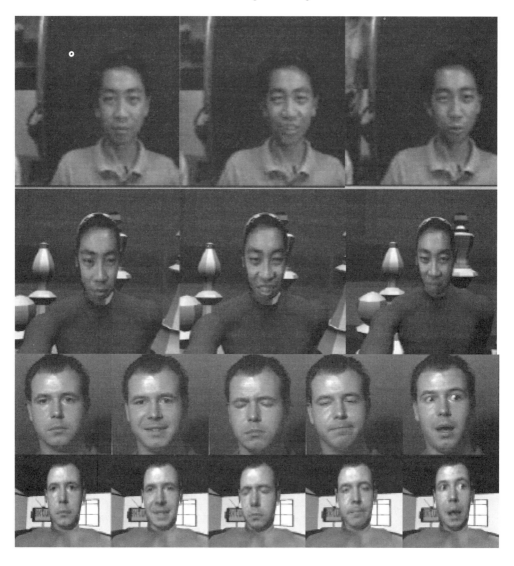

Figure 5-2. Video texturing of the face: some examples

Figure 5-2 illustrates the video texturing of the face, showing the original images of the user and the corresponding images of the virtual human representation.

The video texturing method achieves high quality of reproduced facial expressions. The bandwidth requirements are relatively high, though still lower than for a classical videoconferencing systems because of the small size of the image. The computational complexity is increased because of the compression/decompression algorithms. Notice that this method allows tradeoffs between bandwidth and CPU resources by changing the parameters of the compression algorithm. A potential application is the extension of videoconferencing to 3D virtual spaces with the additional capability of collaborative work on 3D objects.

5.4   Model-Based Coding of Facial Expressions

Instead of transmitting whole facial images as in the previous approach, in model-based coding the images are analysed and a set of parameters describing the facial expression is extracted (Pandzic et al. 1994). As in the previous approach, the user has to be in front of the camera that digitizes the head-and-shoulders video images.

Recognition of facial expressions is a very complex and interesting subject. There have been numerous research efforts in this area. Mase and Pentland (1990) applied optical flow and principal direction analysis for lip reading. Terzopoulos and Waters (1991) reported on techniques using deformable curves for estimating face muscle contraction parameters from video sequences. Waters and Terzopoulos (1991) modelled and animated faces using scanned data obtained from a radial laser scanner and used muscle contraction parameters estimated from video sequences. Saji et al. (1992) introduced a new method called lighting switch photometry to extract 3D shapes from the moving face. Kato et al. (1992) used isodensity maps for the description and the synthesis of facial expressions. Most of these techniques do not perform the information extraction in real time. There have been some implementations of facial expression recognition using coloured markers painted on the face and/or lipstick (Magno Caldognetto et al. 1989; Patterson et al. 1991; Kishino 1994). However, the use of markers is not practical, so methods are required to perform recognition without them. In another approach, Azarbayejani et al. (1993) used an extended Kalman filter formulation to recover motion parameters of an object. However, the motion parameters include only head position and orientation. Li et al. (1993) use the Candid model for 3D motion estimation for model-based image coding. The size of the geometric model is limited to only 100 triangles which is rather low for characterizing the shape of a particular model.

Magnenat-Thalmann et al. (1993) propose a real-time recognition method based on snakes as introduced by Terzopoulos and Waters (1991). The main drawback of this approach is that the method relies on the information from the previous frame in order to extract the next one. This can lead to accumulation of error and the snake may completely lose the contour it is supposed to follow. To improve the robustness, we adopt a different approach where each frame can be processed independently from the previous one.

Accurate recognition and analysis of facial expressions from a video sequence requires detailed measurements of facial features. Currently, it is computationally expensive to perform these measurements precisely. As our primary concern has been to extract the features in real time, we have focused our attention on recognition and analysis of only a few facial features.

The recognition method relies on the soft mask, which is a set of points adjusted interactively by the user on the image of the face. Using the mask, various characteristic measures of the face are calculated at the time of initialization. Colour samples of the skin, background, hair, etc., are also registered. Recognition of the facial features is primarily based on colour sample identification and edge detection. Based on characteristics of the human face, variations of these methods are used in order to find the optimal adaptation for the particular case of each facial feature. Special care is taken to make the recognition of one frame independent from the recognition of the previous one, in order to avoid the accumulation of error. The data extracted from the previous frame is used only for the features that are relatively easy to track (e.g. the neck edges), making the risk of error accumulation low. A reliability test is performed and the data is reinitialized if necessary. This makes the recognition very robust. Here are the extracted parameters:

- Vertical head rotation (nod)
- Horizontal head rotation (turn)
- Head inclination (roll)
- Aperture of the eyes
- Horizontal position of the iris
- Eyebrow elevation
- Distance between the eyebrows (eyebrow squeeze)
- Jaw rotation
- Mouth aperture
- Mouth stretch or squeeze

The following sections describe the initialization of the system and the details of the recognition method for each facial feature, as well as the verification of the extracted data. The recognition of the features and the data verification are presented in the order of execution, as shown schematically in Figure 5-3.

5.4.1   Initialization

Initialization is done on a still image of the face grabbed with a neutral expression. The soft mask is placed over the image as shown in Figure 5-4. The points of the mask are interactively adjusted to the characteristic features of the face, such as mouth, eyes and eyebrows. These points determine the measures of the face with neutral expression and provide colour samples of the background and the facial features. The process of setting the mask is straightforward and usually takes less than half a minute.

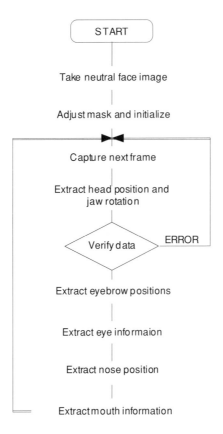

Figure 5-3. Flow chart of the facial recognition method

5.4.2 Head Tracking

The first step is to find the edges of the neck (blue circles in Figure 5-5, points N1 and N2 in Figure 5-6). During the initialization, colour samples are taken at points 1, 2 and 3 of the mask (Figure 5-4). Points 1 and 3 are aligned over background and skin respectively, and point 2 over the hair falling on the side of the face, if any. During recognition, a sample taken from the analysed point of the image is compared with those three samples and identified as one of them. As each colour sample consists of three values (red, green and blue), it can be regarded as a point in a three-dimensional RGB space. The distance in this space between the sample being analysed and each stored sample is calculated. The closest one is chosen to categorize the point. This method of sample identification works fine in the areas where the number of possible different colours is small and where there is sufficient difference between the colours.

The next step is to find the hairline (point M in Figure 5-6). The samples of the hair and skin colour are taken and the edge between the two is detected. The horizontal position of the starting point is halfway between the neck edges, and the vertical position is taken from the previous frame. At a fixed distance below the hairline, the edges of the hair seen on the sides of the forehead are detected (marked with circles in Figure 5-5, points L1, L2, R1, R2 in Figure 5-6) using the sample identification method described above.

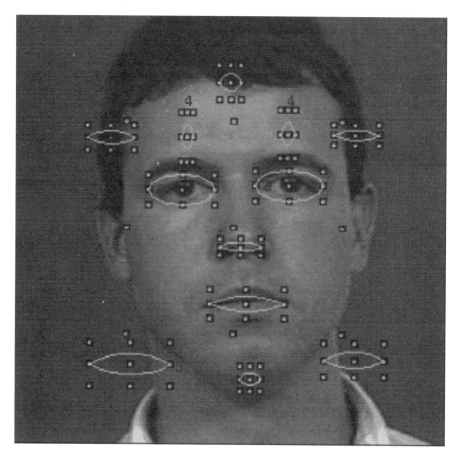

Figure 5-4. Recognition initialization: neutral face with the soft mask

Using the information from points L1, L2, R1, R2, N1, N2 and M (Figure 5-6) we estimate the head orientation for different movements. For example:

head turn = f(L1, L2, R1, R2)
head nod = f(M)
head roll = f(L1, L2, R1, R2, N1, N2)

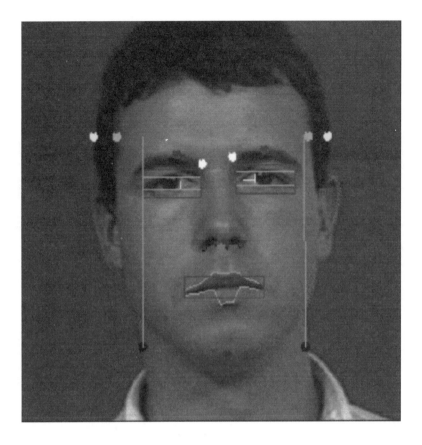

Figure 5-5. Face with recognition markers

5.4.3 Jaw Rotation

To extract the rotation of the jaw, the position of the chin has to be found. We exploit the fact that the chin casts a shadow on the neck, which gives a sharp colour change on the point of the chin. Once again the sample identification is used to track this edge.

5.4.4 Data Verification

The data extracted so far is checked against the measurements of the face made during initialization. If serious discrepancies are observed, the recognition of the frame is interrupted, the warning signal is issued and the data is reinitialized in order to recognize the next frame correctly. This may happen if the user partially or totally leaves the camera field of view or if they take such a position that the recognition cannot proceed.

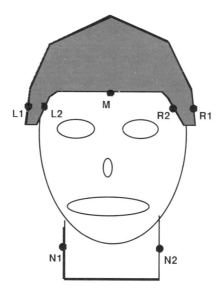

Figure 5-6. Points used in facial feature tracking

5.4.5   Eyebrows

The starting points for the eyebrow detection are above each eyebrow, sufficiently high that the eyebrows cannot be raised above them. They are adjusted interactively during initialization (points marked 4 in Figure 5-4) and kept at fixed positions with respect to the centre of the hairline. Also during initialization, the colour samples of the skin and the eyebrows are taken. The search proceeds downwards from the starting point until the colour is identified as eyebrow. To avoid wrinkles on the forehead being confused with the eyebrows, the search is continued downward after a potential eyebrow is found. If that is the real eyebrow (i.e. not just a wrinkle), the next sample resembling the eyebrow will be in the eye region, i.e. too low. The points on the eyebrows are marked with circles in Figure 5-5. The relative position of each eyebrow with respect to the hairline is compared with the eyebrow position in the neutral face to determine the eyebrow raise. The eyebrow squeeze is calculated from the distance between the left and right eyebrows.

5.4.6   Eyes

During initialization, a rectangle (marked as 5 in Figure 5-4) is placed over each eye and its position relative to the centre of the hairline is measured. During recognition the rectangles (outlined in Figure 5-5) are fixed with respect to the centre of the hairline and stay around the eyes when the user moves.

To determine the aperture of the eye, we exploit the fact that the sides of the iris make strong vertical edges in the eye region. The points lying on vertical edges are found as the local minima of a simplified colour intensity gradient function. The edges are found by searching for the groups of such points connected vertically. The largest vertical edge is a side of the iris. To find the aperture of the eye, we search for the eyelid edges upwards and downwards from the extremes of the vertical edge found earlier. In Figure 5-5 the aperture of the eyes is marked with horizontal lines; the vertical line marks the side of the iris.

To determine the horizontal position of the iris, we find the distance between the iris and the edge of the eye using simple edge detection. This distance is marked with a horizontal line.

5.4.7   Nose and Mouth

The distance between the nose and the hairline is measured during initialization. Using this value the approximate position of the nose is determined. Edge detection is used for locating the nose. A point where the vertical colour intensity gradient is above a certain threshold, is considered to lie on a horizontal edge. A 3×3 pixels gradient operator is used. The threshold value is determined during initialization by exploring the gradient values in the area. A line in Figure 5-5 connects the edge points and a circle marks the nose position.

For acquisition in the mouth region, we search for a horizontal edge downward from the nose point to find a point on the upper lip. At the same horizontal position, the search is performed from the chin in an upward direction to find a point on the lower lip. This process is repeated on the next horizontal position n pixels to the right, n being 1/10 of the mouth width. The search starts in the proximity of the found vertical positions. We continue to move to the right, each time storing in memory the points on the lip edges found, until the corner of the lips is passed. This is detected when no edge is found in the area. The corner of the lips is then tracked more precisely by decreasing the step to $n/2, n/4, n/8, ...,1$. The same process is repeated for the left side. All the points found together thus form the mouth curve, as shown in Figure 5-5. However, due to shadows, wrinkles, beard or insufficient lip–skin colour contrast, the curve is not very precise. Therefore the average height of the points in the middle third of the curve is taken for the vertical position of the lip. The bounding rectangle of the mouth is outlined. This rectangle provides measures for the relative vertical positions of upper and lower lip and squeeze/stretch of the mouth.

The analysis is performed by a special facial expression driver. The extracted parameters are easily translated into minimal perceptible actions, which are passed to the facial representation engine, then to the communication process, where they are packed into a standard VLNET message packet and transmitted.

On the receiving end, the facial representation engine receives messages containing facial expressions described by MPAs and performs the facial animation accordingly. Figure 5-7 illustrates this method with a sequence of original images of the user (with overlaid recognition indicators) and the corresponding images of the synthesized face.

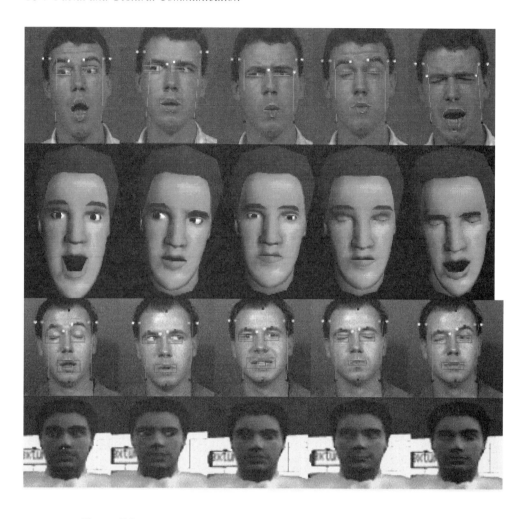

Figure 5-7. Model-based coding of the face: original and synthetic face

This method can be used in combination with texture mapping. The model needs an initial image of the face together with a set of parameters describing the position of the facial features within the texture image in order to fit the texture to the face. Once this is done, the texture is fixed with respect to the face and does not change, but it is deformed together with the face, in contrast to the previous approach where the face was static and the texture was changing. Some texture-mapped faces with expressions are shown in Figure 5-8. The bandwidth requirements for this method are very low. However, considerable computing power is needed, and the complexities of facial expression extraction from video are not yet resolved in a satisfying way; therefore the method yields less quality in reproducing facial expressions than desirable. Providing that the extraction is improved, this method is promising for very-low-bit-rate conferencing in virtual environments.

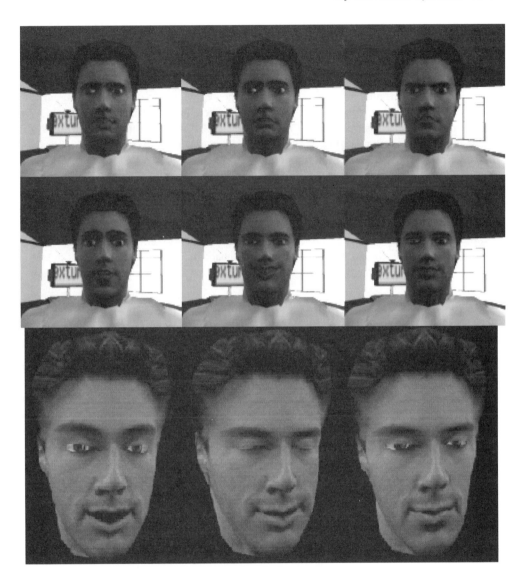

Figure 5-8. Predefined facial expressions: some examples

5.5 Lip Movement Synthesis from Speech

It might not always be practical for the user to be in front of the camera (e.g. if they don't have one, or if they want to use an HMD). Nevertheless, the facial communication does not have to be abandoned. Lavagetto (1995) shows that it is possible to extract visual parameters of the lip movement by analysing the audio signal of the speech. An application which performs such recognition and generates MPAs for controlling the face can be connected to VLNET as the facial expression driver, and the facial representation engine will be able to synthesize the face with the appropriate lip movement corresponding to the pronounced speech. However, currently available software for the segmentation of the audio signal into phonemes does not provide real-time performance, therefore we found it unsuitable for integration in VLNET and we have developed a simpler method that analyses the audio signal and produces a simple open/close mouth movement when speech is detected, allowing the participants in the NVE session to know who is speaking.

This method in its current implementation has very low bandwidth and computing power requirements, but the functionality is limited to the indication of the active speaker. The full implementation of the method, with phoneme extraction from the audio signal and accurate synthesis of visual speech, would still be in a very-low-bit-rate domain; however, the computing complexity is quite high. Nevertheless, the gap to real-time implementation is not too big and it should be possible in the near future. This will allow potential enhancement of speech intelligibility in noisy environments or for hearing-impaired persons.

5.6   Predefined Expressions or Animations

In this approach the user can simply choose between a set of predefined facial expressions or movements (animations). The choice can be made from a menu. The facial expression driver in this case stores a set of defined expressions and animations and just feeds them to the facial representation engine as the user selects them. This method is extensively used in the interface described in Section 5.8. Figure 5-8 shows some examples of predefined facial expressions.

This method is relatively simple to implement and cheap in terms of both bandwidth and computing power. Its potential use is in the virtual chat rooms on the network, where the user community already has a culture of using character-based smileys to express emotions.

5.7   Avatars and Non-Verbal Communication

5.7.1   The Field of Non-Verbal Communication in Social Sciences

We have identified one of the most important functions of embodiments as *tools* in interpersonal communication. The use of the body in interpersonal communication has been studied in psychology under the name of non-verbal communication (NVC). It is useful now to recall the basic ideas about non-verbal communication in the social sciences so that some of our choices can be better explained later on. Non-verbal communication is defined as the whole set of means by which human beings communicate except for the human linguistic system and its derivatives (writings, sign language, etc.). Communication is to be seen in this definition, in short, as the sending by a sender of stimuli which causes a change in the state or behaviour of the recipient. So, for Argyle (1988), 'Non-verbal communication, or bodily communication, takes place whenever one person influences another by means of facial expression, tone of voice, or any of the other channels (except linguistic). This may be intentional or it may not be'. When this production of clues about the state of mind, ideas, etc., of the sender is not conscious, this process is often called non-verbal behaviour.

The encoding/decoding paradigm is central to studies about non-verbal communication and these studies are often divided into looking at the process of encoding the message and looking at the process of decoding. From a system point of view, the process of NVC has the following structure: an event happens in system A, it is processed, encoded and the result is communicated to system B through one or more channels. System B decodes the signal which provokes a change in its state; it then sends a new message to A, etc. The message is sent through structuring a determined physical element, which is the channel, e.g. the body. This process of encoding through the organization of a channel, so that it can be decoded, is realized by following a code, which can be peculiar to a geographic area or more universal.

It is very important to notice that the meaning of non-verbal communication or non-verbal behaviour always varies considerably depending on its context of occurrence; to decide on the meaning of a particular gesture, for example, one has to take into account the specific social settings of the culture of the sender and recipient, the gesture's position in time and its relation to the other signals preceding or accompanying it. The processes of encoding and decoding in NVC are very subtle. They can express things in many different ways and intensity, and require an important skill of global interpretation from the participants to make the interaction a success, which is not always the case.

In most situations, NVC is not used alone but jointly with verbal communication. It is not to be regarded as a concurrent channel but rather as a means for people to strengthen what they say, make it explicit, etc. In the evolution of human communication, verbal communication has not replaced non-verbal communication but they have evolved together. Yet, according to Ekman and Friesen (1967), there is a type of signal which is still independent from language: the affective expression. It seems that non-verbal communication doesn't need any verbal expression in the task of communicating emotional messages, and that it is able to express things that would be very difficult to express using the linguistic system, even in a very powerful way. The communication of emotions is a very important function of non-verbal communication.

Corraze (1980) proposes there are three types of information which are conveyed by NVC: information about the affective state of the sender, as we have just seen, information about its identity, and information about the external world. To communicate this information, three main channels are used: (1) the body and its moves, (2) the artifacts linked to the body or to the environment, (3) the distribution of the individuals in space. The use of artifacts, such as choice of clothes or choice of a car, will not be discussed here because it goes beyond the context of this book.

The study of proxemics analyses the way people handle the space around their body and situate themselves next to other people in space. Proxemic research focuses on the analysis of the distance and angle chosen by the individuals before and during their interactions, the relationships associated with each distance, the permission to touch and its circumstances, etc. For example, Hall uses a classification of distances (Figure 5-9) connected with the degree of intimacy of the individuals: the intimate space goes from 0 to 1.5 feet, the personal space from 1.5 to 4 feet, the social-consultive space to 10 feet, and the public space beyond (Weitz 1974). The smaller the distance, the higher the probability of a physical contact, or of feeling the warmth or the breath of the other person, which may or may not be taboo depending on the relationship of the individuals. The angle chosen by the individuals for their interaction can be used to assert their rejection of the other or to show that they are open to the interaction, demanding it, etc.

Kinesics includes gestures, postures, postural shifts, and movements of the hands, head, trunk, etc.; it analyses what is sometimes called the body language. Three main types of bodily movements have been identified by several authors: the emblems, the illustrators and the postural shifts (Argyle 1988; Corraze 1980). The emblems are gestures having a precise meaning that can be translated by one or two words. Their knowledge is often specific to a group or subculture and their use is mostly conscious. The illustrators are movements which are directly tied to speech, serving to illustrate what is being said verbally. The hands are the part of the body commonly used, and this activity is generally unconscious or half-conscious. Together with the facial expressions, the postures are the best way to communicate emotions and states of mind. A posture is a precise position of the body or some of its parts, compared to a determined system of references. These references can be the orientation of a part of the body compared to some other parts or to the whole body, or the orientation of the body compared to the body of the interlocutor. Later on we'll see some examples which illustrate this point. Some other body focus movements

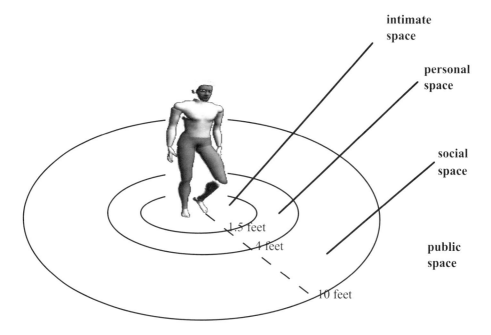

Figure 5-9. Classification of distances connected with the degree of intimacy of the individuals

exist, e.g. scratching the head, but they also happen in a non-interactional context, and their importance in non-verbal communication is weaker.

The purpose of this theoretical part was to highlight the importance of non-verbal communication in human interaction: it can accompany verbal communication allowing the speaker to strengthen, make explicit or weaken the sense of their speech, make it less boring by catching the attention of the recipient, etc. It allows the interlocutors to give each other information about their identity or their environment. And finally it is the best and only efficient way to communicate feelings. For all these reasons, the implementation of a mechanism allowing users to employ non-verbal communication during their interactions in NVEs is important for the quality of the interactions and the immersive aspect of the system.

5.7.2   Introducing Social Science Theories into NVE Systems

The navigation functionalities within NVE systems have allowed the user to handle proxemic signals in a fairly convenient way, but specific existed for the kinesic aspect. By using such devices as the Flock of Birds, the users can add this aspect of non-verbal communication to their interactions unconsciously, in a natural and transparent way, simply by moving their body as they would have done in a natural environment. On the other hand, these devices are rather difficult to use. Currently they are expensive and very inconvenient (heavy, restrictive, time-consuming to install and calibrate, etc.), which means the system is difficult to use and test, so it is rarely employed in practice. It was therefore decided to develop a simple user inerface for VLNET that would allow the user to add informal communication to the interaction, without the need for extra items beyond the basic devices, simply by using the mouse. The functionalities of the application we have developed will be discussed later on, but the proposal of predefined actions can be taken up here.

The use of predefined actions clearly raises some problems. First, it postulates that the actions of non-verbal communication are conscious, which as we have seen is not always the case. Then there is no longer any correspondence between the real posture of the participant and the posture of its avatar, so it can be expected that the immersive aspect of the experience will be weaker. Finally, the control on the action will be restricted and, as in real life, the expression of very subtle contents will be difficult.

The use of the Flock of Birds has its own problems. As explained already, it restricts the user's moves, e.g. a 360° turn is often very problematic. Then navigation is a problem as the area in which the user must stay is always very small. This means a non-immersive way to move in the virtual environment has to be developed, which rather detracts from this solution. If an HMD is used as display device, the interaction cannot last for very long because of the weight and inconvenience (such as motion sickness) and if the display is a 2D screen, the participants must always orient themself for visualizing the scene. And there are other problems, e.g. some people can't use it because of their height or corpulence. Even in the best case, the use of such a device also involves a learning process. All in all, the immersive quality of these devices is still not much better then a 2D interface and a mouse, which nearly everyone knows how to use already.

The choice of developing a 2D interface seemed to us the best compromise between practical constraints and the will to take into account what the social sciences have taught us about non-verbal communication. Moreover, the open architecture of VLNET makes it possible for some users in the network environment to work with trackers while others have the 2D interfaces, so we do not leave out the use of trackers.

After making the choice to use predefined actions, we next had to consider the choice of actions and their organization. We have seen that three types of bodily movements are important for non-verbal communication: the emblem gestures, the postures and the illustrators. In order to make any sense, the illustrators have to be tightly coupled with the speech, illustrating the ideas and their intensity in a way difficult to anticipate and highly synchronized with the verbal expression. Realistic illustrators are difficult to standardize, so we decided to leave them out temporarily, leaving open the possibility to simply include some basic illustrators with the other gestures. The two other categories have been included: the emblem gestures, including all bodily gestures and facial mimics, and the postures grouped with facial expressions. A *posture* or a *facial expression* is an attitude characterizing a state of mind or an emotion, which stays during the interaction until it is replaced by a new one. A *gesture* or *mimic* is an action expressing an idea and whose length is fixed in time (short). This distinction is also important for the user because it reflects a difference in function and in timing, and it was decided to use it for classifying the different actions. The other main classifying criteria chosen are the part of the body that executes the action and the emotional impact of the action. Because they are the most widely used and because of lack of studies on lower body actions currently available, the priority has been given to actions of the upper body.

We started to select a small number of gestures and postures (less than 30), corresponding to a basic palette of actions. Note that it is almost impossible to identify a basic palette of gestures and postures that would allow the user to express all its potential ideas and feelings. First, non-verbal communication does not work as a linguistic system, with an alphabet whose combination permits us to construct whatever meaning we like; instead it should be compared to a language using a great variety of ideogram-like signs. No psychological study has been able to build such a classification for the interactions in the real world. At best, such attempts have been made in more limited fields, like facial expressions, and we have tried to use them. We have only used actions documented in scientific papers, because we wanted to avoid any ethnocentric bias; we did not want to have gestures that were valid only in our local context.

The following criteria have been used to select the actions:

- Documented in scientific papers
- Basic action, commonly used, expresses simple idea
- Different enough to compose a palette of actions
- Can be understood in many places and cultures
- Can be performed in the standing position
- A graphical representation of the action was available

Table 5-2 shows the chosen actions, classified by posture/gesture and part of the body. Each action has the name of the idea or state of mind it expresses.

Table 5-2. Chosen postures/expressions and gestures/mimics

	Postures/expressions	Gestures/mimics
Face	Neutral Caring Happy Unhappy Sad Angry	
Head/face		Yes No Nod Wink Smile
Body	Neutral Attentive Determined Relaxed Insecure Puzzled	Incomprehension Reject Welcoming Angry Joy Bow
Hand/arm		Salute Mockery Alert Insult Good Bad

The body/global postures and gestures are based on work by Rosenberg and Langer (1965), who analysed the reception of basic postures and gestures on a rather large sample of people. The postures we have selected illustrate very well the four fundamental postural attitudes developed by W. James, in which the position of the head and the position of the trunk are essential: attitude of approach with the body bent forward (attentive), attitude of reject with the body turned away from the other (rejection) attitude of pride with the expansion of the head, the trunk and the shoulders (determined), attitude of prostration with the head bent and the shoulders falling (insecure). The open/close dimension showed up by Mehrabian is clearly present too.

The basic facial expressions are based on a description by Miller (1976), who tried to explain the mechanisms that we use to give a sense to facial configurations, and they have also been inspired by Ekman's categories. The source for the main hand gestures is due to Morris et al. (1979), who conducted statistical research on many different and faraway locations to analyse the geographical distribution and plurality of sense for basic gestures (Morris et al. 1979).

Finally, we propose to use a classification of types of interaction in order to better evaluate and determine the design priorities in the development of NVEs. This classification can help developers to make decisions in trade-off situations, such as decisions about the need to use a realistic-looking avatar or to allocate the CPU time for another task (e.g. increasing the frame rate). In the case of non-verbal communication, all studies suggest different uses for it in different situations. So, with such a classification, we can account for the fact that the presence of the non-verbal communication engine is very important for one kind of interaction, and could be dropped in another kind with minimal impact on the quality of the communication. The classification we propose has the advantage that it relies on psychological theories and makes classification of the collaborative applications under one of the categories rather easy. But it is true that this is a model, and real-life situations are always a mix of these categories, to a greater or lesser degree. Here are our categories:

1. *Actional*: this type induces an activity of the users with a precise goal, often a manipulating task, and requires their active collaboration.
2. *Informational*: the users mainly furnish abstract information to each other.
3. *Emotional*: the emotional state of the users is central and constitutes the main content of the messages exchanged.

Specific VR applications correspond to each of the defined types , such as teleworking, teleconferencing and VR chat.

From the viewpoint of non-verbal communication, these categories have been chosen because they correspond to different logics and different uses of the body are to be found in each one of them. The emotional type corresponds to the major function of non-verbal communication, so it needs a specific category. An important difference between the actional and the informational type is the intentionality: the non-verbal communication present in the actional type is intentional and conscious but it lacks some of the aspects in the informational and emotional types. As we have seen, non-verbal communication always has an effect on the recipient. But in the actional type this effect is wanted and explicit. If we use the distinction created by Argyle (1988) between the sign and the signal, which both affect the recipient but respectively in a non-intentional and intentional way, we can say that actional interactions mainly use signals, and informational interactions mainly use signs. The main type of gesture that is used in the actional types is emblems, like yes, no, right, left, come, stop. For the informational interactions, the main use of non-verbal communication will be the use of illustrators to illustrate, carry, and make the speech more attractive. Postures and facial expressions will mostly be used in emotional situations.

Our work started with virtual reality teleconferencing applications which require more interactions of an emotional type. Our ongoing work is to evaluate the VLNET system for all types of interaction. We think that categorizing the applications with respect to their required types of interaction gives us the possibility to evaluate them in a better way than a general approach to all NVE applications.

5.8   Non-Verbal Communication with 2D Interface

In order to fulfil the need for easy and fast usage, and an intuitive and easy-to-learn user interface, we decided to use image buttons, displaying a snapshot of the actual move and a textual label describing the idea or state of mind expressed by the action. The advantage of using a snapshot is that the action can be visually recognized and that it reflects the real action executed (because an angry posture could be represented in many different ways).

We decided to work with three windows (Figure 5-10): the posture panel, the gesture panel and the control panel. The posture panel offers a global view of all postures available, with clickable image buttons. It has two sections containing the postures classified by body part: one section for the face and one for the body. The actions are ordered by emotional impact, and the sections are divided into three columns: positive, negative and neutral. There are four radio buttons allowing the user to choose the mode they prefer: The first mode, automatic selection, lets the software select by default a corresponding facial/body posture to the selected facial/body posture. For example, when the user selects the 'unhappy' facial expression, the body posture 'insecure' is automatically selected. The second mode, automatic body posture selection, gives the priority to the facial expression; when the user selects a body posture, their former choice of facial expression is not replaced. In the third mode, automatic facial expression selection, only the facial expressions are proposed. The last mode, free selection, lets the user freely select the facial expression and the body posture, so they can choose contradictory postures and expressions in order to produce a more complex idea.

The gesture panel is organized in the same way as the posture panel, and offers a global view of all gestures available, with clickable image buttons. It has three sections containing the gestures classified by body part: one section for the head/face, one for the hand/arm and one for the body. The user can execute a gesture directly or sometimes they must confirm it, perhaps if they are in a more delicate interaction. There is a vertical slider that lets the user define the speed of the gesture they want. It is initially set to a default value.

The control panel is a smaller window that is displayed first after loading the software. It manages the posture panel and the gesture panel, and two buttons allow the user to open or close them. There is a representation of the current facial expression and body posture in the centre of the window. For convenience, the panels can all be moved and resized by the user, and similar to the mode changes, they are saved for the next use.

This configuration has the advantage of offering a global view of the available postures and gestures; it is very fast as the panels stay open and are ready to be used at any time, with one single click of the mouse. The high degree of organization of the actions (posture/gesture, part of the body, positive/neutral/negative) coupled with the fact that all actions can be activated immediately, allows the user to rapidly find and execute the action that best fits the situation.

As the application has to handle an arbitrary number of actions without being recompiled, the user interface had to be made dynamic. The posture panel and the gesture panel are fully dynamic in the sense that the size of the window and the number and position of the buttons depend on the actual number of actions and their types. Even the keyboard shortcuts are dynamically generated from the name of the action. When started, the application reads the default configuration file, or another configuration asked, and generates the posture and gesture panels according to the content of the file.

From a VLNET viewpoint, the non-verbal communication program is an external driver. The postures, expressions, gestures and mimics are realized with two animation techniques that correspond to two file formats and several associated functions. The main animation

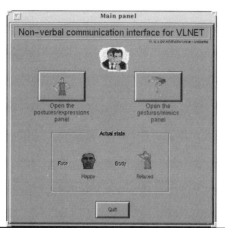

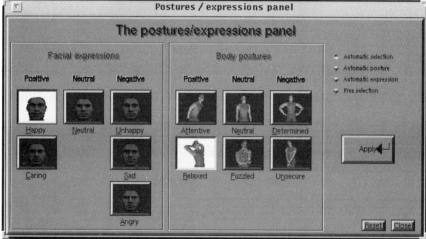

Figure 5-10. Panels to select postures/expressions and gestures/mimics

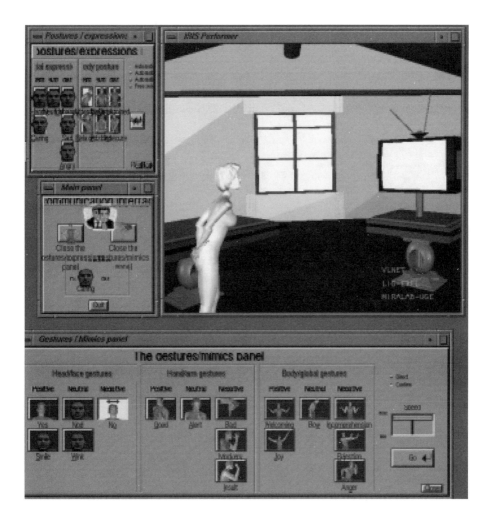

Figure 5-11. A VLNET session

technique used is keyframe animation. This approach was used for every posture and gesture, but not for the facial expressions and mimics. The skeleton of the avatar is animated by modifying its joint angle values according to values linked to a precise timing, which are read from a keyframe file. The computer then interpolates the in-between frames to supply a smooth animation.

In this application, a local body is created first with a skeleton similar to the skeleton of the VLNET avatar. When an action is chosen, the corresponding keyframe file is executed on this body. The joints angle values are then sent to the shared memory through the body posture interface, encapsulated, distributed, performed by the body representation engine and finally displayed. Figure 5-11 shows a VLNET session and Figure 5-12 shows some facial expressions.

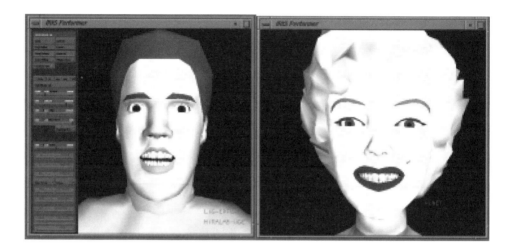

Figure 5-12. A screen snapshot: angry and happy facial expressions

5.9   Non-Verbal Communication with Chat Interface

We have already mentioned that non-verbal communication is generally used together with verbal communication. In order to support interactions with text-based communication, we have developed a driver that connects to the VLNET body, face and text interfaces. Previously, we have discussed how a palette of body postures or gestures can be predefined and then chosen by a user input metaphor. For example, the smileys normally used within emails can be used to set a subset of the joints in the current body using the keyboard. The body posture driver just stores the predefined postures and gestures (i.e. animated postures) and feeds them to the body posture engine as the user selects them.

The approach works as follows: a configuration file exists that describes the keyframe sequence of each smiley (Table 5-3). When the user enters a smiley, the previously running gesture is cancelled, if it exists, and the new gesture is played back. We use a configuration file that relates the posture or gesture to the words that are generated by the autonomous actor.

Table 5-3. Configuration file relates the posture/gesture to words generated by autonomous actor

	POSTURES
Happy	'happy' 'Pretty good' 'I'm fine'
Caring	'excuse me' 'sorry'
Neutral	':-|' 'can't say' 'not sure' 'no idea'
Unhappy	':-('
Sad	'sad'
Angry	'angry'
Attentive	'hmm'
Relaxed	'relax' 'cool down'
Puzzled	'I am confused' 'hesitate'
Determined	'sure not!'
Insecure	
	GESTURES
Yes	'yes'
No	'no'
Smile	':-)' 'hehe' 'haha' 'funny'
Wink	';-)'
Good	'good'
Alert	'be careful' 'attention' 'dangerous'
Bad	'bad'
Mockery	
Insult	'stupid' 'dumb'
Welcoming	'welcome' 'ok' 'sure' 'no prob'
Joy	'cool'
Bow	'hello' 'hi'
Incomprehension	'I don't understand'
Rejection	'I don't want'
Anger	'angry' 'mad' 'upset'

5.10 Autonomous Actor Control with Chat Interface

In the field of artificial life, researchers have built various implementations that mimic the chatting person at the end of the connection. Among them, Eliza is an autonomous agent program that studies natural language communication between real users and autonomous agents (Weizenbaum 1966). The program works by entering and outputting text. We have connected one of the existing Eliza-based implementations, as a driver to VLNET, with the additional gestural interface. The connection again uses text interface, in addition to the body posture interface. When the program outputs a keyword, an associated keyframe sequence is retrieved from a table, and this keyframe is played back. The keywords and associated keyframe sequences are as follows.

This case study demonstrates the use of conversational embodied autonomous actors that depend on textual communication with the participants.

The conversational virtual human has the following characteristics:

- It is based on a previously developed freeware program, called Splotch. Splotch is a freeware C implementation of Eliza, written by Duane Fields.
- The virtual human looks for participants around it; when there is at least one participant around the virtual human, it starts chatting with that participant.
- The conversation takes place textually through a chat window.
- The virtual human uses its non-verbal communication to strengthen and accompany its verbal communication.

The conversational virtual human program is connected to VLNET through the textual, information and body interfaces. The autonomous actor program obtains the participants' textual messages and outputs answers through the text interface.

We provided an initial implementation that is based on detecting the words used within the sentences. A set of keywords are accompanied with gestures that the actor plays. For example, the autonomous actor uttering the word 'hmm' is assumed to be paying attention to the participant's words, therefore the autonomous actor's virtual body is animated with a predefined keyframe sequence for attentive posture.

We have defined a palette of gestures and postures that the autonomous actor can animate. Each keyframe sequence is accompanied with a set of keywords. In the initial implementation, we only looked into which words the autonomous actor speaks. Thus, at each text input from the remote participant, this input is passed to the Eliza program, the Eliza program outputs its answer, the answer text is searched for keywords, and one keyframe sequence is chosen using the found keywords. An extension would be to define the state of the actor in the autonomous behaviour level, and select the gestures from this input, rather than analysing the spoken words. Note that the conversational agent program can use a similar configuration for associating words with keyframes, with the participant using a chat interface, therefore it uses the same configuration file.

6 Networking Data for Virtual Humans

6.1 Introduction

Virtual humans put some additional burdens on the networking strategy of an NVE system. First, there is a need for each participant to provide their personal data to all other participants in the session. Second, the movement and behaviour of the user needs to be transmitted through the network.

The transmission of personal data typically happens when a new user joins the NVE session. The personal data minimally includes some kind of identity (e.g. name) and appearance data. The appearance information might be simply a choice between a number of predefined appearances provided by the system. However, it is desirable for a user to be able to fully customize their appearance in the virtual world: size and shape of the body, face, textures, etc. Depending on the way the system handles user actions, personal data might include behaviour information, for example definition of personalized gestures or facial expressions. When the user joins an NCVE session, their personal data needs to be distributed to all users already in the session, or at least to those that are currently in the vicinity of the newcomer. Obviously, the newcomer must receive the personal data from other participants.

The transmission of user movement and/or behaviour happens all the time during the session as the users move, gesture or emote through facial expressions. A system using primitive user representation without virtual humans needs to update only user positions. When virtual humans are used, body postures and facial expressions need to be updated.

One way of achieving this is through implicit or explicit behaviours. Implicit behaviour means that the body postures are determined from the global motion; for example, if the user is standing, the global motion is interpreted as walking and appropriate walking motion is generated; if the user is lying on the ground, the global motion is interpreted as crawling and crawling motion is generated (Pratt et al. 1997). In this strategy no additional data has to be transmitted as the postures are generated locally at each site. For explicit behaviours, high-level behaviour data is transmitted (e.g. jump, wave, smile) and this data is interpreted locally to provide actions (i.e. jump is translated into a jumping motion of the body, smile into the appropriate facial expression).

The use of implicit and explicit behaviours provides the means to control behaviour at a high level without the need to send a lot of data through the network. However, this approach lacks flexibility because it is constrained to the behaviours already defined in the system. To allow any kind of free movement and facial expression, body postures and facial expressions need to be transmitted through the network in a more general form.

For the body, the usual representation of postures is in terms of joint angles, where each degree of freedom of the body is represented by an angle, as described in Section 4.4.1. Typically, virtual humans are modelled with fewer degrees of freedom than the real human body.

The facial expressions need to be transmitted in terms of basic facial movements (e.g. MPAs as described in Section 5.2) allowing the reproduction of any facial expression as a combination of the basic movements.

In summary, the articulated structure of the human body together with the face introduces a new level of complexity in the use of network resources because the size of a message needed to convey the body posture is greater than for simple, non-articulated objects. This might create a significant overhead in communication, especially as the number of participants in the simulation increases. In order to reduce this overhead, it is possible to communicate the body postures in more compact forms, accepting some loss of accuracy in the posture definition. This is not the only trade-off to be considered when choosing the optimal approach. Conversions between different forms of posture definition require potentially expensive computations which might induce more overhead in computation than was reduced in communication. The choice will also depend on the quality and quantity of raw data available from the input devices, the posture accuracy required by the application, and the projected number of participants in the simulation.

Furthermore, when participants dynamically join and leave the VE during the session, the files defining the embodiment need to be downloaded and loaded to the memory of each client. The size of files defining the embodiment tends to increase with increasing embodiment complexity. We propose a progressive downloading technique together with asynchronous loading, in order to decrease the interaction idle time that clients need for loading new bodies.

For the purpose of discussion, we separate the networking tasks into two stages: *set-up* and *simulation*. Set-up refers to the stage when a new participant connects to the scene, loads the scene, sends the URL of its embodiment information to other clients, and the receiving clients fetch the files and load the new participants. Hence there is no 3D interparticipant interaction involved in this stage. The simulation stage corresponds to the part of the session where transmission of update messages occurs for interaction.

During simulation, we can decompose the communication into a set of steps: (i) transformation of input body parameters to a message to be sent through the network, (ii) compression of this message; and at the receiver site, (iii) decompression of this message, and (iv) inverse transformation to a list of parameters. The transmission lag for a message will be the sum of the lags for all these steps. In addition, each message type contains an accuracy loss of data which is a trade-off to decrease the lag.

In this chapter, we analyze different message types with respect to the following aspects:

- *Transformation computation at the sender site*: We evaluate the amount of computation needed in order to convert the input body posture data into the message format to be sent, at the sending site; and the size of different message types to describe the motion.

- *Compression techniques and bit rate requirements*: We evaluate the techniques and bandwidth requirements for compression of the body animation message into a set of codes.
- *Inverse transformation computation at the receiver site*: We evaluate the amount of computation needed to interpret the message and convert it to the body posture for display at the receiving site. The weight of this computation on the simulation is typically greater than the weight at the sender site because the messages from a potentially large number of participants have to be processed. This is the opposite of transformation which is done only for the locally controlled figure.
- *Accuracy loss*: We evaluate the loss of accuracy of the body posture with respect to the original input data. This is typically the trade-off to be considered against decreasing transformation and compression computations, and transmission overhead.

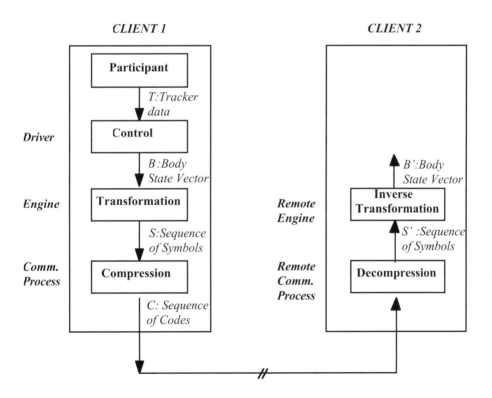

Figure 6-1. Steps for transmitting participant representations

Figure 6-1 illustrates the relationship between the different steps. The VLNET body representation engine, as discussed in Section 3.2.2, performs the transformation of parameters, and the communication process performs compression.

Data compression techniques can be divided into two major classes: lossy and lossless. Lossless data compression consists of techniques which guarantee to generate an exact duplicate of the input data stream after compression and decompression. These techniques are widely used in text compression, databases or spreadsheets. Lossy data compression techniques introduce a certain loss of accuracy for better compression. Lossy data compression techniques have been widely applied to computer graphics images and audio sequences. The success of these techniques in these areas is due to the nature of the initial data: the digitized representations of analogue phenomena already introduce a loss of information, so a degree of mismatch between source and output may be acceptable. Virtual human data also has this lossy nature: either the magnetic trackers introduce a loss of resolution, or the procedural or keyframe animations are designed with certain inaccuracy. The inaccuracy typically varies with respect to the motion control method, among other factors. Dynamics animation might require higher accuracy than a keyframe animation, while keyframe animation may need to be sent more accurately than procedural animation. Therefore, scalable techniques are necessary for sending virtual human data. Most lossy compression techniques can be adjusted to different quality levels, gaining higher accuracy in exchange for less effective compression. In Figure 6-1, if the animation output B is the same as the input to remote copy B', then the compression is lossless. Otherwise, the compression is lossy.

As the number of participants increases, the transmission and decoding overheads will be excessive, and the computations to process remote participants might increase significantly. Therefore, methods should be investigated to decrease the overhead which arises with an increasing number of participants. One solution is not to send the information to a site at all if there is no or little interaction, using various techniques such as filtering and dead reckoning. Filtering removes messages that are not relevant to a given client; the client receives only those messages that concern them. Dead reckoning is applied to extrapolate the human information from the last received information of body and face, and the last speed. Finally, the motion level of detail approach allows the frame rate to be used for sending messages depending on the distance between participants.

As already claimed, we aim to provide mechanisms for efficient virtual human representation in NVEs with varying CPU, network and application requirements in VLNET. For networking aspects, we incorporated into VLNET most of the issues discussed in this chapter, in order to support scalable mechanisms for communicating virtual humans.

6.2   Elements of Networking Scalability

Previously we introduced the term 'networking scalability' that refers to the networking overhead of a virtual human figure. This type of scalability is further divided into three elements:

- *Loading scalability*: the amount of computational and network overhead needed to download a body model and load it in the memory, during the initialization phase of a new participant.
- *Transformation scalability*: the number of computations needed to convert the input from a body driver that controls the representation into a list of symbols that are ready to be sent through the network and back (Figure 6-1).
- *Bandwidth scalability*: the bit rate (kilobits per second) needed to communicate the body state in real time.

6.3 Loading Scalability

Loading complexity defines the network and computation overhead in order to initialize a virtual human in the NVE. This includes (i) downloading the body definition of a new participant through the network to the local disk, and then (ii) loading the contents of the downloaded body files into the host's local memory.

As this step also involves loading the participant's local body, it has to be performed in minimum time so as to minimize the time to join the NVE. Table 6-1 shows the file sizes for different resolutions in a typical (default) body.

Table 6-1. Size in bytes of the different resolutions of the default embodiment

	Very high resolution	High resolution	Low resolution	Rough resolution
Body	255 729	41 296	26 958	14 360
Left hand	66 864	16 992	9 132	8 208
Right hand	66 864	16 992	9 132	8 208
Left foot	15 912	10 628	9 120	7 156
Right foot	15 912	10 628	9 120	7 156
Head	53 268	53 268	29 052	29 052
Total	442 725	149 804	92 514	74 140

Note that these numbers do not contain textures, and other 3D garment objects attached to the body. For these more complex representations, the file sizes will further increase significantly. The overhead to fetch the body files and load them into clients' memory is proportional to the complexity of the body representation files, and efficient techniques are needed for loading new participants.

6.3.1 Asynchronous Loading

The fetching of new participants and loading them into VLNET internal shared memory happens in the database (dbase) process, as discussed in Section 3.2.4. Using this capability, clients already connected can continue their interaction while new participants are loaded, without blocking their rendering and simulation as would be the case for a single-threaded architecture.

The embodiment is defined by a body configuration (.bdy) file. This file contains the URL values of each body file for the participant, and a further information (.inf) file that describes the associated skeleton structure, the levels of detail for their surfaces, and other surfaces attached to the body. In this representation, different levels of detail are stored in different subdirectories, each subdirectory named res*x*, where *x* is the level of resolution from 0 to 4, 0 being the highest resolution. As we discussed in Chapter 4, multiple levels of detail allow us to have graphical scalability in rendering.

Note that we use URLs to locate bodies. The fetching of body files using HTTP is achieved through a library that allows us to open a TCP connection to the destination host, and fetch files using the HTTP protocol. The library also has a caching capability to retrieve the already fetched files from local disk, rather than fetching them again.

The body files are arranged in a directory structure, with the following contents:

```
body_dir/
        skeleton_template.tpl
        res0/
            3D geometry and texture files for body, extremities and garments
        res1/
            3D geometry and texture files for body, extremities and garments
        res2/
            3D geometry and texture files for body, extremities and garments
        res3/
            3D geometry and texture files for body, extremities and garments
        res4/
            3D geometry and texture files for body, extremities and garments
```

The body file contains the URL of each file to be downloaded:

```
BODY
{
        BASE_URL "http://ligwww.epfl.ch/vlnet/BODYDATA/Clerk"
        TRANSFER_FILE "bob_clerk.inf"  /* Information about attachments, LODs */
        TRANSFER_FILE "Buffman.tpl"                /* Skeleton template */
        TRANSFER_FILE "res0/Buffman.dat"           /* Body cross section file */
        TRANSFER_FILE "res0/Buffman_right_foot.sm" /* Feet */
        TRANSFER_FILE "res0/Buffman_left_foot.sm "
        TRANSFER_FILE "res0/Buffman_right_hand.sm" /* Hands */
        TRANSFER_FILE "res0/Buffman_left_hand.sm"
        TRANSFER_FILE "res0/Buffman_head.sm"       /* Head */
        TRANSFER_FILE "res1/Buffman.dat"           /* Body cross section file */
        TRANSFER_FILE "res1/Buffman_right_foot.sm" /* Feet */
        TRANSFER_FILE "res1/Buffman_left_foot.sm "
        TRANSFER_FILE "res1/Buffman_right_hand.sm" /* Hands */
        TRANSFER_FILE "res1/Buffman_left_hand.sm"
        TRANSFER_FILE "res1/Buffman_head.sm"       /* Head */
}
```

6.3.2 Progressive Downloading

For a participant representation with multiple levels of detail, all the body files defining all the resolutions need to be downloaded. Adding the time to fetch and load all resolutions drastically increases the set-up time, hence the delay to start the interaction.

For decreasing the loading overhead, we have designed a *progressive downloading* technique. Remote clients first load a default body that represents the new participant, while the new participant's embodiment files are being fetched and loaded. This body is an articulated representation with the same number of degrees of freedom, with boxes representing body limbs. The files for the default body are part of the VLNET client distribution package, and are stored on the local disk of each host, i.e. they are *not* transmitted over the network when a new participant connects to the VE. Similarly, the newly joining participant loads this body locally, allowing the interaction to be started immediately after loading the default body.

After the default body has been loaded, if there are multiple levels of detail for the same body, the lowest resolution is fetched and loaded first, asynchronously with the interaction. The goal of this selection is to approximate representation, and progressively improve the graphical quality of the embodiment, if multiple levels of detail are defined. The detection of which resolutions are present in the embodiment is done by parsing the .bdy file and choosing URLs containing substring 'res$x$' in them, x being a number between 0 and 4 (Figure 6-2).

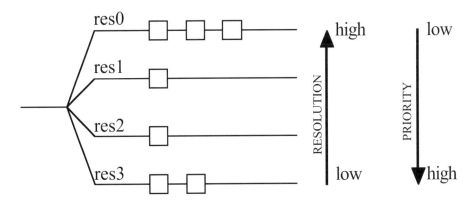

Figure 6-2. Loading of multiple bodies is performed with multiple queues, low resolutions with high priority

Especially with increasing number of participants, or scenes where participants are often joining and leaving, several participants need to be loaded at a time. This means there is a need for a mechanism to arbitrate over the next embodiment resolution to be loaded. We use a number of queues; each one stores the pending body files to be fetched for a different resolution. For example, if there is any embodiment waiting to be loaded in the lowest resolution queue, this embodiment is loaded. If there is no embodiment left in the lowest resolution queue, the next highest resolution queue is checked.

6.4 Transformation Scalability

Transformation scalability refers to the number of computations needed by the engine to convert the parameters that are input from a driver into a list of symbols ready to be transmitted to the server. Ideally, for decreasing the transformation computation overhead, the input parameters and the transformed symbols should be the same (for example, if the driver inputs joint angles, the joint angles will be sent through the network). However, under different conditions, perhaps when the network bandwidth is too low to send joint angles and the application can tolerate posture losses, the state of the body can be recognized and sent through the network with small parameters.

We consider four approaches to define the body posture state (Figure 6-3):

- Global positioning parameters
- Joint angle parameters
- End-effector matrices
- State information

Global Positioning Parameters
The global positioning of 17 body limbs can be sent as independent transformation matrices. This data can be used directly to display the body, bypassing the conversion to joint angles. Each entry in the matrix is represented by a floating-point value.

The homogeneous matrix for representing the transformation contains redundant data: instead of representing the transformation by 16 floating-point numbers, using Euler angles (h, p, r) and translation values (x, y, z), decreases this number to 6 floating-point values. Therefore we select this representation rather than transformation matrices.

Now we can calculate the size of a message defining the body posture in one frame with global positioning parameters:

17 parameters * 6 floats/parameter * 32 bits/float = 408 bytes = 3264 bits

Joint Angles
These values are the degrees of freedom comprising the body; they correspond to the state vector introduced in Chapter 4. Each degree of freedom is represented by a floating-point value, which is an angle between 0 and 360°.

So now we can calculate the size of message defining the body posture in one frame with joint angle parameters:

75 parameters * 32 bits/float = 300 bytes = 2400 bits

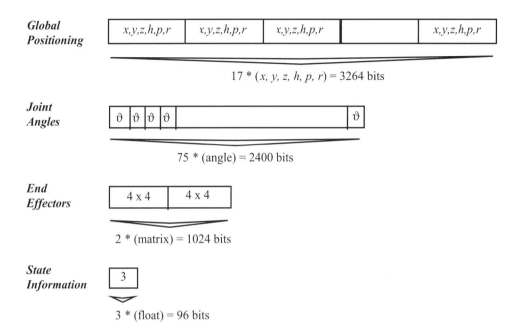

Figure 6-3. Four approaches to define body posture state

End-Effector Matrices

A 4×4 floating-point matrix is used to determine the position of the end-effectors, in this example the head and the right hand. An inverse kinematics algorithm with two end-effectors (head and hand) has to be applied to these two matrices, in the received message, to obtain the final posture.

The size of the end-effector parameters for head and hand end-effectors is

$$2 \text{ parameters} * 16 \text{ floats/parameter} * 32 \text{ bits/float} = 128 \text{ bytes} = 1024 \text{ bits}$$

State Information

Only the high-level state information is conveyed, which makes the messages small. Moreover, the messages are sent only when the state changes. The computation complexity involved to produce the postures from the state information can range from quite simple (in the case of predefined static postures like sitting or standing) through medium (in the case of predefined dynamic states like walking or running) to very complex (in the case of more complex dynamic states like searching an object). In this evaluation, we take the medium-level walking action as an example, which requires an x, y, z walking direction vector as an input, with the *size* of the vector denoting the speed:

$$3 \text{ floats/parameter} * 32 \text{ bits/float} = 24 \text{ bytes} = 96 \text{ bits}$$

Note that we assume the hand parameters are only represented by joint angles, so they are an extension to the joint angle parameters. This choice comes from the fact that almost all the animation programs and VR device-tracking libraries assume joint angle specification for hand postures, and global transformation matrix parameters are not used for hands.

The computational requirements for each transformation type depend on the input device characteristics. For example, if the data is in joint angles, and the parameters to be sent are joint angles, the conversion is minimal. We compare the representation types in the next section.

6.5   Comparison of Representation Types

We have presented various ways for transmitting virtual human posture state, and each technique has advantages over others in different conditions. We analyse three typical situations with respect to various real-time control data conditions: (i) complete body posture data is available, (ii) only head and hand end-effector data is available, (iii) walking motion guiding data is available from an external driver.

Figures 6-4 to 6-7 show the bit rate requirements, transformation and inverse transformation computations per frame, and accuracy loss for different message types. Figure 6-4 is calculated with the assumption of a minimum real-time speed of 10 frames/s. We see that the bit rate requirement varies between 24 kbits/s and 1.92 kbits/s for one human body. Figures 6-5 and 6-6 show the transformation and inverse transformation results on an SGI Indigo2 Impact workstation with 250 MHz processor. The results show there are a wide range of possibilities to define and transmit human figure information with respect to computation and bandwidth requirements. The choice of the control and message type will depend on the application. Where high accuracy is needed (e.g. medical training applications) the transfer of body part matrices or at least end-effector matrices will be required; in the large-scale simulation with many users, it might be efficient to convey small messages containing the state information coupled with filtering and level of detail techniques to reduce the computational overhead. We chose the joint angle transfer as the optimal solution covering a wide range of cases since it offers fair or good results on all criteria, balancing accuracy loss with the network and compression/decompression computational overhead (the traversal of the human hierarchy to convert joint values to transformation matrices of body parts, to be rendered on display).

kbits/s

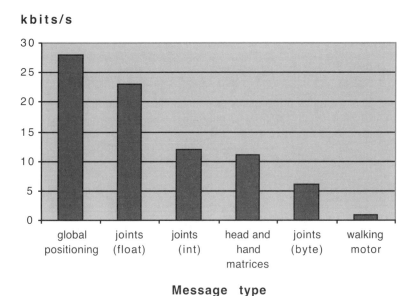

Message type

Figure 6-4. Bit rate requirements for each message type

msec/frame

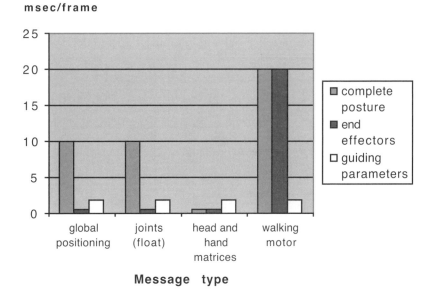

Message type

Figure 6-5. Transformation computations at sender for one frame

msec/frame

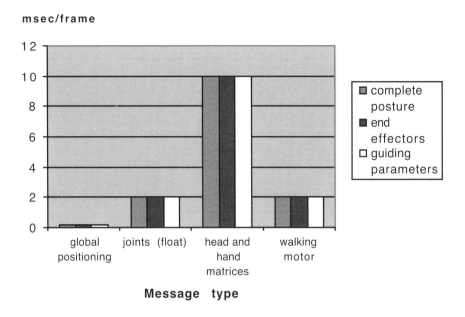

Figure 6-6. Inverse transformation computations at receiver for each body posture

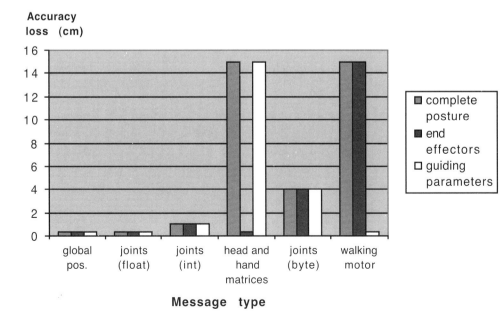

Figure 6-7. Accuracy loss with respect to original input data

Using the state parameters for high-level motions decreases the network bandwidth, but it requires a fast decoding process at the receiving site, and may also require heavy computations to recognize postures at the sending site. The example walking motor shows the possibility of decreasing bandwidth requirements for sending motion data. It also shows the accuracy loss of posture data with varying message types and input methods. The results were computed by averaging the Euclidean distance between the corresponding body parts in the initial body posture at the sender's site and the decoded posture at the receiver's site.

6.6   Bandwidth Scalability

In this chapter, we assume that the bitstream is a temporal sequence of body animation frames (Figure 6-8) which are output from the compression step, therefore the number of bits representing an individual compressed frame can be variable from one frame to another, instead of being fixed.

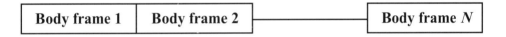

Figure 6-8. Bitstream contains a temporal sequence of body animation frames

Data compression has grown in the last 30 years to a point where there are various techniques that work well for compression of binary programs, data, sound and images. By using special higher-level techniques for the underlying type of objects, a high compression ratio can be achieved. For example, instead of sending the image of a person for a teleconferencing application, if we send their joint angles defining body posture and facial animation parameters, we achieve a much higher compression ratio. By considering the underlying virtual human representation, a higher compression rate can be achieved instead of representing the embodiment as a set of independent 3D surfaces.

Data compression is defined as the procedure that takes a stream of symbols and transforms them into a string of codes that is a compressed version of the input stream. Input symbols are assumed to be drawn from a set of well-defined values, such as ASCII or pixel RGB values. The model is simply a collection of data and rules used to process input symbols, and is a way of determining which codes to output. The coding element takes these data and rules, and generates the codes to be transmitted. Therefore, the data compression consists of two elements: modelling and coding. The model is the particularly interesting point for coding individual objects. Thus, the compression process has the breakdown shown in Figure 6-9.

In the next section, we consider lossless compression. And later on we discuss lossy compression. The virtual human figure representation is suitable for lossy compression, so the techniques considered here are expected to provide better results in terms of bandwidth requirements without any drastic loss in graphical quality.

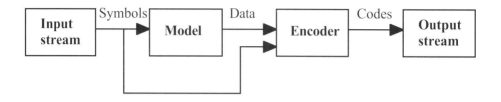

Figure 6-9. Steps of lossy compression

6.7 Lossless Compression of Posture Data

6.7.1 Joint Grouping

In order to further decrease the bandwidth requirements and facilitate communication, the joints comprising the body can be partitioned into a finite set of groups with respect to their interrelationships and importance. For example, joints related to the spine can be grouped. In this way, if the motion affects only one part of the body, only the joints of that part of the body which change in the frame are coded and sent through the bitstream to the server, and then other clients. For example, if the virtual human is waving with their right arm, only joints involved in moving the right arm are sent through the network.

We divide the body degrees of freedom into the groups shown in Table 6-2. Complete degrees of freedoms are given in Table 6-3. Similarly, hand joints can be grouped as shown in Table 6-4 with degrees of freedom detailed in Table 6-5.

The groups can be sent separately by introducing a mask for each group, and inserting this mask in the beginning of the message. The mask has the following format:

<13-bit mask><4-bit mask><dofs for each group in mask>...

Table 6-2. Groups of DOFs for bodies

Pelvis	3 DOFs
Left leg1	4 DOFs
Right leg1	4 DOFs
Left leg2	6 DOFs
Right leg2	6 DOFs
Simple lower spine	10 DOFs
Simple neck	6 DOFs
Head	3 DOFs
Left arm1	5 DOFs
Right arm1	5 DOFs
Left arm2	7 DOFs
Right arm2	7 DOFs
Detailed spine	72 DOFs
Global position	6 DOFs

Table 6-3. Degrees of freedom for bodies

GROUP 1: PELVIS (3 DOFs)
pelvic_tilt, pelvic_torsion, pelvic_roll
GROUP 2: LEFT LEG1 (4 DOFs)
l_hip_flexion, l_hip_abduct,
l_knee_flexion,
l_ankle_flexion
GROUP 3: RIGHT LEG1 (4 DOFs)
r_hip_flexion, r_hip_abduct,
r_knee_flexion,
r_ankle_flexion
GROUP 4: LEFT LEG2 (6 DOFs)
l_hip_twisting, l_knee_twisting,
l_ankle_twisting,
l_subtalar, l_mid_foot, l_toe_flexion
GROUP 5: RIGHT LEG2 (6 DOFs)
r_hip_twisting,
r_knee_twisting, r_ankle_twisting,
r_subtalar, r_mid_foot, r_toe_flexion
GROUP 6: SIMPLE LOWER SPINE (10 DOFs)
vl1_tilt,
vl2_roll, vl2_tilt,
vl3_roll, vl3_tilt,
vt4_roll, vt4_torsion, vt4_tilt,
vt5_roll, vt5_torsion

GROUP 7: SIMPLE NECK (6 DOFs)
vt6_roll, vt6_torsion, vt6_tilt,
vc7_roll, vc7_torsion, vc7_tilt,
GROUP 8: HEAD (3 DOFs)
vc8_roll, vc8_torsion, vc8_tilt
GROUP 9: LEFT ARM1 (5 DOFs)
l_shoulder_flexion, l_shoulder_abduct,
l_shoulder_twisting, l_elbow_flexion,
l_wrist_flexion
GROUP 10: RIGHT ARM1 (5 DOFs)
r_shoulder_flexion, r_shoulder_abduct,
r_shoulder_twisting, r_elbow_flexion,
r_wrist_flexion
GROUP 11: LEFT ARM2 (7 DOFs)
l_clav_abduct, l_clav_rotate,
l_scap_abduct, l_scap_rotate,
l_elbow_twisting, l_wrist_pivot,
l_wrist_twisting
GROUP 12: RIGHT ARM2 (7 DOFs)
r_clav_abduct, r_clav_rotate,
r_scap_abduct, r_scap_rotate,
r_elbow_twisting, r_wrist_pivot,
r_wrist_twisting
GROUP 13: GLOBAL POSITION (6 DOFs)
tr_vertical, tr_lateral, tr_frontal,
rt_body_turn, rt_body_roll, rt_body_tilt

Table 6-4. Groups of DOFs for hands

Left hand1	16 DOFs
Right hand1	16 DOFs
Left hand2	9 DOFs
Right hand2	9 DOFs

Table 6-5. Degrees of freedom for hands

GROUP 1: LEFT HAND1 (16 DOFs) l_pinky_flexion1, l_pinky_flexion2, l_pinky_flexion3, l_ring_flexion1, l_ring_flexion2, l_ring_flexion3, l_middle_flexion1, l_middle_flexion2, l_middle_flexion3, l_index_flexion1, l_index_flexion2, l_index_flexion3, l_thumb_flexion1, l_thumb_abduct, l_thumb_flexion2, l_thumb_flexion3 **GROUP 2: RIGHT HAND1 (16 DOFs)** r_pinky_flexion1, r_pinky_flexion2, r_pinky_flexion3, r_ring_flexion1, r_ring_flexion2, r_ring_flexion3, r_middle_flexion1, r_middle_flexion2, r_middle_flexion3, r_index_flexion1,	r_index_flexion2, r_index_flexion3, r_thumb_flexion1, r_thumb_abduct, r_thumb_flexion2, r_thumb_flexion3 **GROUP 3: LEFT HAND2 (9 DOFs)** l_pinky_twisting, l_pinky_pivot, l_ring_twisting, l_ring_pivot, l_middle_twisting, l_middle_pivot, l_index_twisting, l_index_pivot, l_thumb_twisting **GROUP 4: RIGHT HAND2 (9 DOFs)** r_pinky_twisting, r_pinky_pivot, r_ring_twisting, r_ring_pivot, r_middle_twisting, r_middle_pivot, r_index_twisting, r_index_pivot, r_thumb_twisting

For example, to send only arm joints, the message has the following format:

<0000000011000><0000><5 floats><7 floats>

This decreases the size of the message from 408 bytes to 60 bytes. Thus, with an additional overhead of 3 bytes, we can decrease the message size significantly.

6.7.2 Downloadable Drivers

Downloadable drivers are useful tools to implement autonomous and guided virtual human control, as introduced in Chapter 4, with fewer bandwidth requirements. Remember that autonomous control is achieved by specifying a smaller set of inputs than direct control, such as goals to achieve (e.g. *walk to <loc>*), and guided control specifies high-level parameters to define motor skills (e.g. *walk <speed>*, *breathe<intensity><timelength>*). These parameters may not change at each frame (for example, the destination point to walk will remain constant until the virtual human reaches this point). The downloadable drivers further make use of this fact to decrease the interclient communication.

Both guided and autonomous control techniques assume an underlying virtual human control. This control is typically defined by a compiled program written by the developer of the virtual human behaviour. The complexity of the program defining behaviour may be large or small, depending on the behaviour.

An example of bandwidth reduction is 'breathing' behaviour, as introduced in Chapter 4. Normally, this behaviour would change the joint angles every frame; this means sending joint angles every frame. Additionally, sending low-level messages with low resolution results in more discrete body motion, and this can be overcome by computing joint angles locally at each client.

The downloadable drivers are specified in the command line of the new client (for the sake of discussion, call it client 1):

% vlnet -w http://ligwww.epfl.ch/vlnet/test.vlw -B http://ligwww.epfl.ch/vlnet/breathe

Client 1 downloads the file from URL http://ligwww.epfl.ch/vlnet/breathe and starts this program locally. Then, client 1 sends a message containing this URL to other clients. If there is another client in the same world, say client 2, it will also fetch the program file and spawn it on its local host using the correct parameters for VLNET external interface IDs. An example is shown in Figure 6-10.

Then multiple copies of the same program run asynchronously and in parallel at each host, communicating only small high-level messages occasionally or with lower frequency.

Communication during the Session
During the session, the high-level control parameter of the downloadable driver will normally change. The change will be input from the participant, hence the host that stores the master copy of the driver. This change needs to be sent to the other copies of the driver, through the VLNET protocol.

We use the text interface to control the communication between different versions of the driver. Driver 1 sends the text message with contents:

<char1: special message tag:'#'><char2:clientid:'1'> <char3:drivertype:'B'><char4-char8 domain-specific data for drivers>

For example, if the master client 1 breathing driver wants to inform the remote slave drivers to breathe with intensity 1.2 and time length 3, it can send a text message:

'#1B 1.3 2'

Note that it is completely left to the drivers to define their domain-specific message structure and contents. This provides generality to implement new drivers without changing the VLNET core, with the extra cost of not compressing this already small message.

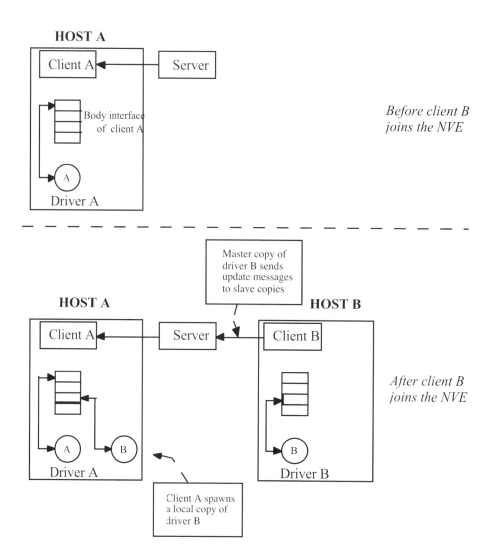

Figure 6-10. When client B connects to the server with a downloadable driver, other clients spawn a local copy of driver B. Client B sends user-defined messages during simulation to update high-level behaviours of remote copies.

6.8 Lossy Compression of Posture Data

Lossy compression can generally be seen as a two-step process: first a lossy step to reduce the number of bits required for storing the joint angles, and then a lossless compression step to convert the resulting data vector to a list of codes (Figure 6-11).

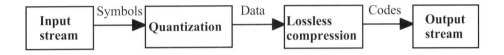

Figure 6-11. Lossy compression process

For transmitting body postures through the network during the simulation phase, the first task is to decide the format of codes for defining body animation parameters defining the body posture, what is sent through the network. This section discusses lossless compression of body animation parameters, mainly for the joint angles.

Our lossy compression techniques typically decreases the resolution of the joint angles in order to transmit posture information with lower bit rates. In this section, we first discuss the effect of using lower joint angle resolutions, then the effect of transmitting a subset of joints, and then a scalable solution to transmit angles with different bit rates by varying compression parameters.

6.8.1 Multiple Levels of Resolution for Joint Angles

The most straightforward approach for lossy compression is to send messages with lower resolution, decreasing the size for each parameter.

We evaluate three possibilities for sending the joint angle message type:

- The actual 4-byte floating-point representation for each degree of freedom.
- A 2-byte integer representation for each degree of freedom, discretized over 0–360°.
- A 1-byte representation for each degree of freedom, discretized over 0–360°.

The discretization for the 2-byte integer representation is performed as follows:

$$\text{integer value} = (2^{16} - 1) * \text{deg} / 360$$

Similarly, the discretization for the 1-byte representation is

$$\text{byte value} = (2^8 - 1) * \text{deg} / 360$$

Remember that the joint angle representation requires

$$75 \text{ parameters} * 32 \text{ bits/float} = 300 \text{ bytes} = 2400 \text{ bits}$$

for one frame. Assuming that the frame rate is 10 frames/s, we need a bandwidth of 24 kbits/s for transmitting joint angles in floating-point form, for one embodiment.

The 2-byte representation decreases the bandwidth requirements to 12 kbits/s, and the 1-byte representation decreases it to 6 kbits/s. Therefore, with some accuracy loss, the compression ratio of 4:1 is achieved.

This discretization introduces an accuracy loss in the final body posture. We present the experimental results of this accuracy loss in the next chapter.

6.8.2 Transmission of a Subset of Joints

Note that the previous techniques assume the transmission of all body joints comprising the body. It is also possible to further group the joints with respect to their visual influence on the resulting posture, from highest priority to lowest priority:

1. Global position and global orientation of the body (6 values)
2. Joint angles with a higher visual influence: thigh (2*3 DOFs), knee (2*2 DOFs), shoulder (2*3 DOFs), elbow (2*2 DOFs), and fl1 and fl2 flexion values of hands as shown in Chapter 5 (2*10 DOFs). This gives a total of 20 values or 40 values
3. Other joint angles with smaller visual influence: 42 values (= 62 – 20) or 82 (=112 – 40) values

As discussed before, the bandwidth requirements for body transmission are assumed with an interactive speed of 10 frames per second. We think that this scalable level of detail for the posture information, with the fast posture updates, allows us to provide fast compression of body data in low-bandwidth networks (Table 6-6).

Table 6-6. Bandwidth requirements for body posture transmission with subset of joints

	Full body transmission with and without hand mobilities		Transmission of a subset of joints
	Without	With	
Very high quality	21.76 kbits/s	37.76 kbits/s	6.4 kbits/s
Good quality	11.30 kbits/s	19.36 kbits/s	3.2 kbits/s
Reduced quality	6.40 kbits/s	10.40 kbits/s	1.6 kbits/s

6.9 Data Compression Tools

This section describes a scalable compression technique, based on ideas in Section 6.8.2. Compression takes place in two steps. First comes a lossy quantization step, then comes a lossless arithmetic coding (Figure 6-12).

For each joint in the state vector, the quantization module stores a quantum value between 1 and 255. The quantum value indicates what the step size is going to be for that joint angle in the compressed representation of the joint angle parameter. Thus, a quantum value of 1 indicates the angle will be encoded with the most precision, and 255 indicates the least precision. Note that each degree of freedom has a different precision requirement. Therefore different quantization step sizes are applied to each degree of freedom. The base quantization step sizes for each joint angle are presented in the next chapter.

The actual formula to obtain quantized state vector S' (Figure 6-12) from S is

Quantized Value (i) = (StateVector(i)/(Quantum(i)*Global_Quantization_Value)
$$\rightarrow \text{Rounded to the nearest integer}$$
(for each joint angle i)

During decoding, the dequantization formula works in reverse:

StateVector' (i) = QuantizedValue(i) * Quantum (i)
(for each joint angle i)

Encoder:

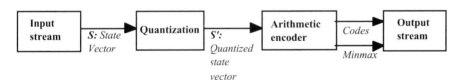

Decoder:

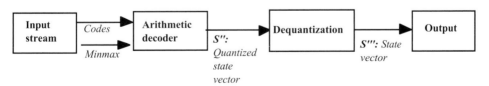

Figure 6-12. Dataflow of the scalable compression technique

The bit rate is controlled by adjusting the quantization step via the use of a quantization scaling factor called *Global_Quantization_Value*. This value is applied uniformly to all DOFs. The magnitude of the quantization parameter ranges from 1 to 255. By modifying this value, we can control the bit rate requirements. For example, a global quantization value of 1 requires higher bit rates, changing it to 255 gives less accurate quantized values, letting the next step, arithmetic coding, to compress for lower bit rates. We measure the precision requirement for *Quantum(i)* of each joint angle in Chapter 8.

The lossy step of coding is performed using the well-defined quantization process. This approach is better than other lossy coding techniques such as the discrete cosine transform (DCT) for body data compression, as it needs fewer computations and it is easy to implement.

Arithmetic Coder

The most well-known lossless coding techniques are Huffman coding and arithmetic coding. Arithmetic coding gives better results than Huffman coding, as it gives greater compression, is faster for adaptive models, and clearly separates the underlying model from the codes. Therefore this approach was selected for the lossless step of the coding.

The adaptive arithmetic coding algorithm developed by Witten et al. (1987) is adopted to code the body state vector. The arithmetic coding method depends on an array of probabilities, with one entry for each possible quantized value. The chosen implementation is an improvement on the initial technique, in that it performs adaptive coding by gathering a table of frequencies for each of the body joint angles. Initially, all joint angle frequencies are set to 1 (reflecting no initial information), but they are updated as each symbol is seen to approximate the observed frequencies. This method requires that both encoder and decoder use the same initial values and the same updating algorithm. The encoder receives the next symbol, encodes it and updates its model. The decoder identifies the symbol according to its current model and then updates its model.

In our MPEG-4 standardization work (Chapter 7), we combine this method with joint grouping. We refer the reader to MPEG (1998) for further details on our syntax.

Predictive Coding

Once the individual frames are defined as above, the entries in the body state vector, that is the degrees of freedom, can be further quantized and coded in the in-between frames, by a predictive coding scheme. This is the approach we have taken in the body animation tool of the forthcoming MPEG-4 standard. For each parameter to be coded in the current frame, the decoded value of this parameter in the previous frame is used as the prediction (Figure 6-13). Then the prediction error, i.e. the difference between the current parameter and its prediction, is computed and coded by arithmetic coding. This predictive coding scheme prevents the coding error from accumulating.

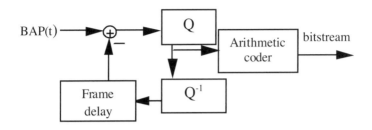

Figure 6-13. BAP predictive coding

6.10 Dead Reckoning

The dead-reckoning algorithm is a way to decrease the number of messages communicated among the participants, and is used for simple non-articulated objects in popular systems such as DIS (IEEE 1993) and NPSNET (Macedonia et al. 1994).

To describe the dead-reckoning algorithm, similar to Gossweiler et al. (1994), we can give an example of a space dogfight game with n players. Each player is represented by their own ship which they control. When player X moves their ship, a message is sent to the other $n-1$ players to tell them the new position. When all players move once, a total of $n(n-1)$ messages are communicated. To reduce the communication overhead, player X sends the ship's position and velocity to other participants. The other participants will use the velocity information to extrapolate the next position of player X. This extrapolation operation is called *dead reckoning*.

In this technique, each participant also stores another copy of its own model, called a *ghost* model, to which it applies the dead reckoning algorithm. If the difference between the real position and this additional copy is greater than a predefined maximum, then player X sends the real position and velocity to the other participants, so they can correct their copy of player X's object. Note that player X sends messages if and only if there is a big difference between the real position and extrapolated one.

The performance of the dead-reckoning algorithm depends on how it correctly predicts the next frames. Therefore, the characteristics of the simulation, and the body model should be taken into account for developing the algorithm (Figure 6-14).

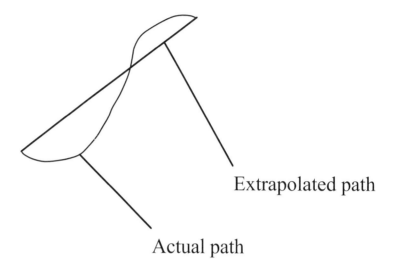

Extrapolated path

Actual path

Figure 6-14. Dead-reckoning technique extrapolates the next path

6.10.1 Dead Reckoning for Virtual Human Figures

The dead-reckoning algorithm on virtual human figures works on their position and body joint angles. There are different possible levels for dead reckoning of virtual humans:

- *Joint-level dead reckoning*: This approach requires no knowledge about the type of action the figure is executing (e.g. walking, grasping) and no information about the motion control method (e.g. inverse kinematics, dynamics, real-time motion capture). The joint angles of the virtual body are considered to be the only available information; and the dead-reckoning computations are performed on this information.
- *Action-level dead reckoning*: The algorithms within this approach know that the actor is performing a particular action (e.g. walking), and the parameters of the actor's state (e.g. tired). There has been some work on the automatic recognition and synthesis of the participants' actions (Unuma et al. 1995; Tosa and Nakatsu 1996; Emering et al. 1997). In this type of dead reckoning, the algorithm uses the parameters of the current motion (e.g. speed and direction for walking); and it uses higher-level motion control mechanisms to obtain the motion, e.g. walking motor (Boulic et al. 1990).

In this chapter, we provide a joint-level dead-reckoning algorithm (Capin et al. 1997a). In order to predict in-between postures, we use a Kalman filter.

6.10.2 Kalman Filtering

The Kalman filter is an optimal linear estimator that minimizes the expected mean-square error in the estimated state variables. It provides a means to infer the missing information using noisy measurements, and is used in predicting the future courses of dynamic systems. Its efficient recursive formulation allows the algorithm to keep up with the real-time requirements of posture prediction. For further information on Kalman filtering, see Welch and Bishop (1995). Previously, in the virtual reality field, the Kalman filter has been applied to decrease the lag between tracking and display in the head trackers; for an overview see Azuma and Bishop (1995) and Foxlin (1996).

The Kalman filter tries to estimate the n-dimensional state vector x of a first-order, discrete-time controlled process governed by the linear difference equation

$$x_{k+1} = A_k x_k + Bu_k + w_k$$

together with a measurement vector z given by

$$z_k = H_k x_k + v_k$$

The random variables w_k and v_k represent the process and measurement noise respectively, and they are assumed to be independent of each other. The $n \times n$ matrix A relates the state x at time step k (x_k) to the state at time step $k + 1$ (x_{k+1}). The $n \times l$ matrix B relates the control input to the state x. The $m \times n$ matrix H relates the measurements z_k to the state variable x_k. At each time step, the filter applies two stages of computation using feedback control: time update computations and measurement update computations.

The time update computations consist of the following steps:

$$\hat{x}_{k+1}^- = A_k \hat{x}_k + Bu_k$$

$$P_{k+1}^- = A_k P_k A_k^T + Q_k$$

where $\hat{x}_k^-$ denotes the *a priori* state estimate at step k given knowledge of the process before step k, and $\hat{x}_k$ is *the a posteriori* state estimate at step k given measurement. P_{k+1}^- and P_k respectively denote the *a priori* and *a posteriori* estimate error covariance, formulating how accurate the filter believes the state variables are.

The measurement update computations consist of the following steps:

$$K_k = P_k^- H_k^T (H_k P_k^- H_k^T + R_k)^{-1}$$

$$\hat{x}_k = \hat{x}_k^- + K(z_k - H_k \hat{x}_k^-)$$

$$P_k = (I - K_k H_k) P_k^-$$

where K_k, called the *Kalman gain matrix*, controls the blending of measurement with the state variables. The filter parameters, the process noise Q_k and measurement error covariance matrix R_k can be tuned by providing constant values computed off-line. See Welch and Bishop (1995) for details.

There is considerable freedom in modelling the system, depending on the knowledge of the modelled processes. In our system, we make the following assumptions: at a time frame, only the joint angles of the body are available, and their velocities are to be computed. The 75 degrees of freedom can be decomposed into 75 independent 1-dof values, each using a separate predictor (Figure 6-15). This makes the system simpler although less accurate. Moreover, we assume that joint angle changes across the prediction interval are small, therefore it is possible to represent joint rotations by yaw, pitch and roll operations where the order of operations is not important. Based on these assumptions, we use a linear discrete Kalman filter of Markov–Gaussian type for each degree of freedom. This allows us to have a simple solution without having any further information or make assumptions on the type of action that the virtual body is performing. The wide range of motions in the body make it difficult to build a model for predicting whole body motions. In this chapter, we built the Kalman filter based on the filter previously developed for predicting the sensor rotations mounted on the head-mounted display. Although it would be ideal to use specific parameters for each degree of freedom in the body, for the initial implementation, we selected uniform parameters for all the filters. The filters that we use are based on the Markov–Gaussian process in the form

$$x'' = -\beta x' + \sqrt{2s^2 \beta} w(t)$$

where

x', x'' = first and second derivatives of x
$w(t)$ = white noise
β = a time factor
s^2 = a variance

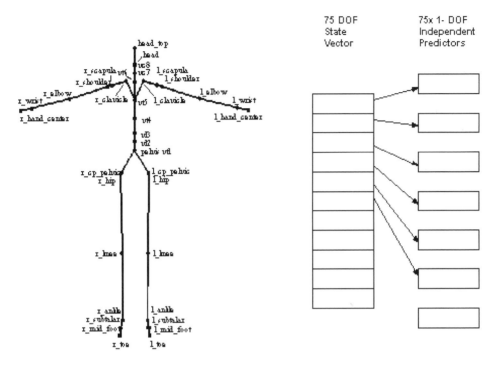

Figure 6-15. Dead-reckoning algorithm divides the state vector into 75 independent joints, each using a separate predictor

This model has been proposed by Liang et al. (1991) for modelling head orientations. They make two assumptions:

- The user's head movement remains static except bursty movements.
- The speed and angular acceleration are non-zero only during the infrequent changes in orientation.

Depending on these assumptions, the filter models head orientation as a random variable which changes at random times, and has limited range of change during these times.

We have assumed that all the body limbs have the same behaviour (relatively stable with bursty changes). Depending on this assumption, we apply the same model parameters for each component. After experimental evaluation, we found that the best values were $\delta = 50$ ms, $\tau = 150$ ms, $\beta = 8.7$ and $\sigma^2 = 0.2$.

The filter algorithm as described by Liang et al. (1991) is shown in Figure 6-16.

Kalman $(\beta, s^2, \gamma, \delta, \tau)$ {

$$x = \begin{bmatrix} z_0 \\ 0 \end{bmatrix}$$

$$H = \begin{bmatrix} 1 & 0 \\ 0 & 1/\delta \end{bmatrix}$$

$P = I$

$R = \gamma^2 H^T H$

$$q_{11} = \frac{2\sigma^2}{\beta} \left[\delta - \frac{2}{\beta}\left(1 - e^{-\beta\delta}\right) + \frac{1}{2\beta}\left(1 - e^{-2\beta\delta}\right) \right]$$

$$q_{12} = 2\sigma^2 \left[\frac{1}{\beta}\left(1 - e^{-\beta\delta}\right) - \frac{1}{2\beta}\left(1 - e^{-2\beta\delta}\right) \right]$$

$q_{21} = q_{12}$

$q_{22} = \sigma^2 \left(1 - e^{-2\beta\delta}\right)$

$$Q = \begin{bmatrix} q_{11} & q_{12} \\ q_{21} & q_{22} \end{bmatrix}$$

$$\Phi = \begin{bmatrix} 1 & \frac{1}{\beta}\left(1 - e^{-\beta\delta}\right) \\ 0 & e^{-\beta\delta} \end{bmatrix}$$

$$\Psi = \begin{bmatrix} 1 & \frac{1}{\beta}\left(1 - e^{-\beta\tau}\right) \\ 0 & e^{-\beta\tau} \end{bmatrix}$$

while not end of session do {

$\qquad K = PH^T \left(HPH^T + R\right)^{-1}$

$$z = \begin{bmatrix} z_i - z_{i-1} \\ z_i \end{bmatrix}$$

$\qquad x = x + K(z - Hx)$

$\qquad P = \Phi(I - KH)P\Phi^T + Q$

$$\begin{bmatrix} y_i \\ \dot{y}_i \end{bmatrix} = \Psi x$$

$\qquad output(y_i)$

$\qquad x = \Phi x$

$\qquad$ }

}

Figure 6-16. Kalman filter

6.10.3 Dead-Reckoning Algorithm for Virtual Body

The dead-reckoning algorithm is detailed in Figure 6-17. Note that, even if the participant Y receives a message from participant X at time frame i, it still performs Kalman filter computations for participant X. This is due to the delay between the time that participant X's body posture is obtained, and the time that participant Y receives the message containing this information.

One important decision is to select the metrics to compare two body postures. The common practice to compare two postures has been to compare them with the eye. However, the dead-reckoning algorithm requires mathematical comparison of joint angles. There are many possibilities to decide on a comparison metric; here are three:

1. Maximum of differences between corresponding angles:

       max (body[mybody][joint] - ghost_body[joint])   joint = 1 to 75

2. Maximum of differences between corresponding angles, with a different coefficient for each joint:

       max(coef(i)*(body[mybody][joint]-ghost_body[joint])) joint = 1 to 75

3. 3D distance between corresponding joints

Approach 1 assumes that every angle has equal importance for the posture. However, in most cases, some angles have a small effect on the overall posture (for example, in the hand-waving posture, the wrist angles have small effect). Approach 2 tries to take this into consideration by assigning a coefficient to each degree of freedom. The third approach uses the 3D position of each joint, and computes the Euclidean distance between corresponding joints. The third approach is expected to achieve better results in providing a metric to compare two postures; this is because it takes into consideration the 3D positions similar to comparison by the eye, and the overall posture of the body. In the next section, we compare the performance of these actions on some examples.

In the VLNET implementation, the dead-reckoning technique is implemented in the body engine, therefore the details of the filter are transparent to the body drivers.

6.11 Filtering

To further reduce the total network load, message filters are applied so that update messages are not sent to every other client at every update. These filters take into consideration the users' viewing frusta in the VE, and make sure that the clients receive only the updates for participants they see. An example of frustum-based filtering is presented in Figure 6-18.

```
for each participant p do
        /* initialize Kalman filters for body p */
At each time step do
    for each participant p do
        if (p == mybody) then
            /* Compute measured body joints -> store in body[p] */
            body[p] = Measure()
            /* Compute predicted body joints of local body: */
            ghost_body = Kalman( ghost_body)
            /* Compare body[p] and ghost_body joint angles */
            delta = compare( body[p], ghost_body)
            if (delta > maximum_allowed_data)  then
                    Send message  m with body joints of body[p]
                    Copy body[p] joints to ghost_body joints
            endif
        endif
        else
            if (message m arrived from participant p)
                    Copy message m joint angles to body[p]
            endif
            body[p] = Kalman( body[p])
        end
    endfor
end
```

Figure 6-17. Dead-reckoning algorithm for virtual body

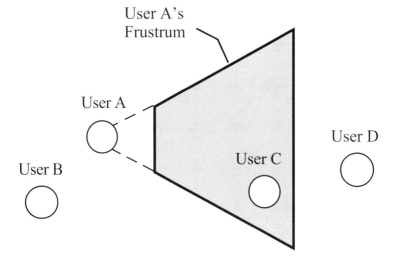

Figure 6-18. Example of frustum-based filtering: users B and D are outside client A's frustum, therefore client A does not receive updates from B and D.

Message filtering is performed within the VLNET world server. The server maintains a list of frusta, which move with the participants. When a new update is received from a client, it performs tests to determine whether this update is within the frustum of any clients, and sends this update to the list of clients which pass this test. Performing this test on the world server rather than the clients, relieves the client hosts to perform other critical tasks such as rendering and interaction.

But we need to send system messages, such as leaving from the VE, to all remote clients regardless of their intervisibility. And for dead reckoning, we need to send messages for participants occasionally, in order to keep the state of the body up to date. For this purpose, we make use of the *heartbeat* messages, which are not filtered.

7 Standards for NVEs and Virtual Humans

Currently, a number of standardization efforts are continuing to solve different aspects of representing virtual humans in NVEs. Among them, the most significant are MPEG-4 Face and Body Animation (FBA), and VRML 2.0 Humanoid Animation (HAnim) specifications. The VRML 2.0 HAnim group attempts to define a standard humanoid that can be exchanged between different users, or programs. The MPEG-4 FBA group aims at streaming virtual human bodies and faces with very low bit rates (less than 10 kbits/s for the whole body).

7.1 MPEG-4 Face and Body Animation Specification

In this section, we introduce our work in ISO/IEC JTC1/SC29/WG11—better known as MPEG. MPEG is traditionally committed to coding and compression of audiovisual data from natural sources. However, the emerging MPEG-4 standard aims not only at multiple natural audiovisual objects composing the scene, but also synthetic audio and video to be integrated with the natural. It will also allow more interaction with both synthetic and natural objects. Within the MPEG-4 ad hoc group on face and body animation we have provided a major contribution to the specification of face and body animation and definition parameters. This experience has led us to believe there is a strong potential relation of the MPEG-4 standard to NVEs and that it will be possible in the near future to build rich multimedia 3D networked environments based on this standard. We analyse the potential use of MPEG-4 for NVE systems. In Section 7.1.1 we briefly introduce the MPEG-4 standard, with more concentration on the face and body animation part of the standard. In Section 7.3 we systematically present the requirements on the bitstream contents encountered in NVE applications, and in Section 7.4 we analyse how these requirements can be met by the MPEG-4 standard. The last section is a conclusion.

7.1.1 Introduction to MPEG-4

ISO/IEC JTC1/SC29/WG11 (Moving Pictures Expert Group, MPEG) is currently working on the new MPEG-4 standard, scheduled to become an International Standard in February 1999. In a world where audiovisual data is increasingly stored, transferred and manipulated digitally, MPEG-4 sets its objectives beyond 'plain' compression. Instead of regarding video as a sequence of frames with fixed shape and size and with attached audio information, the video scene is regarded as a set of dynamic objects. Thus the background of the scene might be one object, a moving car another object, the sound of the engine yet another object, and so on. The objects are spatially and temporally independent and therefore can be stored, transferred and manipulated independently. The composition of the final scene is done at the decoder, potentially allowing great manipulation freedom to the consumer of the data.

Video and audio acquired by recording from the real world is called natural. In addition to the natural objects, synthetic, computer-generated graphics and sounds are being produced and used in ever increasing quantities. MPEG-4 aims to enable integration of synthetic objects within the scene. It will provide support for 3D graphics, synthetic sound, text to speech, as well as synthetic faces and bodies. Figure 7-1 shows an overview of MPEG-4 and its relation to VRML 2.0.

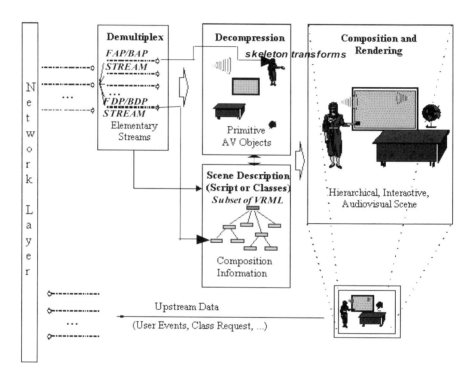

Figure 7-1. Overview of MPEG-4 and its relation with VRML 2.0

Currently there are four groups that work on producing MPEG-4 standards: systems, audio, video and synthetic/natural hybrid coding (SNHC). The standard will finally consist of systems, audio and video parts, and the specifications produced by SNHC will be integrated in either audio or video.

The systems layer supports demultiplexing of multiple bitstreams, buffer management, time identification, scene composition and terminal configuration.

MPEG-4 video provides technologies for efficient storage, transmission and manipulation of video data in multimedia environments. The key areas addressed are efficient representation, error resilience over a broad range of media, coding of arbitrarily shaped video objects, and alpha map coding.

MPEG-4 Audio standardizes the coding of natural audio at bit rates of 2 kbits/s to 64 kbits/s, addressing different bit rate ranges with appropriate coding technologies.

Synthetic/natural hybrid coding (SNHC) deals with coding of synthetic audio and visual data. In particular, a subgroup of SNHC deals with the animation of human faces and bodies. We present in more detail the activities of this group and their current draft specification in the following subsection.

7.1.2   Face and Body Animation (FBA)

The face and body animation ad hoc group (FBA) deals with coding of human faces and bodies, i.e. efficient representation of their shape and movement. This is important for a number of applications ranging from communication, entertainment to ergonomics and medicine. Hence there exists quite a strong interest in standardization. The group has defined in detail the parameters for both definition and animation of human faces and bodies. This draft specification is based on proposals from several leading institutions in the field of virtual humans research. At the time of writing, it is being updated within the current MPEG-4 committee draft (MPEG-N1901; MPEG-N1902).

Definition parameters allow detailed definition of shape, size and texture for bodies and faces. Animation parameters allow facial expressions and body postures to be defined. The parameters are designed to cover all naturally possible expressions and postures, as well as exaggerated expressions and motions to some extent (e.g. for cartoon characters). The animation parameters are precisely defined in order to allow accurate implementation on any facial or body model.

7.1.2.1   Facial Animation Parameter Set

The facial animation parameters (FAPs) are based on the study of minimal facial actions and are closely related to muscle actions. They represent a complete set of basic facial actions, and therefore allow the representation of most natural facial expressions. The lips are particularly well defined and it is possible to precisely define the inner and outer lip contour. Exaggerated values make it possible to define actions that are normally not possible for humans, but could be desirable for cartoon-like characters.

All the parameters involving translational movement are expressed in terms of the facial animation parameter units (FAPUs). These units are defined in order to allow interpretation of the FAPs on any facial model in a consistent way, producing reasonable results in terms of expression and speech pronunciation. They correspond to fractions of distances between some key facial features (e.g. eye distance). The fractional units used are chosen to allow enough precision.

The parameter set contains two high-level parameters. The viseme parameter visemes to be rendered on the face without having to express them in terms of other parameters or to enhance the result of other parameters, ensuring the correct rendering of visemes. The full list of visemes is not defined yet. Similarly, the expression parameter allows the definition of high-level facial expressions.

7.1.2.2 Facial Definition Parameter Set

An MPEG-4 decoder supporting facial animation must have a generic facial model capable of interpreting FAPs. This ensures that it can reproduce facial expressions and speech pronunciation. When it is desired to modify the shape and appearance of the face and make it look like a particular person or character, FDPs are necessary.

The FDPs are used to personalize the generic face model to a particular face. The FDPs are normally transmitted once per session, followed by a stream of compressed FAPs. However, if the decoder does not receive the FDPs, the use of FAPUs ensures that it can still interpret the FAP stream. This ensures minimal operation in broadcast or teleconferencing applications.

The facial definition parameter set can contain the following items:

- 3D feature points
- Texture coordinates for feature points (optional)
- Face scene graph (optional)
- Face animation table (FAT) (optional)

The feature points are characteristic points on the face allowing salient facial features to be located. They are illustrated in Figure 7-2. Feature points must always be supplied, but the rest of the parameters are optional.

The texture coordinates can be supplied for each feature point. The face scene graph is a 3D polygon model of a face including potentially multiple surfaces and textures, as well as material properties. The face animation table (FAT) contains information that defines how the face will be animated by specifying the movement of vertices in the face scene graph with respect to each FAP as a piecewise linear function. We do not deal with FAT in this chapter. The feature points, texture coordinates and face scene graph can be used in four ways:

- If only feature points are supplied, they are used on their own to deform the generic face model.
- If texture coordinates are supplied, they are used to map the texture image from the face scene graph on the face deformed by feature points. Obviously, in this case the face scene graph must contain exactly one texture image and this is the only information used from the face scene graph.
- If feature points and face scene graph are supplied, and the face scene graph contains a non-textured face, the facial model in the face scene graph is used as a calibration model. All vertices of the generic model must be aligned to the surfaces of the calibration model.
- If feature points and face scene graph are supplied, and the face scene graph contains a textured face, the facial model in the face scene graph is used as a calibration model. All vertices of the generic model must be aligned to the surfaces of the calibration model. In addition, the texture from the calibration model is mapped onto the deformed generic model.

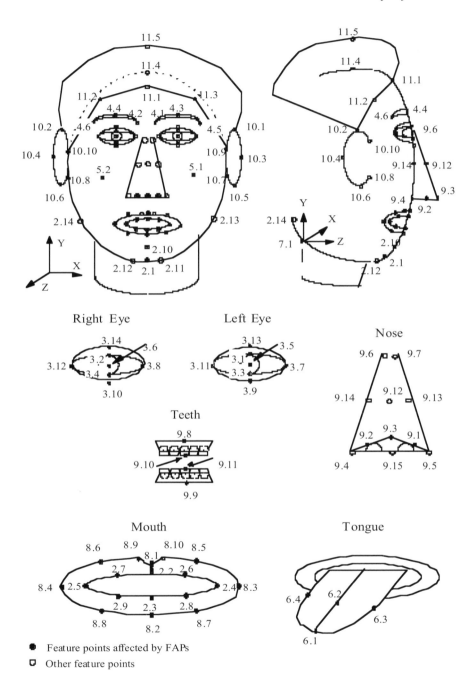

Figure 7-2. FDP feature foints

7.1.2.3   Body Animation Parameter Set

Similar to facial animation parameters, body animation parameters (BAPs) are used to modify the posture of the virtual body during animation. The same BAPs can be applied to different models in order to produce reasonably similar high-level results in terms of body posture and animation, without the need to initialize and calibrate the model. The BAP set contains the joint angles connecting different body parts; these include toe, ankle, knee, hip, spine (C1–C7, T1–T12, L1–L5), shoulder, clavicle, elbow, wrist and the fingers. The body contains a total of 175 degrees of freedom, including 25 degrees of freedom for each hand. In particular, the spine contains five levels of detail, and models can be constructed with varying complexity: a total of 9, 24, 42, 60, 72 degrees of freedom. Thus, the models can have variable complexity depending on the target application.

Although an initial effort attempted to provide a set of high-level parameters similar to the high-level FAPs (such as walking and running), during the standardization process they had to be removed as the body has significantly more body actions than facial actions, and it is difficult to specify a minimal set of actions.

7.1.2.4   Body Definition Parameter Set

Similar to the face, an MPEG-4 decoder is assumed to have a default body model. The body definition parameter (BDPs) allow this local model of the receiver site to be customized by a particular body model. It contains the following items:

1. Body surface geometry (with texture coordinates if texture is used)
   The body surface geometry is downloaded using the 3D mesh transmission mechanism. The body geometry surfaces are specified using the VRML 2.0 HAnim PROTO SEGMENT definitions, as discussed below.
2. Joint centre locations
   The positions of the joints are specified using an augmented version of the VRML PROTO JOINT definitions.
3. Texture images (optional)

The VRML 2.0 ad hoc group on humanoid animation is working on a standard specification of bodies, which fulfils most of these specifications. The BDP syntax is strongly based on HAnim Version 1.1 specification (http://ece.uwaterloo.ca/~h-anim/spec.html). The texture images can be defined for each surface. Note that the texture images are part of the VRML PROTO SEGMENT geometry, defined by the VRML 2.0 syntax.

In addition to downloading the whole body model, it is also possible to calibrate the default body model of the decoder by sending a subset of humanoid definition in VRML 2.0 HAnim syntax. Typically, the decoder will scale its default humanoid skeleton using the joint centres (centre field in the Joint node in the downloaded .wrl file). The decoder can also optionally calibrate its default humanoid model shape, using the Segment node in the downloaded VRML scenegraph.

Thus, three types of behaviours are defined for the decoder:

- *Simple*: the decoder ignores the BDP parameters.
- *Calibration*: the decoder customizes its default body using downloaded BDP parameters.
- *Predictable*: the decoder replaces its default body using downloaded BDP parameters.

Here are the basic assumptions in the BDP:

1. Basic postures to initialize a human body model
   Standing posture: according to the definition, the feet should point to the front direction, the two arms should be placed at the sides of the body with the palm of the hands facing inward. This posture also implies that all joint angles have value zero.
2. Establishing a coordinate system
   The body coordinate system's origin is located at ground ($y = 0$) level, between the humanoid's feet, with the lateral and frontal position the same as the spine origin (l1tilt). The orientation of the coordinate is x points to the left of the humanoid, y up, z front.
3. Calibration or initial parameter set to specify joint centres and segments

More information on the parameters and their syntax can be found at the MPEG web site (http://drogo.scelt.stet.it/mpeg.).

7.2   VRML 2.0 HAnim Specification

The VRML 2.0 HAnim specification aims to provide a standard representation   of virtual human bodies in VRML 2.0 syntax. Virtual humans created with this specification can be animated using various motion control techniques—keyframing, procedural animation, inverse kinematics, etc. – as well as MPEG-4 Face and Body Animation stream.   Therefore, it complements the MPEG-4 standardization effort rather than conflicting with it.

A VRML humanoid consists of three types of nodes: *Joint*, *Segment* and *Humanoid*. Joint nodes are used to create a skeleton hierarchy of joints. The Segment nodes are attached to the Joint nodes, and typically contain the geometry of the body surfaces or the deformable skins, clothes, etc. Finally, the Humanoid node allows information to be included such as the author of the file, copyright information and name.

The Joint PROTO looks as follows:

```
PROTO Joint [
    exposedField    SFString    name                    " "
    exposedField    SFVec3f     translation             0 0 0
    exposedField    SFRotation  rotation            0 0 1 0
    exposedField    SFVec3f     scale                   1 1 1
    exposedField    SFRotation  scaleOrientation    0 0 1 0
    exposedField    SFVec3f     center                  0 0 0
```

```
            exposedField    MFNode      children              [ ]
            exposedField    MFFloat     ulimit                [ 0 0 0 ]
            exposedField    MFFloat     llimit                [ 0 0 0 ]
    ]
```

Notice that most of the fields correspond to those of the Transform node. This is because the typical implementation of the Joint PROTO will be

```
    {
        Transform {
                translation IS translation
                rotation IS rotation
                scale IS scale
                scaleOrientation IS scaleOrientation
                center IS center
                children IS children
        }
    }
```

The u_limit and l_limit fields are upper and lower bounds on the degrees of freedom in the joint. The eulerSequence field specifies the sequence in which the angles must be composed. The default sequence is assumed to be 'XYZ'.

There is one Joint node for each joint. Each joint node can contain other joint nodes, and may also contain a segment node. The segment node describes the body part associated with that joint.

```
    PROTO Segment [
        exposedField    SFString    name            " "
        exposedField    SFFloat     mass            0
        exposedField    SFVec3f     centerOfMass    0 0 0
        field           SFVec3f     bboxCenter      0 0 0
        field           SFVec3f     bboxSize        -1 -1 -1
        exposedField    MFNode      children        [ ]
    ]
```

Both bboxCenter and bboxSize, if supplied, may provide information that can be used during the rendering process, or for calibrating the shape of the default model of the decoder. If bboxCenter and bboxSize are not defined, then the children field containing the shape geometry can be used by the decoder to calibrate the shape.

The children field contains the geometry for the segment. Any geometry node may be attached. A joint may contain between one and three BAPs.

Table 7-1 presents the joints, and associated BAPs and segment names.

Table 7-1. Joints, and associated BAPs and segment names

Joint	BAPs	Segment
sacroiliac	pelvic_tilt, pelvic_torsion, pelvic_roll	pelvis
l_hip	l_hip_flexion, l_hip_abduct, l_hip_twisting	l_thigh
r_hip	r_hip_flexion, r_hip_abduct, r_hip_twisting	r_thigh
l_knee	l_knee_flexion, l_knee_twisting	l_calf
r_knee	r_knee_flexion, r_knee_twisting	r_calf
l_ankle	l_ankle_flexion, l_ankle_twisting	l_hindfoot
r_ankle	r_ankle_flexion, r_ankle_twisting	r_hindfoot
l_subtalar	l_subtalar	l_midproximal
r_subtalar	r_subtalar	r_midproximal
l_midtarsal	l_mid_foot	l_middistal
r_midtarsal	r_mid_foot	r_middistal
l_metatarsal	l_toe_flexion	l_forefoot
r_metatarsal	r_toe_flexion	r_forefoot
vl5	l5roll, l5torsion, l5tilt	l5
vl4	l4roll, l4torsion, l4tilt	l4
vl3	l3roll, l3torsion, l3tilt	l3
vl2	l2roll, l2torsion, l2tilt	l2
vl1	l1roll, l1torsion, l1tilt	l1
vt12	t12roll, t12torsion, t12tilt	t12
vt11	t11roll, t11torsion, t11tilt	t11
vt10	t10roll, t10torsion, t10tilt	t10
vt9	t9roll, t9torsion, t9tilt	t9
vt8	t8roll, t8torsion, t8tilt	t8
vt7	t7roll, t7torsion, t7tilt	t7
vt6	t6roll, t6torsion, t6tilt	t6
vt5	t5roll, t5torsion, t5tilt	t5
vt4	t4roll, t4torsion, t4tilt	t4
vt3	t3roll, t3torsion, t3tilt	t3
vt2	t2roll, t2torsion, t2tilt	t2
vt1	t1roll, t1torsion, t1tilt	t1
vc7	c7roll, c7torsion, c7tilt	c7
vc6	c6roll, c6torsion, c6tilt	c6
vc5	c5roll, c5torsion, c5tilt	c5
vc4	c4roll, c4torsion, c4tilt	c4
vc3	c3roll, c3torsion, c3tilt	c3
vc2	c2roll, c2torsion, c2tilt	c2
vc1	c1roll, c1torsion, c1tilt	c1
skullbase		skull
r_wrist	r_wrist_pivot, r_wrist_twisting	r_wrist
r_thumb1	r_thumb1_flexion, r_thumb1_abduct	r_thumb_metacarpal
r_thumb2	r_thumb2_flexion	r_thumb_proximal
r_thumb3	r_thumb3_flexion	r_thumb_distal
r_index1	r_index1_abduct, r_index1_flexion	r_index_proximal
r_index2	r_index2_flexion	r_index_middle
r_index3	r_index3_flexion	r_index_distal
r_middle1	r_middle1_abduct, r_middle1_flexion	r_middle_proximal
r_middle2	r_middle2_flexion	r_middle_middle
r_middle3	r_middle3_flexion	r_middle_distal
r_ring1	r_ring1_abduct, r_ring1_flexion	r_ring_proximal
r_ring2	r_ring2_flexion	r_ring_middle
r_ring3	r_ring3_flexion	r_ring_distal
r_pinky1	r_pinky1_abduct, r_pinky1_flexion	r_pinky_proximal
r_pinky2	r_pinky2_flexion	r_pinky_middle
r_pinky3	r_pinky3_flexion	r_pinky_distal
l_wrist	l_wrist_pivot, l_wrist_twisting	l_wrist
l_thumb1	l_thumb1_flexion, l_thumb1_abduct	l_thumb_metacarpal

Table 7-1. *Continued*

l_thumb2	l_thumb2_flexion	l_thumb_proximal
l_thumb3	l_thumb2_flexion	l_thumb_distal
l_index1	l_index1_abduct, l_index1_flexion	l_index_proximal
l_index2	l_index2_flexion	l_index_middle
l_index3	l_index3_flexion	l_index_distal
l_middle1	l_middle1_abduct, l_middle1_flexion	l_middle_proximal
l_middle2	l_middle2_flexion	l_middle_middle
l_middle3	l_middle3_flexion	l_middle_distal
l_ring1	l_ring1_abduct, l_ring1_flexion	l_ring_proximal
l_ring2	l_ring2_flexion	l_ring_middle
l_ring3	l_ring3_flexion	l_ring_distal
l_pinky1	l_pinky1_abduct, l_pinky1_flexion	l_pinky_proximal
l_pinky2	l_pinky2_flexion	l_pinky_middle
l_pinky3	l_pinky3_flexion	l_pinky_distal

Note that the body can be defined by a subset of Joint nodes. The body is typically built as a series of nested Joints, each of which may have a Segment associated with it. For example:

...

```
     DEF hanim_l_shoulder Joint {   name "l_shoulder"
       center 0.167 1.36 -0.0518
       children   [
         DEF hanim_l_elbow Joint {   name "l_elbow"
           center 0.196 1.07 -0.0518
         children      [
           DEF hanim_l_wrist Joint {   name "l_wrist"
             center 0.213 0.811 -0.0338
             children   [
               DEF hanim_r_hand Segment {   name "r_hand"
                ...
               }
             ]
           }
           DEF hanim_l_forearm Segment {   name "l_forearm"
            ...
           }
         ]
       }
       DEF hanim_l_upperArm Segment {   name "l_upperArm"
        ...
       }
     ]
   }
   ...
```

Many Joints may be omitted, such as most of the vertebrae, the midtarsal, and the acromioclavicular. The spinal joints that belong to first spine groups are the ones that should be given priority if a full spine is not implemented.

The most up-to-date specification of a VRML 2.0 humanoid can be found at the HAnim specification homepage, http://ece.uwaterloo.c/~h-anim/spec.html.

Figure 7-3 shows an example of virtual humans represented in a VRML environment.

Figure 7-3. Virtual humans in VRML

7.3 Bitstream Contents in NVE Applications

We analyse various data types that are transmitted through the network in NVE systems. Figure 7-4 presents an overview of all data types usually encountered. Current systems usually support only a subset of the data types presented here.

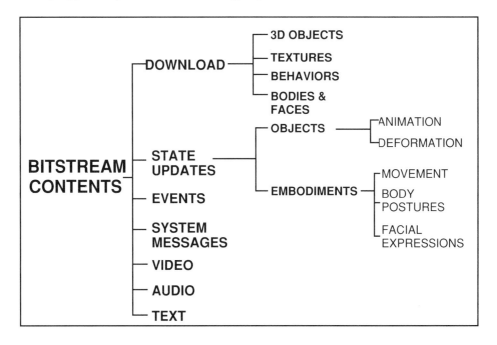

Figure 7-4. Bitstream contents breakdown for NVE systems

7.3.1 Download

The main need for download arises when a new user joins an NVE session. At this moment the complete description of the virtual environment has to be downloaded to the new user. This includes 3D objects structured in a scene hierarchy, textures and possibly behaviours in the form of scripts or programs. The new user also has to download the embodiment descriptions of all users and send their own to everyone. The embodiment might be a simple geometrical object, but in a more sophisticated system it should be a body and face description in a form that allows later animation of both body and face.

Downloads are not restricted to the session establishment phase, they can also occur anytime during the session if new objects are introduced in the scene—they have to be distributed.

7.3.2 State Updates

All state changes for both the environment itself and the users' embodiments as a special part of the environment have to be propagated through the network.

For the objects in the environment, this commonly involves the change of position and orientation, i.e. animation of rigid objects. Objects in non-networked VEs are not only animated rigidly, they are often also deformed. Free deformation of objects is not commonly supported in NVE systems because of increased bandwidth needs—all displaced vertices have to be updated. It is, however, a very desirable feature to be included in NVE systems.

For user embodiments, state updates also involve basic movement, and in the case of simple, rigid embodiments this is enough. For articulated, human-like embodiments means must be provided to communicate body postures and facial expressions to allow the simulation of natural body movements and actions.

7.3.3 Events

These are typically short messages about events happening in the environment. The basic difference from state updates is that a state message makes all previous state messages for the same object obsolete (e.g. a new position of the object makes all previous positions obsolete) (Kessler and Hodges 1996), which is not the case with event messages. An event is sent only once and can influence the environment state potentially for a long time. Therefore the security of event messages must be higher then for state updates.

7.3.4 System Messages

These messages are typically used during session establishment and log-off. Their security is essential because errors can cause serious malfunction of the system.

7.3.5 Video

Video can be streamed and texture-mapped onto any object in the environment, producing real-time video textures. This can be used in different ways for various applications. Examples include virtual video presentations, facial texture mapping for facial communication as presented in Section 5.3, as well as mixing of real and virtual worlds for augmented reality applications or virtual studios.

The requirements on the video quality may vary from application to application.

7.3.6 Audio

The most common use of audio in NVEs is for speech communication. However, synthetic 3D sound can also be an important part of a virtual environment.

7.3.7 Text

The most common use of text is for text-based chat between users. There are, however, more interesting ways to use it. As explained in Chapter 4, autonomous virtual humans with built-in AI decision-making algorithms can also be participants in NVEs. The best way to communicate orders, questions or dialogues to them is through text, and that is also the easiest way for them to respond. Speech recognition and text-to-speech (TTS) systems (possibly coupled with facial animation for lip sync) can be used to interface naturally with the users.

7.4 How MPEG-4 Can Meet NVE Requirements

Based on the requirements laid out in the previous section and MPEG-related documentation (MPEG-N1886; MPEG-N1901; MPEG-N1902; Koenen et al. 1997; Doenges et al. 1997) we study how MPEG-4 tools can be deployed to solve the problems of NVE systems.

As for the network topologies, the solutions are outside the scope of MPEG, which mostly concentrates on bitstream contents. It is, however, worthwhile noting that an MPEG-4 system will be capable of receiving objects from up to eight different sources, a fact to be considered when planning network topologies for particular applications.

In the following subsections we study various components of bitstream contents with respect to MPEG-4.

7.4.1 Download

The MPEG-4 standard provides the means to download and store audio, video and synthetic objects. Furthermore, progressive transmission based on scalable coding techniques are supported.

MPEG-4 supports a VRML-like 3D geometry hierarchy with all attributes, as well as behaviour data. It provides means for efficient compression of 3D meshes. Efficient still texture coding is supported, as well as spatial- and quality-scalable coding to fit available bandwidth and rendering capabilities.

MPEG-4 supports body and face objects. Using body definition parameters (BDPs) and face definition parameters (FDPs) it is possible to define body and face representation. BAPs and FAPs are scalable, offering a wide choice of trade-offs between definition quality and bandwidth requirement. In the absence of FDPs and/or BDPs, generic bodies and faces can be used.

7.4.2 State Updates

MPEG-4 supports scaling, rotation and translation of any video object (natural or synthetic, i.e. 3D objects included) about any axis in 2D or 3D space. Changes in audio objects' localization are also supported.

MPEG-4 supports efficient coding of face and body animation. The parameters are defined to express body postures and facial expressions in an efficient manner and independently of a particular face or body model. The BAPs are quantized and coded by a predictive coding scheme, similar to the FAPs. For each parameter to be coded in the current frame, the decoded value of this parameter in the previous frame is used as the prediction. Then the prediction error, i.e. the difference between the current parameter and its prediction, is computed and coded by arithmetic coding. This predictive coding scheme prevents the coding error from accumulating. The BAPs are grouped with respect to their visual effect on the final posture of the virtual body; and within a BAP group, individual BAPs can be masked in order to obtain further compression. Using these techniques, the parameters are compressed to obtain very small bit rates (approximately 2 kbits/s for facial expressions and 5 kbits/s for body postures).

7.4.3 Events and System Messages

These messages are specific to a particular NVE system, hence they are not explicitly covered by MPEG-4.

7.4.4 Video

Video is a traditional part of MPEG, and the video tools are mature and extensive. MPEG-4 video supports all types of pixel-based video with high compression efficiency. Tools are provided to achieve error-resilient video streams over a variety of networks with possibly severe error conditions, including low-bit-rate networks. Scalability in terms of content and spatial and temporal quality are also one of the goals. Various delay modes, including low delay modes for real-time communication are also supported. MPEG-4 tools are optimized for the following bit rate ranges: < 64 kbits/s (low), 64 to 384 kbits/s (intermediate) and 384 to 1800 kbits/s (high). MPEG-4 also supports various video formats.

7.4.5 Audio

MPEG-4 supports the following types of audio content: high-quality audio (> 15 kHz), intermediate quality audio (< 15 kHz), wideband speech (50 Hz to 7 kHz), narrowband speech (50 Hz to 3.6 kHz) and intelligible speech (300 Hz to 3.4 kHz). Tools are provided to achieve error-resilient audio streams, including support for low-bit-rate applications. In particular, speech coding compression supports intelligible speech at 2 kbits/s. A number of audio formats are supported, as defined by sampling frequency, amplitude resolution, quantizer characteristics and number of channels.

7.4.6 Text

Simple text is not explicitly supported by MPEG-4. However, there are tools for text-to-speech functionality which requires at least simple text, and possibly auxiliary information such as phoneme duration and amplitude of each phoneme. MPEG-4 supports the capability to synchronize TTS output with a facial animation system visualizing the pronounciation.

7.4.7 Integration

For NVE systems it is not only important to support all the data types described in previous sections, but also to achieve an orderly integration of all data types with respect to relative priorities and synchronization.

MPEG-4 includes dynamic multiplexing of all objects. It provides means to identify the relative importance of parts of coded audiovisual information with at least 32 levels of priority. Synchronization between all objects is supported, with specified maximal differential delays (e.g. between two video objects or between an audio object and a video object).

7.5 Concluding Remarks

We have analysed the networking requirements of NVEs, and how MPEG-4 tools can be used to fulfil these requirements.

The building of network topology, session establishment and destruction, and system-particular message passing are outside the scope of MPEG-4 and should be dealt with on another level. However, most of the data types that are important for NVE systems will be very well supported by MPEG-4 tools (video, audio, 3D objects, textures, bodies, faces). On top of this, MPEG-4 will offer reliable multiplexing, mechanisms for establishing priorities among data, as well as synchronization. We believe that MPEG-4 tools should play an important role in building future NVE systems.

8 Applications and Experiments

8.1   Potential Applications

Networked virtual environment systems are suitable for numerous collaborative applications ranging from games to medicine (Doenges et al. 1997):

- Virtual teleconferencing with multimedia object exchange
- All sorts of collaborative work involving 3D design
- Multi-user game environments
- Teleshopping involving 3D models, images, sound (e.g. real estate, furniture, cars)
- Medical applications (distance diagnostics, virtual surgery for training)
- Distance learning and training
- Virtual studio/set with networked media integration
- Virtual travel agency

This chapter presents some different techniques developed using the VLNET system, and evaluation of the results.

8.2   Example Applications and Programming Results

In order to test the efficiency of the VLNET architecture, and its contribution in rapid prototyping of applications, we developed a number of pilot applications, and made demonstrations of these applications at various exhibitions and conferences. Note that all the applications use the same VLNET core, and only the application-specific drivers are written or reused from a list of default drivers.

Virtual Chess
We think that a main subset of the most driving applications for NVEs are multi-user games. To demonstrate the use of VLNET for this purpose, we have developed a variety of games. The first application was a 3D chess table (Figure 8-1), with the chess pieces having the size of participants. This scaling gave an impression of presence in a room, and allowed face-to-face interaction of participants in addition to the object interactions for the game, giving a sense of being together. This application was a demonstration of how embodiments can be used in a different way. The participants were represented by guided virtual humans, controlling their embodiment by SpaceBall and mouse; and walking and grasping motor

skills combined with global constraints. However, the users of the game said that it was difficult to have an overall view of the game, which is required for chess playing.

Figure 8-1. Virtual chess application

We also tried a smaller-scaled chess table. In this version, we needed a precise movement of the hand and precise picking capabilities, otherwise the participants could pick different piece than they wanted to. This needs further techniques for finer manipulation of the objects, and as discussed at the beginning of this book, fine manipulation is a growing research topic by various groups, and we have not included it in our work.

Networked Virtual Tennis Game
At the Computer Graphics Laboratory of EPFL and MIRALab at the University of Geneva, we developed a virtual tennis game over the network (Molet et al. 1998). This was shown at the opening and closing ceremonies of Telecom Interactive '97; the videotapes were demonstrated at the opening ceremony of the Virtual Humans '97 Conference at Los Angeles, at the Virtual Technologies booth of SIGGRAPH '97 and at various other conferences.

The tennis game (Figure 8-2) involved two participants and one referee. The participants, one in Geneva, the other in Lausanne, were represented by directly controlled virtual humans, wearing Flock of Birds magnetic trackers attached to their bodies. They were using immersive head-mounted displays for visualizing the scene. The autonomous referee used her synthetic vision to watch the game and decided the state of the game and the score. She updates the state of the match when she 'hears' a ball collision event (ball–ground, ball–net, ball–racket) according to what she sees and her knowledge of the tennis   game, and   she communicates her decisions and the state of the game by 'spoken words' (sound events).

Figure 8-2. Virtual tennis application

Figure 8-3 shows the configuration used for the application. For this purpose, a Flock of Birds program, a tennis ball simulation program, a virtual camera control program, and an autonomous referee program, each written by different persons in different cities, needed to be integrated within the same environment. Furthermore, new versions of each software item were developed simultaneously, so it was difficult to integrate the separate items within one application. Additionally, the time to develop the whole application was only 4 months. VLNET architecture allowed each developer to work independently, and make tests every week for half a day with new versions of other programs. The system could satisfy the requirements of this demonstration within the time constraints, and the resulting NVE simulation speed was sufficient for the high interactivity requirements of the game.

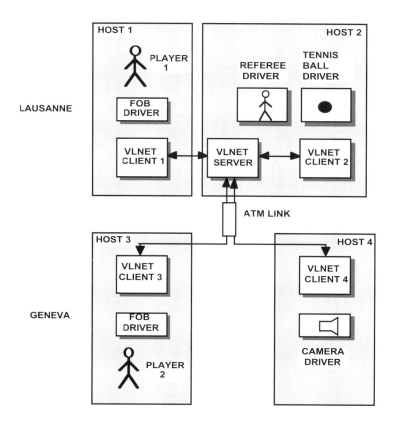

Figure 8-3. Process configuration of the virtual tennis application

Virtual Tennis Game against an Autonomous Actor

A version of the tennis game against an autonomous actor was also developed (Noser et al. 1996; Noser and Thalmann 1997). Figure 8-4 shows the configuration of this version. Note that this version uses the same driver for Flock of Birds, referee, and the ball. Only one driver for one participant was replaced by an autonomous player program. Figure 8-5 shows a typical scene.

The environment of the autonomous virtual humans is modelled and animated by L-systems which are timed production systems designed to model the development and behaviour of static objects, plant-like objects and autonomous creatures. They are based on timed, parameterized, stochastic, conditional environmentally sensitive and context-dependent production systems, force fields, synthetic vision and audition (Noser and Thalmann 1996). Prusinkiewicz and Lindenmayer (1990) present the Lindenmayer systems, or L-systems for short, as a mathematical theory of plant development with a geometrical interpretation based on turtle geometry. The authors explain mathematical models of developmental processes and structures of plants and illustrate them with computer-generated images. Our behavioural L-system is based on the general theory about L-grammars described in this work.

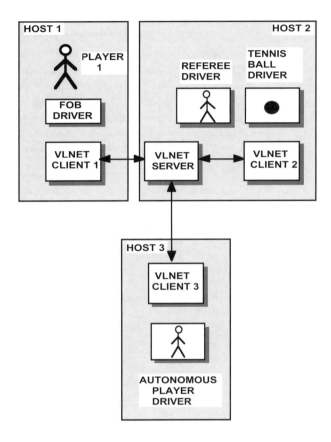

Figure 8-4. Process configuration for virtual tennis against autonomous player

An L-system is given by an axiom, which is a string of parametric and timed symbols, and some production rules specifying how to replace corresponding symbols in the axiom during the evolution of time. The L-system interpreter associates to its symbols basic geometric primitives, turtle control symbols or special control operations necessary for an animation. Basic geometric primitives are cubes, spheres, trunks, cylinders terminated at their ends by half-spheres, line segments, pyramids and imported triangulated surfaces. We define the non-generic environment as the ground, the tennis court and the walls, and we do this directly in the axiom of the production system. The generic parts such as growing plants are defined by production rules having only their germ in the axiom. The virtual actors are also represented by a special symbol. Their geometric representation can vary from some simple primitives like some cubes and spheres, over a more complicated skeleton structure to a fully deformed triangulated body surface.

Through VLNET clients and the VLNET server, the L-system interpreter shares with the participant client the important environment elements such as the tennis court, the tennis ball, an autonomous referee, the autonomous player and the participants. Each virtual human has its own VLNET client, and the L-system interpreter program controls the referee and the autonomous player through the external interfaces of the VLNET system. The representation of the real participant in the L-system interpreter is reduced to a simple racket, whose position is communicated through the network and obtained from the local VLNET client's object behaviour interface at each frame. The racket and head positions and orientations of the autonomous virtual human player are communicated at each frame to the participant's VLNET client where they are mapped to an articulated, guided virtual human. This guided human is animated through inverse kinematics using the racket position. The referee is also represented by a guided virtual human in the user client, getting their position at each frame from the L-system animation process.

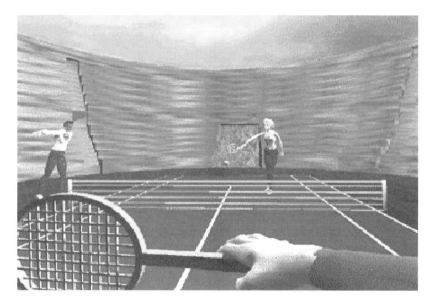

Figure 8-5. Virtual tennis with autonomous player and referee

In the tennis game simulation the different behaviours of the autonomous virtual humans are modelled by automata controlled by a universal stack-based control system. As the behaviours are severely based on synthetic sensors being the main channels of information capture from the virtual environment, we obtain a natural behaviour which is mostly independent of the internal environment representation. By using a sensor-based concept, the distinction between an autonomous virtual human and an interactive user merged into the virtual world becomes small, and they can easily be exchanged as demonstrated with the interactive game facility. The autonomous referee, represented by Virtual James, judges the game by following the ball with his vision system. He updates the state of the match when he 'hears' a ball collision event (ball–ground, ball–net, ball–racket) according to what he sees and his knowledge of a tennis match, and he communicates his decisions and the state of the game by 'spoken words' (sound events). The autonomous player, represented by Virtual Marilyn, can also hear sound events and obeys the decisions of the referee. Her game automata use synthetic vision to localize the ball's position and her opponent's position and adaptively estimates the future ball–racket impact point and position. She uses her partner's position to fix her game strategy and to plan her stroke and her path to the future impact point.

This application involves the critical issues discussed before: interaction of a real user with an autonomous virtual human over the network, real-time requirement for natural ball simulation, synthetic vision necessary for the autonomous virtual humans, multilevel control of the synthetic human figures.

Teleshopping

This pilot application was developed for a demonstration at Telecom '95, together with Chopard, a watch company in Geneva. In the same virtual shop, a participant in Singapore, representing the customer, was connected in the same virtual shop, with a participant in Geneva, representing the seller.

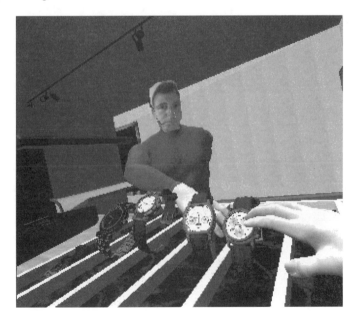

Figure 8-6. Teleshopping application

The users examined the watches on show (Figure 8-6), and the participant chose the watch that he liked. They were represented by guided actors, and had walking and picking behaviour. Navigation was heavily used in the application, particularly while the seller was showing the way to the customer, and using virtual human embodiments could provide the customer with clues about the seller's next direction of walking. The watch models were actual 3D CAD models created by the company for production

An ATM connection of 8 Mbits/s in both directions was provided during the demo, and this bandwidth was mainly used for video and audio communication in addition to the VLNET message transmission. This demonstration showed the effect of using complex models within 3D NVEs together with participant representation, and using a high-speed link for communicating different media together with VLNET protocol over a very long distance.

Collaborative Virtual Presentation

In this application, two participants, one in Geneva and the other in Lausanne, made a presentation of a scientific paper in 3D. The embodiments were guided by SpaceBall. The scene consisted of a virtual blackboard, which changed its slide to the next one when a participant selected it (Figure 8-7). In this way, the 3D presentation was merged within the same natural multimedia NVE, with images representing slides along with 3D objects.

Figure 8-7. Collaborative virtual presentation application

Medical Education

This was a scenario demonstrating medical education to distant students, using 3D models and animated architectures. The goal was to teach a student the position, properties and function of a particular muscle. First, the student chooses the place of a particular muscle on an anatomical slice image that is texture-mapped onto an object attached to the wall. Then the student shows the place of the muscle on a 3D model (Figure 8-8). This model is the output of the European CHARM medical project (Beylot et al. 1996), which includes 3D reconstruction of human organs, muscles and skeleton from MRI images. Finally, an autonomous virtual human was used as a mannequin that demonstrates the action resulting from the use of the muscle. In this scenario, the student and teacher participant embodiments were controlled by the standard human motion involving walking and arm motion, and the autonomous actor was controlled by a driver that plays a keyframe sequence. This application demonstrated the effect of integrating autonomous actors with virtual human embodiments for various uses.

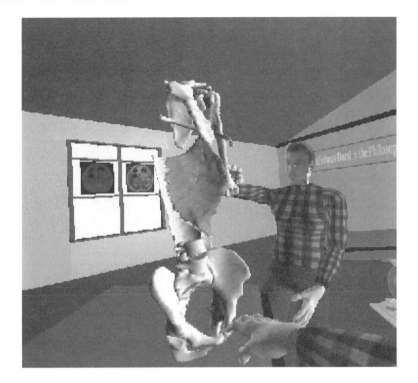

Figure 8-8. Medical education application

Virtual Helper Program

We have also developed an autonomous virtual helper program that communicates with the real participants through text (Figure 8-9). As described in Chapter 5, we use an implementation of the Eliza program, which uses natural language for communication. It waits for questions by the real participant, and answers using natural language. The details were given in Chapter 5.

This application demonstrated the effect of using textual communication with autonomous actors, while using non-verbal communication as an addition to the interaction.

Additionally, various other applications are under development, or will be started soon, such as a virtual entertainment part, networked multi-user adventure game, and a foreign language learning VE.

Figure 8-9. Eliza-based helper application

Stock exchange

An application has been developed to visualize in 3D the real-time updates of stock exchange data and allow interactions of users with the data (buy, sell) and with each other. A particular appeal of the virtual 3D marketplace is in the representation of participants' actions. The users can intuitively visualize the interest of others in certain markets as they see the avatars move from one market area to the other (Figure 8-10). This can potentially create a real feeling of the market.

8.3 Evaluation of Virtual Human Embodiment in NVEs

From the outset we have attempted to evaluate the immersive aspect of the VLNET system and the contribution of the non-verbal communication in realistic situations with people that formerly knew nothing about it. After some tests, it appeared to be a rather difficult but promising task.

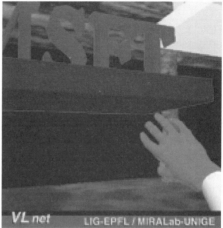

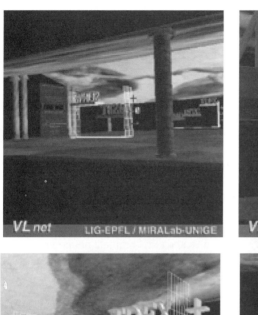

Figure 8-10. Stock market

The first decades of research in the field of non-verbal communication have seen a great use of laboratory experiments (Argyle 1988). In these experiments, the subjects were placed in very precise situations and asked to do specific things. But many researchers, since about the 1960s, have expressed doubts about the validity of these experiments, and about the fact that the resulting behaviour would occur and be reproduced in more normal situations (Argyle 1988). Nowadays there is an increasing preference among psychologists for observing real and spontaneous behaviour. But experimenting with non-verbal communication in virtual environments is a special case and the laboratory context clearly cannot be replaced by a simple real-life observation. What can be done to avoid the crucial impact of the researcher on the results is simply to teach different people how to use the system, put them together in a virtual environment, give them total freedom of action and carefully observe what happens. This is what we have done. This nearly anthropological methodology presents the advantage that the participants are not too much influenced, and makes the experiment a lot easier to organize. We also collected the participant's impressions with a survey at the end of the experiment.

Ideally, a representative sample of the population could have been built and a large number of experiments conducted. The observations could then have been referred to the variables that appear as important, such as the age, which seems to be central in all technology-related inquiries. However, for practical reasons, we have chosen a more qualitative paradigm, testing only a few subjects but with very close observation and for a rather long time. In this kind of experiment, the researchers try to identify crucial issues or behaviours, but it would not be accurate to give any number as a result. The hypothesis built on this small-scale experiment can then be verified on a greater sample and quantitative analysis can be done.

We have chosen six subjects: two females and four males, two very familiar with each other, two having already seen each other some times, and two complete unknowns. After an introduction to the system, they have been given a total freedom of action, being allowed to talk with each other or stay silent, to explore the scene or stay at the same place, to use non-verbal communication or not. The experiment lasted for two hours. Three systems were at their disposal for interacting: a navigation system allowing their avatar to walk freely in the environment, rotate, etc.; the non-verbal interaction application with its 30 actions as discussed in Chapter 5; a microphone and headphones for verbal communication. The scene we used represented a square with a bar in its centre and was chosen for its public and socially oriented characteristics (Figure 8-11). Here are some of the interesting points that have been observed.

First, a very important point for the immersive quality of the system: the users agreed that the avatar they saw on their screen maybe was not really their interlocutor, but at least could work as the real person and was a credible representation of the other. This is very clear in the words chosen by the subjects: they never spoke about 'your representation', 'your character', etc., but always used the 'you' particle as in I can see you; Why don't you move; You look funny; and so on. The same is true with their own avatar: I'm coming in front of you, etc. A sentence that was used shows very well the particular relationship that showed up between the individual and its avatar: Look how I'm smiling! One can see very well here the acceptance of the avatar as a representation of the 'self' but also some distance because clearly such a sentence cannot be heard in real life.

Then it is interesting to notice that, through the mechanisms of non-verbal communication, the users have been able to reproduce their relationship of the real world in the virtual environment. The subjects that didn't know each other before the experiment situated themselves at a bigger interactional distance than those who were familiar, and this is typical of what proxemics has shown. Moreover, they carefully avoided all the aggressive gestures, whereas the other subjects (who knew each other) used several times the mockery gesture or the forearm jerk. They also respected social rules in their use of the kinesics.

Figure 8-11. Virtual bar scene for testing non-verbal communication

At another level, the non-verbal communication application allowed them also to respect the formal structure of the social interactions. At the beginning of the interaction, they all used one of the actions to greet the other (bow, welcoming) and to signal that they were ready to begin the exchange. The end of the interaction followed that logic too, and has always been confirmed by non-verbal means. The normative sanction present when someone doesn't respect these rules in real life has showed up: R was speaking with J. R suddenly decided to explore the world and left J abruptly. R became angry and used verbal and non-verbal means to express it. R came back and they left to explore the world together. This funny example shows very well that even in virtual environments, when minimal means are provided to control of the interaction, the individuals can't do anything and must respect some rules, or the other individuals don't appreciate it. In their structure the interactions become realistic.

Many other elements confirm this point. During the experiment, the avatars of J and L collided with each other. They naturally apologized and then laughed about the experience. Later the avatar of J (who is male) and the avatar of L (who is female) were very close, nearly touching each other in a position that could have been interpreted as very intimate. A strong emotion was then noticed on the participants, first in the form of uneasiness and then laughter. This behaviour is typical of the relationship of J and L: they have different sexual identities and know each other slightly. The movements and positions of their avatars weren't free because they had real consequences, and this scene had nearly the same effect as if it had happened in real life. A final example illustrates this real effect of virtual interactions: during the experiment, J became really angry because R wanted him to do something that he didn't want to. R refused to speak for a moment but used the forearm jerk gesture in a totally sincere way.

Globally, the participants used gestures more than postures. A posture was always chosen at the beginning of the interaction, but often it stayed a long time as the participants didn't think of changing it. This can be easily explained by the fact that gestures are mostly conscious actions, while postures are often chosen unconsciously. The users also had difficulties in identifying what useful gesture or posture was missing. Their method was mainly to examine what was at their disposal and then use it, rather than searching for what would be best suited and looking to see whether the application had it. What has been strongly asked but is technically difficult, is to be able to touch the other avatars, a tap, a punch or simply shaking hands. This suggests the addition of new actions that involve physical touch.

The subjects used the scene in different ways. The bar was used by R and J in a proxemic approach. They tried to lean on the bar next to each other as if they were having a drink, and they used, in this position, mainly facial expressions. It appears that they were trying to use the bar as a non-verbal communication artifact and this also shows that they were able to adapt the channel used to the position of the avatar. T and P, and J and L organized a race around the building. They all wanted to be able to open the doors and interact with the objects.

A fundamental need emerged from the collection of impressions of the participants: the presence of a visual feedback. Without being able to feel the posture of their avatar, they strongly asked for the possibility to view their own body. But this solution could take away some of the immersive feeling because the user can see themselves as if they were totally exterior to the situation. Another strategy they used was to ask the other participants about their own appearance. Some participants told us that the fact they used a screen and could see the laboratory around was distracting them from the interactions. This 'parasite' information could be removed by the use of an HMD. The caricature-like aspect of the gestures and postures has also been emphasized. But the probability is high that any predefined action would be considered so, or would not be understood easily enough if the visual clues were to be weakened. The main point is that predefined actions cannot, by definition, be finely adjusted to the specific ongoing interaction, suggesting an adaptive gesture representation scheme.

Finally, we have to recognize that, beyond these encouraging results, the quantity of non-verbal information the user can provide with a palette of actions, and the subtlety of the proposed actions, should be a lot greater. The subjects always wanted to decode signals that were not present or just suggested. The sentence 'It's not funny, you're not moving!' is typical from that record. In real life you cannot stop communicating. But that is what happens in the virtual environment, and it gives a somewhat unrealistic aspect to one subject's vision of another. Currently it is a lot more difficult to have an interaction in a virtual environment than in the real world, because several mechanisms are still missing: illustrators should be present, lip movements should follow speech, and orientation of eyes and head should be properly controlled. The posture that was most commonly used during the experiment was the attentive posture, as shown in Chapter 5. The users explained to us that it was their only way to express their interest in what the other was saying, as they could not use their gaze to do so. They accepted this attitude was largely beyond what they wanted to express, because they felt the feedback it gave to the speaker was crucial for continuing the interaction. This example illustrates very well the current state of our work: we have given users the opportunity to send important messages to their interlocutors that they couldn't send before, but in a rather raw and limited way.

8.4 Performance of the System

In this section, we measure the computational and display overhead of different parts of the system, with varying conditions. Unless stated otherwise, the results were taken on a VLNET client running on an SGI Onyx with 4×200 MHz R4000 processors and Reality Engine 2 graphics, and the VLNET server running on an SGI Indy with 100 MHz R4000 processor. The VLNET server needs to be run on the same machine as an HTTP server. Considering the graphical and computational complexity of the human representations used in VLNET, we are currently not aiming for a system scalabe to large numbers of users, but rather trying to obtain a high-quality experience for a small number of users.

8.4.1 Display Rate for Different Resolutions

In order to evaluate the overhead created by a high-level body representation in the NVE, we have undertaken three series of measurements: with full body representation, simplified body representation and without a body representation. The full body representation involves complex graphical representation (about 10 000 polygons) and deformation algorithms. The simplified body representation consists of a body with reduced graphical complexity (about 1500 polygons), with facial deformations and with a simplified body animation based on displacement of rigid body elements (no deformation). The tests without the body representation were made for the sake of comparison. To mark the positions of users, we used simple geometric shapes. No facial or body animation is involved. Figure 8-12 shows some snapshots from the measurement sessions.

Table 8-1 and Figure 8-13 show the display rate of the VLNET client, with varying number and resolution of virtual humans visible in an empty scene (i.e. no object display overhead). The table shows that, when there are four highly complex virtual humans in the view, the VLNET client obtains a graphics rate lower than the minimum 10 frames/s. When the virtual humans have low resolution, the client displays six virtual humans in real time; and with the lowest resolution, we achieve a display rate of 9 frames/s with seven virtual humans. These results show that having multiple resolutions of the body representation leads to twice the frame rate for complex representations.

(a)

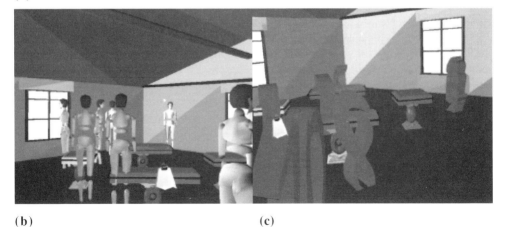

(b)   (c)

Figure 8-12. Snapshots from performance and network measurements: (a) full bodies, (b) simplified bodies, (c) no body representation

There are two important aspects to consider while interpreting the display results. These results do not measure the display performance with respect to the number of virtual humans *in the VE*, but those which are *inside the viewing volume*. For example, if there are six other virtual humans in the scene, and two of them are visible to the viewer, the frame rate is 20 frames/s, not 9 frames/s. When a virtual human is outside this volume (e.g. behind the viewer, or too far to be seen), then the virtual human is *culled* before drawing. Therefore, the display overhead for invisible virtual humans is negligible. Thus, the VLNET client can display up to seven bodies in real time with an acceptable quality.

The second important aspect involves the effect of the display computations on the other parts of the VLNET core processes and the driver. As the display is run in parallel with other parts on different processors, this effect is minimal. However, on uniprocessor systems, there will be a slowdown in the frame rate as the computational resources are shared.

Finally, as seen in Figure 8-13, the display overhead is linear with respect to number of virtual humans visible, for a single resolution. In our experiments, each high-resolution body contributed approximately 35 ms, and each rough-resolution representation contributed an additional 10 ms to the display overhead.

Table 8-1. Display rate of the VLNET client with varying number and resolution of virtual human figures

Number of virtual humans	Resolution	Frames per second	Display time (ms)
1	High	20	50
2	High	15	66
3	High	11	90
4	High	8	125
1	Low	25	40
2	Low	18	55
3	Low	17	58
4	Low	15	67
5	Low	11	90
6	Low	10	100
7	Low	7	142
1	Rough	30	33
2	Rough	20	50
3	Rough	17	58
4	Rough	14	71
5	Rough	12	83
6	Rough	11	90
7	Rough	9	111
8	Rough	8	125

8.4.2   Computations at the Body Representation Engine

Table 8-2 and Figure 8-14 show the computational requirements of different stages of the body representation engine. As we discussed in Chapter 3, the engines need to process each frame in four steps: synchronization, preframe, frame, postframe. Synchronization and frame steps are standard low-latency IRIS Performer mechanisms to handle the rendering pipeline. At each preframe step, the body representation engine checks for local drivers' updates, merges them, and passes the final posture in terms of state vector to the outgoing queue of the communication process. At each postframe step, the engines read data containing other clients' updates, make updates in the shared memory, and perform deformation of the bodies.

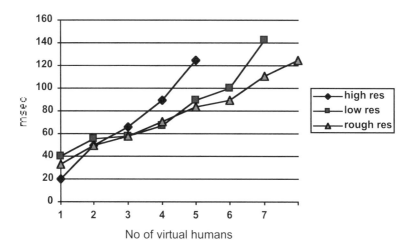

Figure 8-13. Display overhead with varying number and resolution of virtual humans

Table 8-2. Performances of various steps of engine computations at each frame

Number of virtual humans *visible*	Resolution (ms)	Preframe (ms)	Postframe (ms)	Deformation, internal shmem update (ms)	Total (ms)	Frames per second
1	High	4	1	15	20	50
2	High	4	8	33	45	22
3	High	4	13	47	64	16
4	High	4	20	62	86	12
5	High	4	29	76	109	9
6	High	4	35	99	138	7
1	Rough	3	1	3	7	142
2	Rough	3	7	6	16	62
3	Rough	4	12	10	26	38
4	Rough	3	21	13	37	27
5	Rough	4	28	18	50	20
6	Rough	4	34	22	60	17

The preframe computations need to be minimal to decrease frame latency time, and should not depend on the complexity of the VE. For this purpose, the preframe computations only involve sending local body posture. Table 8-2 demonstrates that the implementation achieves these goals: the preframe computations (the third column in the table) take only 4 ms, which is negligible compared to other steps and other processes, and does not change with varying number of virtual humans.

The postframe computations, however, depend on the number of participants. The fourth column in the table represents computations except deformation of bodies. As seen in Figure 8-14, the overhead for this step depends on the number of virtual humans, not their geometrical resolution; each virtual human requires 5 ms of overhead on average. The reason for the independence of geometrical resolution comes from the fact that we use the same underlying skeleton structure for different resolutions.

The fifth column, deformation, refers to the step where the body surfaces are deformed based on the current body postures for all virtual humans. Table 8-2 shows that the computational complexity of deformations is also linearly proportional to the number of virtual humans, but the performance of this step depends on the resolution of the body. The results show that a maximum of five high-resolution virtual humans can be supported for real-time speed of 10 frames/s, i.e. a frame delay of 100 ms. However, using lower resolution allows up to eight virtual humans to be supported.

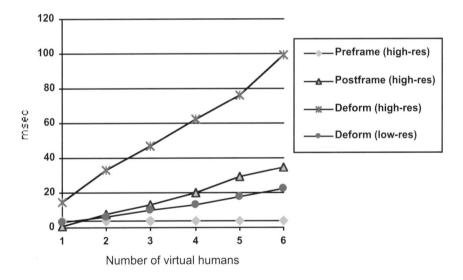

Figure 8-14. Engine computations with varying number of virtual humans

8.4.3 Computations at the Body Driver

The computations for the body driver are also critical; the speed of the body driver needs to match the speed of the client. If the driver computes a frame faster than the VLNET frame rate, then the driver waits for a period of time which is the VLNET client computation time minus the driver computation time for one frame. For example, if the VLNET client runs at 10 frames/s with 100 ms per frame, and if the driver computations take 70 ms, the driver waits for an extra 30 ms in order to have the same rate as the client and to leave the CPU resources for other drivers or VLNET core processes. However, if the driver frame computations take longer than the client computations for one frame, the displayed motion of the virtual body will be aliased.

The results shown here belong to the default standard body driver that includes walking, grasping and head motion actions. The participant uses a mouse to guide the embodiment. The state of the body can be in three modes: navigation (by walking generator), hand motion (by inverse kinematics generator) and head motion (by simple Euler computations). Therefore, depending on the state of the body, the mouse input is interpreted differently. If there is no user input in one frame, the driver does not perform any computations for that frame. If the driver is in the walking state, inverse computations for the right arm are not necessary; therefore the final joint values for the right arm are copied from a table to avoid extra computation.

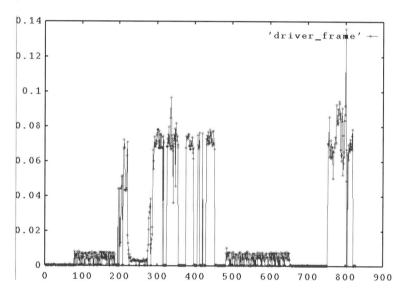

Figure 8-15. Computations for standard desktop driver have a bursty nature

Figure 8-15 demonstrates that driver computations generally take no more than 100 ms. Therefore, it is not possible for the driver computations to take longer then the client computations when running at interactive speeds with the default driver. Figure 8-15 also shows that the computation graph is bursty: a sequence of idle time followed by a period of computations.

Figure 8-16 demonstrates separate components of the driver. From the figure, we see that walking computations only need 10 ms per frame. Note that while the walking motor is active, the inverse kinematics computations are almost 0 ms, as the right arm joints are copied from a table. Walking behaviour sets the joint angle procedurally, therefore excessive computations are not necessary. On the other hand, inverse kinematics computations may take 70 ms on the average, still below 100 ms for real-time interaction.

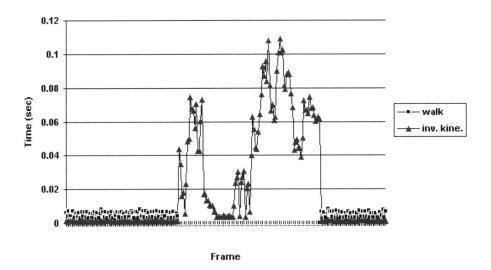

Figure 8-16. Computational requirements for components of the default driver

8.4.4   Performance of the Architecture

Table 8-3 compares heterogeneous parallelism with a monolithic VE architecture. As we discussed in Chapter 4, the frame period of the parallel architecture is the maximum of driver, engine, and display computations. The table assumes that all virtual humans can see each other. The results show that a monolithic solution processes one frame in 0.251 s with four virtual humans. With heterogeneous parallelism, this figure decreases to 0.125 s. Therefore, heterogeneous parallelism improves the speed of the VE simulation. Additionally, if one component of the system uses excessive computations beyond what is required to display one frame, the display rate will not be affected, but the motion will be updated every few frames.

Table 8-3. Comparison of monolithic and parallel architecture performances

Number of virtual humans in the scene	Driver (ms)	Preframe (ms)	Display (ms)	Postframe (ms)	Deformation (ms) (low/high res)	Monolithic (ms)	Parallel (ms)
1	60	4	50	1	3 / 15	115	60
2	60	4	60	8	6 / 33	132	60
3	60	4	90	13	10 / 47	167	90
4	60	4	125	62	23 / 63	251	125

8.5 Networking Results

8.5.1 Loading Results

Table 8-4 demonstrates fetching and loading times for different resolutions of the default representation. As expected, fetching time is higher for more complex representations, and lower network bit rates. We measured the downloading speed over a local Ethernet network, and over an Internet server in Geneva; the measured speed was 584 kbits/s.

Note that downloading times go up to 24 s. This corresponds to approximately 240 frames before starting interaction. We expect that, especially with slower Internet speeds, the start-up of one client will take minutes. On the other hand, loading the fetched files to the local memory takes place in shorter time, from 4 to 7 s.

Table 8-4. Time needed to fetch and load body representation files, with different network capabilities

	Very high resolution	High resolution	Low resolution	Rough resolution
Local fetch (Ethernet)	15.28 s	14.04 s	10.70 s	9.82 s
Remote fetch (Internet)	24.04 s	17.10 s	15.03 s	13.12 s
Load to memory	7.35 s	5.33 s	4.64 s	3.99 s

Table 8-5 shows the improvement when using the progressive loading technique, compared with the naive loading technique which involves fetching and loading all resolutions before starting interaction. Remember that progressive downloading loads a default body first, then asynchronously fetches different resolutions, starting with the lowest resolution. This solution decouples loading from interaction, as discussed in Chapter 6. As seen in Table 8-5, progressive loading takes a fixed amount of time, as a locally stored default body is loaded first, and fetching takes place while interaction continues. Thus, using progressive loading drastically decreases the start-up overhead for bodies.

Table 8-5. Initialization time for one body before starting interaction

	Naive loading	Progressive loading
Local fetch	71.15 s	7.35 s
Remote fetch	90.6 s	7.35 s

8.5.2   Traffic Measurement during Interaction

This section discusses the networking requirements during the interaction phase, once all the bodies are loaded. Note that the results will change for dynamic joining of participants, as this involves loading at the same time as interaction.

8.5.2.1   Output Traffic from VLNET Client

In Chapter 5 we discussed how immersive participants, and participants using desktop configurations have different requirements for representation. This is also true for network traffic generated by their clients. Figure 8-17 compares the output traffic from an immersive client and a desktop client. The desktop client generates bursty traffic, because when the participant does not generate input using the mouse or other input devices, the client does not generate output messages. However, for immersive participants, the trackers attached to the body generate a new update every frame, as the participant moves every frame. Therefore, the immersive client generates more continuous traffic, approximately equal to the peak rate of the desktop client.

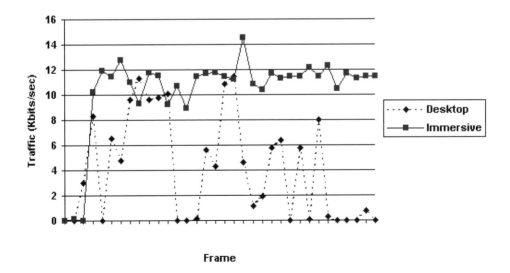

Figure 8-17. Traffic generated by desktop and immersive participants

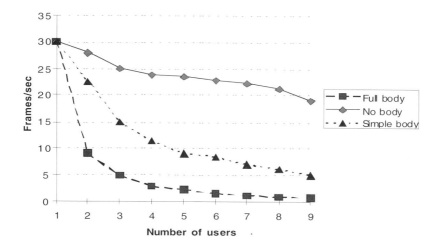

Figure 8-18. Minimal performance with respect to the number of users in the session

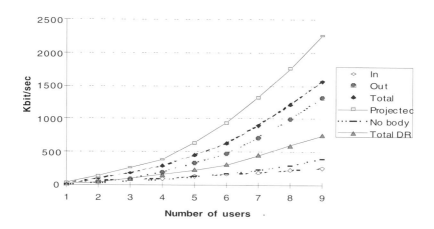

Figure 8-19. Network traffic measurements with respect to the number of users in the session

8.5.2.2   Network Traffic at the VLNET Server

The graphs of performance and network traffic (Figures 8-18 and 8-19) show that the system is indeed not scalabe to any larger number of participants. Nevertheless, the results are reasonable for a small number of users and, more importantly, their analysis helps to give insight into the steps required for better scaleability.

The network traffic (Figure 8-19) was measured on the server. We have measured incoming and outgoing traffic in kilobits per second.

For the performance measures, we connected one standard user-controlled client so we could control the point of view. The rest of the clients were user simulations as described above. Performance is measured in number of frames per second. The culling causes it to vary depending on the point of view (both rendering and computation are culled), so we needed to ensure consistent results. We chose to take measurements with a view where all the user embodiments were within the field of view; this represents the highest strain and the minimal performance for a given number of users in the scene. The performance was measured on a Silicon Graphics Indigo Maximum Impact workstation with 200 MHz R4400 processor and 128M RAM.

Figure 8-18 shows the variation of performance with respect to the number of users in the simulation for different complexities of body representation as explained in the previous subsection. Notice that this is the minimal performance, i.e. the performance measured at the moment when all the users' embodiments are actually within the field of view. Rendering and computation culling boost the performance when the user is not looking at all the other embodiments; this is because they are not rendered and the deformation calculations are not performed for them. The embodiments that are outside the field of view do not decrease performance significantly, which means that Figure 8-18 can also be interpreted as the peak performance when looking at N users, regardless of the total number of users in the scene. This makes the system much more usable than might be apparent at first glance.

We have also measured the percentage of time spent on two main tasks: rendering and application-specific computation. With any number of users, the rendering takes about 65% of the time, and the rest is spent on the application-specific computation, i.e. mostly the deformation of faces and bodies. For the case of simplified body representation, the fraction is 58%. On machines with less powerful graphics hardware, an even greater percentage of the total time is dedicated to rendering.

The results show that the use of complex body representation induces a considerable overhead on the rendering side and somewhat less on the computation side. The fact that the performance can be boosted significantly by simply changing the body representation proves that the system framework does not induce an overhead in itself. The system is scalabe in the sense that, for a particular hardware and requirements, a set-up can be found to produce satisfying performance by varying the complexity of the chosen body and face representation. Most importantly, this proves that the system should lend itself to the implementation of extended level of detail (Rohlf and Helman 1994) techniques automatically managing the balance between performance and quality of the human representation.

8.5.3 Analysis of the Network Results

Figure 8-19 plots the bit rates measured on the VLNET server during a session against the number of simulated users walking within a room, as described in the subsection on experiment design. We measured the incoming and outgoing traffic separately, then calculated the total.

The incoming traffic obviously grows linearly with the number of users, each user generating the same bit rate. The bit rate generated per user is roughly 30 kbit/s, covering the transmission of body positions, body postures and facial expressions.

And notice that the curve for incoming traffic measured at the server corresponds to the maximal incoming traffic for a client. The client will receive the incoming bitstream corresponding to the graph in the situations where all the embodiments of other users are in the viewing frustum of the local user, i.e. in the worst case. Otherwise, when looking at N users the incoming traffic will correspond to N users on the graph. This is similar to the situation with performance measurements.

The outgoing traffic represents the distribution of the data to all the clients that need it. The total traffic is the sum of the incoming and outgoing traffic. The projected traffic curve represents the traffic calculated mathematically for the case of total distribution (all to all). The AOIM technique at the server (Section 2.2.2.5) ensures that the messages are distributed only as they are required and it keeps the total curve well below the projected curve. Further reduction is achieved using the dead-reckoning technique (Capin et al. 1997a), as illustrated by the curve labelled 'Total DR'.

Network traffic is the same when using full and simplified body representations, because the same messages are transferred. In the case when no body representation is used, less network traffic is generated because there is no need to send messages about body postures and facial expressions. A user without a body representation sends only position updates, generating approximately 8 kbit/s. The total traffic curve without a body representation is labelled 'No body'.

The results show that a considerable overhead is introduced by sending face and body data. But there is certainly a great potential for improvement, because the face and body animation parameters are sent in their raw form, i.e. without any coding or compression. The results obtained within the MPEG-4 ad hoc group on face and body animation indicate that full facial animation can be transmitted at approximately 2 kbit/s by using a relatively simple arithmetic coding algorithm. More information on MPEG-4 is given in Chapter 7.

8.5.3.1 Computations at the VLNET Server

Figure 8-20 shows an example of the percentage CPU usage for the VLNET server on the SGI Indy workstation with a 100 MHz processor, with four participants connecting sequentially.

The total CPU requirement is not excessive—less than 30% of the CPU. And the CPU is already busy with other services such as the HTTP server and the mail server. However, there is still an additional 5% of CPU overhead per participant on the VLNET server. This is due to visibility computations between participants, and processing for handling outgoing messages. However, this percentage is higher than normally expected because of one factor: we use IRIS Performer utilities for visibility computations, and the IRIS Performer library itself uses low-level routines to get higher priority to achieve real time. Therefore, using other simulation libraries would decrease the server CPU overhead.

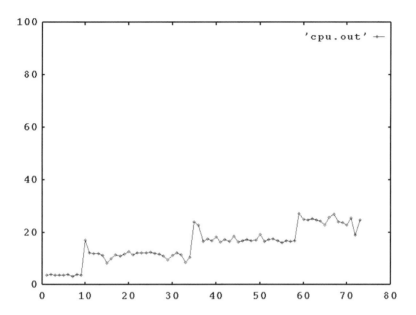

Figure 8-20. CPU requirements for VLNET server

8.5.4 Downloadable Drivers

Here we present the results of using downloadable drivers, and we take breathing as an example. The downloadable drivers technique is explained in Section 6.7.2, and guided control for breathing in Section 4.6.1.8. Remember that downloadable drivers implement guided and autonomous actors in a network-efficient way. As discussed in Section 4.6.1.8, the breathing driver modifies a set of joint angles in the upper torso and shoulders to give the impression of a living entity. If the low-level body state information is used to communicate postures, then a message needs to be sent every frame. However, using a downloadable driver decreases this requirement.

Figure 8-21 compares the resulting traffic at the source client when a downloadable driver is not used, compared to sending joint angle messages.

8.5.5   Compression Results

8.5.5.1   Quality Loss for 2-Byte Integer and Byte Representation

As discussed in Chapter 6, joint angles can be represented in lower resolutions: e.g. 2-byte short integer and 1-byte representation per joint angle. This decreases the bit rate requirements by up to 25% of the original floating-point format, without further compression.

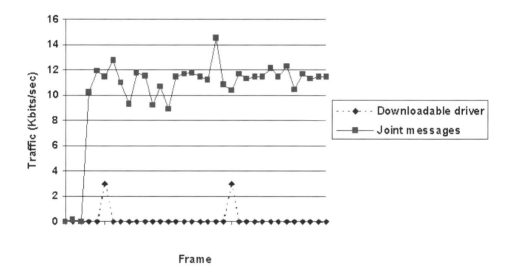

Figure 8-21. Traffic generated by downloadable driver compared to sending joint angles, taking breathing control as an example

We measured the resulting accuracy loss with these two representations. We took two shoulder angles as an example, and selected two keyframe sequences that modify these joints. Then we quantized the 4-byte floating-point representation to 2-byte and 1-byte representations, and dequantized back to a floating-point representation. We measured the error of the resulting values with respect to the original values. Integer representation introduces negligible error in the representation. On the other hand, the byte representation introduces an error of 2° in joint angles. Although this representation is sufficient for many applications, it may generate visual problems with motions involving slight joint changes within frames, such as breathing. Integer representation, on the other hand, does not create these problems.

8.5.5.2   Scalable Compression

In Chapter 6 we introduced the scalable compression technique that requires different bit rates depending on a quantization parameter. Table 8-6 presents the bit rate requirements as a percentage of the original representation requirements for different quantization values. Remember that the quantization was obtained as follows:

Quantized Value (i) = round(StateVector(i)/(Quantum(i)*Global_Quantization_Value)
for each joint angle i

Table 8-6. Percentage of the compressed bitstream traffic, compared to original sequence (%)

Sequence	Quantization values								
	1	2	4	8	16	32	64	128	256
Waving	5.11	5.19	5.40	5.85	5.88	6.13	6.39	6.69	6.95
Curious	7.15	7.51	7.87	8.43	9.49	10.05	10.76	11.48	12.33
Attentive	7.32	7.62	8.05	8.62	9.56	10.02	10.76	12.23	12.30
Walk	10.31	11.35	12.71	14.46	16.07	18.59	20.49	23.36	27.87

Here we assume that all joints have the same quantum values. By modifying the global quantization value between 1 and 256, we get quantized values in the intervals [0, 256] and [0, 65536], respectively. Thus, the representation quality varies between 1-byte and 2-byte values, depending on the global quantization value. Therefore, the higher this value, the higher the compression rates.

Table 8-6 demonstrates the compression ratios for four sequences: the waving sequence involves only moving the left arm, and all the other joints retain their original values; the curious sequence moves only two arms; the attentive sequence moves joints in the upper body; and the walking sequence moves all joints in the body with different non-repetitive behaviour. The table shows that the fewer the changes contained in the sequence, the higher the values for the compression ratio. The walking sequence moves almost all the joints in the body, so it may be considered as the worst case.

Finally, Figure 8-22 shows the bit rate requirements of the scalable compression technique, with an assumption of 10 frames per second. In the worst case, 8 kbit/s is needed for highest quality. Compare this against the uncompressed representation with constant 24 kbit/s for floating-point, and constant 12 kbit/s integer representation. Although 8 kbit/s still seems high, using a quantization value of 16 decreases the bit rate requirements to 4 kbit/s with quality better than byte representation.

8.5.6   Dead-Reckoning Results

We have implemented the algorithm presented in Chapter 6, and investigated its performance with varying conditions. As representative examples, we selected three actions: a *football kick* sequence, a *jump* sequence, and a *hello* sequence.

Figure 8-23 shows the three actions and their joint angle values with respect to time. All motions were created using the Flock of Birds trackers and without prefiltering. The football kick action consists of a slightly jerky motion, due to the nature of the behaviour and the tracking noise. The jumping sequence is more predictive, except for the beginning of the action. The hand-wave sequence mainly involves the right arm joints created by keyframe animation, plus various joint behaviours with respect to time. We chose a prediction interval of 100 ms. The computational overhead for running 75 Kalman filters at the same time for a single virtual human figure did not appear to create a significant overhead; the total computations for a single virtual human took 0.5 ms on an Indigo-2 Impact workstation with 250 MHz processor.

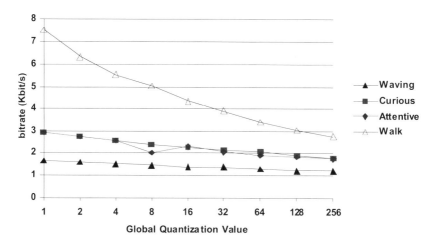

Figure 8-22. Bit rate requirements of scalable compression, with varying global quantization values

Figure 8-24 shows the performance of the dead-reckoning algorithm applied to the three actions, using the posture comparisons as discussed in the previous section. The x-axes in Figure 8-24(a) and (b) show the maximum angle difference between corresponding joint angles of local body and ghost body; and the x-axis in Figure 8-24(c) shows the maximum Euclidean distance between corresponding joints. The y-axis denotes the fraction of time steps where the actions caused message transfer, expressed as a percentage of the whole period of the motion. A percentage of 100% denotes that the dead-reckoning operation has not been performed, and 70% shows that the dead-reckoning technique could successfully predict 30% of the time steps. Figure 8-24 shows the results for the basic algorithm, with varying maximum allowed angle differences between joints. As the limit increases, the algorithm prediction rate increases, hence the message communication decreases.

The results in Figure 8-24(c) were taken using the second of our posture comparison techniques by decreasing the coefficient of twisting angles, with the assumption that they have less effect on the final posture. Figure 8-24(c) shows the results of approach 3 with varying maximum Euclidean distances. The resulting animation was also similar to the original motion, when observed with the eye. The results show that using a distance metric for comparison achieves better performance in dead reckoning than using joint angles. With an error estimate of up to 15 cm, it is possible to achieve a 50% decrease in exchange of messages. Figure 8-25 shows resulting dead-reckoning postures with different bit rates.

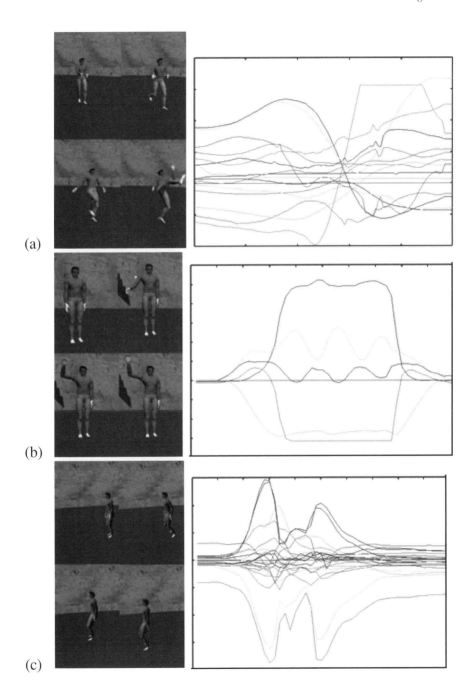

Figure 8-23. Example sequences and the joint value changes with respect to time: (a) football, (b) hello, (c) jump sequence

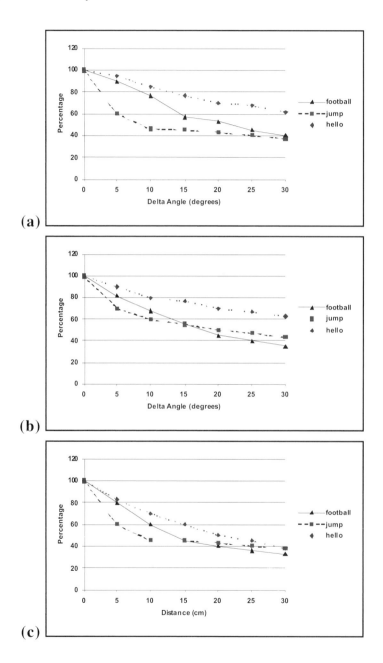

Figure 8-24. Performance of the Kalman filter with varying delta values; the *y*-axis shows the percentage of message communication: (a) approach 1 for comparison (maximum of joint angle difference), (b) approach 2 (maximum of joint angle difference with corresponding angle coefficients, (c) approach 3 (Euclidean distance between corresponding joints)

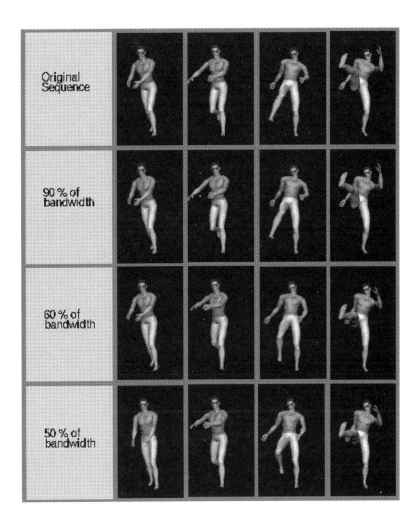

Figure 8-25. Resulting dead-reckoning postures with different bit rates

9 Conclusion

In this book, we have investigated the problems and solutions for inserting virtual human figures into NVEs. There is an increasing interest in shared graphical spaces that allow people to interact with each other in remote locations, or with programs and virtual objects. Using virtual humans increases presence and collaboration in NVEs, as it provides a direct relationship between how we control our avatar in the virtual world and how our avatar moves related to this control.

The survey of previous work and existing NVE systems has shown that most existing systems use relatively simple graphical models to represent users in the VE. The survey of related research has also shown expectations of increased quality and usability of NVE systems with the introduction of more sophisticated human-like representations. We have analysed the challenges and requirements for introducing virtual humans as participant representation in NVEs, and developed the Virtual Life Network (VLNET) system. VLNET provides a modular, open system architecture with a set of extension interfaces. These interfaces provide easy access not only to functions related to virtual human support, but to all other functions of NVEs. Therefore VLNET offers flexible support for different functions and applications, and also lends itself very well as a research test bed.

Virtual human representation in NVEs is a multidimensional problem. Firstly the system architecture should allow easy development of multi-user 3D simulations, and easy integration of embodiment control within these 3D environments. Multiprocess architecture is necessary for efficient simulation and rapid application development involving multi-user NVEs, and the VE architecture should be developed considering the participant virtual human representation as the central element. Secondly, virtual human control has a wide range of characteristics depending on the user input devices and the application. A multiple-level control classification is necessary for different configurations. Thirdly, the protocol used for transmitting virtual human data should make use of the underlying model, and should be scalable, depending on the underlying network, the CPU requirements and the application.

We have analysed the networking requirements of NVEs, and how MPEG-4 and VRML tools can be used to fulfil these requirements. This analysis is based on our active participation in the development of the MPEG-4 standards. Most of the data types that are important for NVE systems will be very well supported by MPEG-4 and VRML tools (video, audio, 3D objects, textures, bodies, faces). On top of this, MPEG-4 will offer reliable multiplexing, mechanisms for establishing priorities among data, as well as synchronization. We believe that MPEG-4 and VRML tools should play an important role in building future NVE systems.

Bibliography

Allan J.B., Wywill B., Witten I.A. (1989) A Methodology for Direct Manipulation of Polygon Meshes, *Proc. Computer Graphics International '89*, Leeds, pp. 451–469.

Argyle M. (1988) *Bodily Communication*, Methuen, New York.

Armstrong W.W., Green M., Lake R. (1987) Near Real-Time Control of Human Figure Models, *IEEE Computer Graphics and Applications*, Vol.7, No.6, pp. 28–38.

Arnaldi B., Dumont G., Hegron G., Magnenat Thalmann N., Thalmann D. (1989) Animation Control with Dynamics, in *State of the Art in Computer Animation*, Springer, Tokyo, pp. 113–124.

Astheimer P., Göbel M., Kruse R., Müller S., Zachmann G. (1994) Realism in Virtual Reality, in Magnenat Thalmann N., Thalmann D. (Eds.), *Artificial Life and Virtual Reality*, John Wiley, Chichester, pp. 189–209.

Azarbayejani A., Starner T., Horowitz B., Pentland A. (1993) Visually Controlled Graphics, *IEEE Transaction on Pattern Analysis and Machine Intelligence*, Vol.15, No.6, pp. 602–605.

Azuma R., Bishop G. (1995) A Frequency-Domain Analysis of Head-Motion Prediction, *Proc. ACM SIGGRAPH '95*, pp. 401–408.

Badler N.I., Morris M.A. (1982) Modelling Flexible Articulated Objects, *Proc. Computer Graphics '82*, Online Conf., pp. 305–314.

Badler N.I., Smoliar S.W. (1979) Digital Representation of Human Movement, *ACM Computing Surveys,* March, pp. 19–38.

Badler N.I., Korein J.D., Korein J.U., Radack G.M., Brotman L.S. (1986) Positioning and Animating Figures in a Task-oriented Environment, *The Visual Computer*, Vol.1, No.4, pp. 212–220.

Badler N.I., Phillips C.B., Webber B.L. (1993) *Simulating Humans: Computer Graphics Animation and Control*, Oxford University Press, Oxford.

Bandi S., Thalmann D. (1998) Space Discretization for Efficient Human Navigation, *Proc. Eurographics '98*.

Barfield W., Weghorst S. (1993) The sense of presence within virtual environments: a conceptual framework, in Salvendy G., Smith M.J. (Eds.), *Human–computer interaction: software and hardware interfaces*, Amsterdam, Elsevier.

Barfield W., Zeltzer D., Sheridan T., Slater M. (1995) Presence and performance within virtual environments, in Barfield W., Furness T. (Eds.), *Virtual environments and advanced interface design*, Oxford University Press, New York, pp. 473–513.

Barr A. (1984) Global and Local Deformations of Solid Primitives. *Proc. SIGGRAPH '84*, Computer Graphics, Vol.18, No.3, pp. 21–30.

Barrus J.W., Waters R.C., Anderson D.B. (1996) Locales and Beacons: Efficient and Precise Support For Large Multi-User Virtual Environments, *Proc. IEEE VRAIS*, pp. 204–213.

Bécheiraz P., Thalmann D. (1996) A Model of Nonverbal Communication and Interpersonal Relationship between Virtual Actors, *Proc. Computer Animation '96*, IEEE Computer Society Press, pp. 58–67.

Benford S., Bowers J., Fahlen L.E., Greenhalgh C., Mariani J., Rodden T. (1995) Networked Virtual Reality and Cooperative Work, *Presence: Teleoperators and Virtual Environments*, Vol.4, No.4, pp. 364–386.

Beylot P., Gingins P., Kalra P., Magnenat-Thalmann N., Maurel W., Thalmann D., Fasel J. (1996) 3D Interactive Topological Modeling using Visible Human Dataset, *Proc. Eurographics '96*, Poitiers, pp. 33–44.

Birman K. (1991) *Maintaining Consistency in Distributed Systems*, Technical Report TR91-1240, Dpt CS, Cornell University, 1991.

Birman K., Cooper R., Gleeson B. (1991*) Programming with process groups: group and multicast semantics*, Technical Report TR-91-1185, Dpt CS, Cornell University.

Blum R. (1979) Representing Three-dimensional Objects in Your Computer, *Byte,* pp. 14–29.

Blumberg B.M., Galyean T.A. (1995) Multi-Level Direction of Autonomous Creatures for Real-Time Virtual Environments, *Proc. SIGGRAPH '95*, ACM Press, pp. 47–54.

Boulic R., Magnenat Thalmann N.,Thalmann D. (1990) A Global Human Walking Model with Real-Time Kinematic Personification, *The Visual Computer*, Vol.6, No.6, pp. 344–358.

Boulic R., Capin T., Huang Z, Kalra P., Lintermann B., Magnenat-Thalmann N., Moccozet L., Molet T., Pandzic I., Saar K., Schmitt A., Shen J., Thalmann D. (1995) The Humanoid Environment for Interactive Animation of Multiple Deformable Human Characters, *Proc. Eurographics '95*, pp. 337–348.

Boulic R., Rezzonico S., Thalmann D. (1996) Multi-Finger Manipulation of Virtual Objects, *Proc. ACM VRST '96*, pp. 67–74.

Bowers, J.M. (1992) Modelling Awareness and Interaction in Virtual Spaces, *Proc. 5th MultiG Workshop*, Kista, Stockholm.

Breen D.E. (1989) Choreographing Goal-oriented Motion Using Cost Functions, in Magnenat Thalmann N., Thalmann D. (Eds.), *State of the Art in Computer Animation*, Springer, Tokyo, pp. 141–152.

Bricken W., Coco G. (1993) *The VEOS Project*, Technical Report R-93-3, Human Interface Technology Laboratory, University of Washington.

Brooks F.P. Jr. (1986) Walkthrough—a dynamic graphics system for simulating virtual buildings, *Proc. Workshop on Interactive 3D Graphics*, Computer Graphics, Vol.21, No.1, pp. 9–21.

Brotman L.S., Netravali A.N. (1988) Motion Interpolation by Optimal Control, *Proc. SIGGRAPH '88*, Computer Graphics, Vol.22., No.4., pp. 179–188.

Bryson S., Levit C. (1992) The Virtual Wind Tunnel, *IEEE Computer Graphics and Applications*, Vol.12, No.4, pp. 25–34.

Butterworth J., Davidson A., Hench S., Olano T.M. (1992) 3DM: A Three-Dimensional Modeler Using a Head-Mounted Display, *Proc. 1992 Symposium on Interactive 3D Graphics*, Vol.25, No.2, pp. 135–138.

Calvert T.W., Chapman J. (1978) Notation of Movement with Computer Assistance, *Proc. ACM Annual Conf.*, Vol.2, pp. 731–736.

Capin T.K., Pandzic I.S., Magnenat Thalmann N., Thalmann D. (1995) Virtual Humans for Representing Participants in Immersive Virtual Environments, *Proc. FIVE '95*, London.

Capin T.K., Pandzic I.S., Thalmann D., Magnenat Thalmann N. (1997a) A Dead-Reckoning Algorithm for Virtual Human Figures, *Proc. VRAIS '97*, IEEE Press, pp. 161–169.

Capin T.K., Pandzic I.S., Noser H., Magnenat Thalmann N., Thalmann D. (1997b) Virtual Human Representation and Communication in VLNET Networked Virtual Environments, *IEEE Computer Graphics and Applications*, Vol.17, No.2, pp. 42–53.

Capin T.K., Pandzic I.S., Magnenat Thalmann N., Thalmann D. (1998) Realistic Avatars and Autonomous Virtual Humans in VLNET Networked Virtual Environments, in Earnshaw R. and Vince J. (Eds.), *WWW and Virtual Environments,* forthcomming.

Carignan M., Yang Y., Magnenat Thalmann N., Thalmann D. (1992), Dressing Animated Synthetic actors with Complex Clothes, *Proc. SIGGRAPH '92, Computer Graphics*, Vol.26, No.2, pp. 99–104.

Carlsson C., Hagsand O. (1993) DIVE—A Multi-User Virtual Reality System, *Proc. IEEE VRAIS '93,* Seattle WA, pp. 394–400.

Chadwick J., Haumann D.R., Parent R.E. (1989) Layered Construction for Deformable Animated Characters, *Proc. SIGGRAPH '89, Computer Graphics,* Vol.23, No.3, pp. 234–243.

Cohen M.F. (1989) Gracefulness and Style in Motion Control, *Proc. Mechanics, Control and Animation of Articulated Figures*, MIT.

Corraze J. (1980) *Les communications nonverbales*, Presses Universitaires de France, Paris.

Crowley J.L. (1987) Navigation for an Intelligent Mobile Robot, *IEEE Journal of Robotics and Automation,* Vol.1, No.1, pp. 31–41.

Curtis P. (1992) Mudding: Social Phenomena in Text-Based Virtual Realities *Proc. Directions and Implications of Advanced Compuing (DIAC '92) Symposium*, Berkeley CA, Ftp://parcftp.xerox.com/pub/MOO/papers/DIAC'92.txt. Also published in Intertek, 3, pp. 26–34. Also available as Xerox PARC technical report CSL-92-4.

Daldegan A., Magnenat Thalmann N., Thalmann D. (1993) An Integrated System for Modeling, Animating and Rendering Hair, *Proc. Eurographics '93, Computer Graphics Forum*, Vol.12, No.3, 1993, pp. 211–221.

Das T.K., Singh G., Mitchell A., Kumar P.S., McGee K. (1997) NetEffect: A Network Architecture for Large-Scale Multi-User Virtual Worlds, *Proc. ACM VRST '97*, pp. 157–163.

Davies C., Harrison J. (1996) Osmose: Towards Broadening the Aesthetics of Virtual Reality, *Computer Graphics*, Vol.30, No.4.

Dawes R. (1980) Social Dilemmas, *Annual Review of Pyschology,* Vol.31, pp. 169–193.

Doenges P.K., Capin T.K., Lavagetto F., Ostermann J., Pandzic I.S., Petajan E.D. (1997) MPEG-4: Audio/Video and Synthetic Graphics/Audio for Mixed Media, *Image Communication Journal,* Vol.5, No.4, pp. 433–463.

Durlach N.I., Mavor A.S. (Eds.) (1995) *Virtual Reality: Scientific and Technological Challenges*, Committee on Virtual Reality Research and Development, National Research Council, National Academy of Sciences Press, ISBN 0-309-05135-5.

Ekman P., Friesen W.V. (1967) Head and Body Cues in the Judgement of Emotion: A Reformulation, *Perceptual Motor Skills*, No.24, pp. 711–724.

Ellis S.R. (1991) Nature and Origin of Virtual Environments: A Bibliographic Essay, *Computing Systems in Engineering*, Vol.2, No.4, pp. 321–347.

Emering L., Boulic R., Balcisoy S., Thalmann D. (1997) Real-Time Interactions with Virtual Agents by Human Action Identification, *Proc. ACM Conference on Autonomous Agents '97*, ACM Press, pp. 476–477.

Fahlen L.E., Brown C.G., Stahl O., Carlsson C. (1993) A Space-Based Model for User Interaction in Shared Synthetic Environments, *Proc. InterCHI '93*, Amsterdam.

Fontaine G. (1992) The experience of a sense of presence in intercultural and international encounters, *Presence: Teleoperators and Virtual Environments*, Vol.1, pp. 482–490.

Forsey D., Wilhelms J. (1988) Techniques for Interactive Manipulation of Articulated Bodies using Dynamics Analysis, *Proc. Graphics Interface '88*, pp. 8–15.

Foxlin E. (1996) Inertial Head-Tracker Sensor Fusion by a Complementary Separate-Bias Kalman Filter, *Proc. IEEE VRAIS '96*, pp. 185–194.

Frécon E., Stenius M. (1998) DIVE: A scalable network architecture for distributed virtual environments, *Distributed Systems Engineering Journal*, Vol.5., No.3., pp. 91–100

Funkhouser T.A. (1995) RING: A Client–Server System for Multi-User Virtual Environments, *ACM SIGGRAPH Special Issue on 1995 Symposium on Interactive 3D Graphics*, Monterey CA, pp. 85–92.

Funkhouser T.A. (1996) Network Topologies for Scaleable Multi-User Virtual Environments, *Proc. VRAIS '96*, pp. 222–228.

Gibson W. (1984) *Neuromancer*, Ace Books, New York.

Girard M. (1987) Interactive Design of 3D Computer-Animated Legged Animal Motion, *IEEE Computer Graphics and Applications*, Vol.7, No.6, pp. 39–51.

Girard M., Maciejewski A.A. (1985) Computational Modeling for Computer Generation of Legged Figures, *Proc. SIGGRAPH '85, Computer Graphics*, Vol.19, No.3, pp. 263–270.

Gossweiler R., Laferriere R.J., Keller M.L., Pausch R. (1994) An Introductory Tutorial for Developing Multiuser Virtual Environments, *Presence: Teleoperators and Virtual Environments*, Vol.3, No.4, pp. 225–264.

Gourret J.P., Magnenat Thalmann N., Thalmann D. (1989) Simulation of Object and Human Skin Deformations in a Grasping Task, *Proc. SIGGRAPH '89, Computer Graphics*, Vol.23, No.3, pp. 21–30.

Greenhalgh C. (1996) *Dynamic, embodied, multicast groups in MASSIVE-2*, Technical Report NOTTCS-TR-96-8, Department of Computer Science, University of Nottingham.

Greenhalgh C., Benford S. (1995) MASSIVE: A Distributed Virtual Reality System Incorporating Spatial Trading, *Proc. 15th International Conference on Distributed Computing Systems*, Los Alamitos CA, ACM, pp. 27–34.

Grimsdale C. (1991) dVS—Distributed Virtual Environment System, *Proc. Computer Graphics '91 Conference*, Blenheim Online, London ISBN 0 86353 282 9.

Hagsand O. (1991) Consistency and concurrency control in virtual worlds, *Proc. Second MultiG Workshop*.

Hagsand O. (1996) Interactive Multi-User VEs in the DIVE System, *IEEE Multimedia* Vol. 3, No.1, pp. 30–39.

HAnim, http://ece.uwaterloo.ca/~h-anim/spec.html.

Heeter C. (1992) Being there: the subjective experience of presence, *Presence: Teleoperators and Virtual Environments*, Vol.1, pp. 262–271.

Hendrix C., Barfield W. (1996) Presence within Virtual Environments as a Function of Visual Display Parameters, *Presence: Teleoperators and Virtual Environments*, Vol.5, No.3, pp. 274–289.

Hodgins J.K., Wooten W.L., Brogan D.C., O'Brien J.K. (1995) Animating Human Athletics, *Proc. SIGGRAPH '95*, pp. 71–78.

Horswill I. (1993) A Simple, Cheap, and Robust Visual Navigation System, *From Animals to Animats 2, Proceedings of the 2nd International Conference on Simulation of Adaptive Behavior*, MIT Press, Cambridge MA, pp. 129–136.

Huang Z., Boulic R., Magnenat Thalmann N., Thalmann D. (1995) A Multi-Sensor Approach for Grasping and 3D Interaction, *Proc. CGI '95*, Academic Press, New York, pp. 235–254.

Hunter I.W., Tilemachos D.D., Lafontaine S.R., Charette P.G., Jones L.A., Sagar M.A., Mallinson G.D., Hunter P.J. (1993) A Teleoperated Microsurgical Robot and Associated Virtual Environment for Eye Surgery, *Presence*, Vol.2, No. 4, pp. 265–280.

IEEE (1993) Institute of Electrical and Electronics Engineers, International Standard, ANSI/IEEE Standard 1278-1993, *Standard for Information Technology, Protocols for Distributed Interactive Simulation*.

Kalawsky R. (1993) *The Science of Virtual Reality and Virtual Environments*, Addison-Wesley, Wokingham, UK.

Kalra P. (1993) An Interactive Multimodal Facial Animation System, PhD Thesis 1183, EPFL.

Kalra P., Mangili A., Magnenat Thalmann N., Thalmann D. (1992) Simulation of Facial Muscle Actions Based on Rational Free-Form Deformations, *Proc. Eurographics '92*, pp. 59–69.

Kato M., So I., Hishinuma Y., Nakamura O., Minami T. (1992) Description and Synthesis of Facial Expressions Based on Isodensity Maps, in Tosiyasu L (Ed.), *Visual Computing*, Springer-Verlag Tokyo, pp. 39–56.

Kessler G.D., Hodges L.F. (1996) A Networked Communication Protocol for Distributed Virtual Environment Systems, *Proc. IEEE VRAIS '96*, pp. 214–221.

Kishino F. (1994) Virtual Space Teleconferencing System—Real-Time Detection and Reproduction of Human Images *Proc. Imagina '94*, pp. 109–118.

Koenen R., Pereira F., Chiariglione L. (1997) MPEG-4: Context and Objectives, *Image Communication Journal*, Vol.9, No.4.

Kollock P., Smith M. (1996) Managing the Virtual Commons: Cooperation and Conflict in Computer Communities, in Herring S. (Ed.), *Computer-Mediated Communication*, John Benjamins, Amsterdam.

Komatsu K. (1988) Human Skin Model Capable of Natural Shape Variation, *The Visual Computer*, Vol.3, No.5, pp. 265–271.

Korein J., Badler N.I. (1982) Techniques for Generating the Goal-directed Motion of Articulated Structures, *IEEE Computer Graphics and Applications*, Vol.2, No.9, pp. 71–81.

Kurihara T., Anjyo K., Thalmann D. (1993) Hair Animation with Collision Detection, *Proc. Computer Animation '93*, Springer, Tokyo, pp. 128–138.

Lafleur B., Magnenat-Thalmann N., Thalmann D. (1991) Cloth Animation with Self-Collision Detection, *Proc. IFIP Conf. on Graphics Modeling*, Tokyo, Japan, pp. 179–188.

Lamotte W., Flerackers E., Van Reeth F., Earnshaw R., De Matos J.M. (1997) VISINET: Collaborative 3D Visualization and VR over ATM Networks, *IEEE Computer Graphics and Applications*, Vol.17, No.2, pp. 66–75.

Lavagetto F. (1995) Converting Speech into Lip Movements: A Multimedia Telephone for Hard of Hearing People, *IEEE Trans. on Rehabilitation Engineering*, Vol.3, No.1, pp. 90–102.

Leblanc A., Thalmann D., Turner R. (1991) Rendering Hair using Pixel Blending and Shadow Buffers, *Journal of Visualization and Computer Animation*, Vol.2, No.3, pp. 92–97.

Lee M.W., Kunii T.L. (1989) Animation Design: A Database-Oriented Animation Design Method with a Video Image Analysis Capability, in Magnenat Thalmann N., Thalmann D. (Eds.), *State of the Art in Computer Animation*, Springer, Tokyo, pp. 97–112.

Li H., Roivainen P., Forchheimer R. (1993) 3-D Motion Estimation in Model-Based Facial Image Coding, *IEEE Trans. on Pattern Analysis and Machine Intelligence*, Vol.15, No. 6, pp. 545–555.

Liang J., Shaw C., Green M. (1991) On Temporal-Spatial Realism in the Virtual Reality Environment, *Proc. ACM UIST '91*, pp. 19–25.

Macedonia M.R., Zyda M.J. (1997) A Taxonomy for Networked Virtual Environments, *IEEE Multimedia*, Vol.4, No.1, pp. 48–56.

Macedonia M.R., Zyda M.J., Pratt D.R., Barham P.T., Zestwitz (1994) NPSNET: A Network Software Architecture for Large-Scale Virtual Environments, *Presence: Teleoperators and Virtual Environments*, Vol.3, No.4, pp. 265–287.

Macedonia M.R., Brutzman D.P., Zyda M.J., Pratt D.R., Barham P.T., Falby J., Locke J. (1995) NPSNET: A Multi-Player 3D Virtual Environment Over the Internet, *Proc. Symposium on Interactive 3D Graphics*, ACM, New York, pp. 93–94.

Magnenat Thalmann N., Thalmann D. (1987) The Direction of Synthetic Actors in the Film 'Rendez-vous à Montreal', *IEEE Computer Graphics and Applications*, Vol.7, No.12, pp. 9–19.

Magnenat Thalmann N., Thalmann D. (1993) The Artificial Life of Synthetic Actors, *IEICE Transactions*, J76-D-II, 8, pp. 1506–1514.

Magnenat Thalmann N., Thalmann D. (1995) Digital Actors for Interactive Television, *Proc. IEEE*, Special Issue on Digital Television, Part 2, July 1995, pp. 1022–1031.

Magnenat Thalmann N., Laperriere R., Thalmann D. (1988) Joint-Dependent Local Deformations for Hand Animation and Object Grasping, *Proc. Graphics Interface '88*, pp. 26–33.

Magnenat Thalmann N., Minh H.T., de Angelis M., Thalmann D. (1989) Design, Transformation and Animation of Human Faces, *The Visual Computer*, Vol.5, No.3, pp. 32–39.

Magnenat Thalmann N., Cazedevals A., Thalmann D. (1993) Modeling Facial Communication Between an Animator and a Synthetic Actor in Real Time, *Proc Modeling in Computer Graphics*, Genoa, pp. 387–396.

Magno Caldognetto E., Vagges K., Borghese N.A., Ferrigno G. (1989) Automatic Analysis of Lips and Jaw Kinematics in VCV Sequences, *Proc. Eurospeech '89,* Vol.2, pp. 453–456

Mapes D.P., Moshell J.M. (1995) A Two-Handed Interface for Object Manipulation in Virtual Environments, *Presence*, Vol.4, No.4, pp. 403–416.

Mas S.R., Thalmann D. (1994) A Hand Control and Automatic Grasping System for Synthetic Actors, *Proc. Eurographics '94*, pp. 167–178.

Mase K., Pentland A. (1990) Automatic Lipreading by Computer, *Trans. Inst. Elec. Info. and Comm. Eng.* , Vol.J73-D-II, No.6, pp. 796–803

Miller G.R. (1976) *Explorations in Interpersonal Communication*, Sage, London.

Mine M.R. (1997) ISAAC: A Meta-CAD System for Virtual Environments. *Computer-Aided Design*, forthcomming.

Moccozet L., Magnenat Thalmann N. (1997) Dirichlet Free-Form Deformations and their Application to Hand Deformation, *Proc. Computer Animation '97*, pp. 93–102.

Moccozet L., Huang Z., Magnenat Thalmann N., Thalmann D. (1997) Virtual Hand Interactions with 3D World, *Proc. Multimedia Modeling '97*, Singapore, pp. 307–322.

Molet T., Boulic R., Thalmann D. (1996) A Real-Time Anatomical Converter for Human Motion Capture*, Proc. Eurographics Workshop on Computer Animation and Simulation*, Boulic R. (Ed.), Springer, Vienna, pp. 79–94.

Molet T., Aubel A., Capin T., Carion S., Lee E., Magnenat Thalmann N., Noser H., Pandzic I., Sannier G., Thalmann D. (1998) Anyone for Tennis, *Presence*, MIT Press, Cambridge MA.

Morris D., Collett P., Marsh P., O'Shaughnessy M. (1979) *Gestures*, Jonathan Cape, London, p. XXII.

MPEG, http://drogo.cselt.stet.it/mpeg.

MPEG-4 System Committee Draft (this is available through the MPEG homepage: http://www.cselt.stet.it/mpeg).

MPEG-N1886, MPEG-4 Requirements Version 5, ISO/IEC JTC1/SC29/WG11 N1886, MPEG97/November 1997.

MPEG-N1901, Text for CD 14496-1 Systems, ISO/IEC JTC1/SC29/WG11 N1886, MPEG97/November 1997.

MPEG-N1902, Text for CD 14496-2 Video, ISO/IEC JTC1/SC29/WG11 N1886, MPEG97/November 1997.

Noser H., Thalmann D. (1995) Synthetic Vision and Audition for Digital Actors, *Proc. Eurographics '95*, pp. 325–336.

Noser H., Thalmann D. (1996) The Animation of Autonomous Actors Based on Production Rules, *Proc. Computer Animation '96*, Geneva, IEEE Computer Society Press, Los Alamitos CA, pp. 47–57

Noser H., Thalmann D. (1997) Sensor-Based Synthetic Actors in a Tennis Game Simulation, *Proc. Computer Graphics International '97*, IEEE Computer Society Press, pp. 189–198.

Noser H., Pandzic I.S., Capin T.K., Magnenat Thalmann N., Thalmann D. (1996) Playing Games through the Virtual Life Network, *Proc. Artificial Life V*, Nara, pp. 114–121.

Ohya J., Kitamura Y., Kishino F., Terashima N. (1995) Virtual Space Teleconferencing: Real-Time Reproduction of 3D Human Images, *Journal of Visual Communication and Image Representation*, Vol.6, No.1, pp. 1–25.

Olson M. (1965) *The Logic of Collective Action: Public Goods and the Theory of Groups*, Harvard University Press, Cambridge MA.

Ostrom E. (1990) *Governing the Commons: The Evolution of Institutions for Collective Action*, Cambridge University Press, New York.

Ousterhout J.K. (1994) *TCL and TK Toolkit*, Addison-Wesley, Reading MA, ISBN 0-201-63337-X.

Pandzic I.S. (1998) *Facial Communication in Networked Virtual Environments*, PhD Thesis, University of Geneva.

Pandzic I.S., Kalra P., Magnenat Thalmann N., Thalmann D. (1994) Real-Time Facial Interaction, *Displays*, Vol.15, No 3.

Pandzic I.S., Çapin T.K., Magnenat Thalmann N., Thalmann D. (1995) VLNET: A Networked Multimedia 3D Environment with Virtual Humans, *Proc. Multi-Media Modeling MMM '95*, Singapore, pp. 21–32.

Pandzic I.S., Capin T.K., Magnenat Thalmann N., Thalmann D. (1996a) Motor functions in the VLNET Body-Centered Networked Virtual Environment, *Proc. 3rd Eurographics Workshop on Virtual Environments*, Monte Carlo, pp. 94–103.

Pandzic I.S., Capin T.K., Magnenat Thalmann N., Thalmann D. (1996b) Towards Natural Communication in Networked Collaborative Virtual Environments, *Proc. FIVE 96*, Pisa, pp. 37–47.

Pandzic I.S., Capin T.K., Lee E., Magnenat Thalmann N., Thalmann D. (1997a) A Flexible Architecture for Virtual Humans in Networked Collaborative Virtual Environments, *Proc. Eurographics '97*, pp. 177–188.

Pandzic I.S., Capin T.K., Magnenat Thalmann N., Thalmann D. (1997b) A Versatile Navigation Interface for Virtual Humans in Networked Collaborative Virtual Environments, *Proc. ACM Symposium on Virtual Reality Software and Technology*, Lausanne, pp. 45–49.

Pandzic I.S., Capin T.K., Magnenat Thalmann N., Thalmann D. (1997c) MPEG-4 for Networked Collaborative Virtual Environments, *Proc. International Conference on Virtual Systems and Multimedia*, IEEE, Geneva, pp. 19–25.

Pandzic I.S., Capin T.K., Magnenat Thalmann N., Thalmann D. (1997d) VLNET: A Body-Centered Networked Virtual Environment, *Presence: Teleoperators and Virtual Environments*, Vol.6, No.6, pp. 676–686.

Parke F.I. (1982) Parametrized Models for Facial Animation, *IEEE Computer Graphics and Applications*, Vol.2, No.9, pp. 61–68.

Patterson E.C., Litwinowich P.C., Greene N. (1991) Facial Animation by Spatial Mapping, *Proc. Computer Animation '91*, Magnenat Thalmann N., Thalmann D. (Eds.), Springer-Verlag, pp. 31–44

Pausch R., Snoddy J., Taylor R., Watson S., Haseltine E. (1996) Disney's Aladdin: First Steps Toward Storytelling in Virtual Reality. *Proc. SIGGRAPH '96*, pp. 193–202.

Pearce A., Wyvill B., Wyvill G., Hill D. (1986) Speech and Expression: A Computer Solution to Face Animation, *Proc. Graphics Interface '86*, pp. 136–140.

Pope A.R., Schaffer R.L. (1991) *The SIMNET Network and Protocols*, BBN Systems and Technologies Corporation Report 7627.

Pratt D.R., Pratt S.M., Barham R.E., Waldrop M.S., Ehlert J.F., Chrislip C.A. (1997) Humans in Large-Scale, Networked Virtual Environment, *Presence: Teleoperators and Virtual Environments*, Vol.6, No.5, pp. 547–564.

Prusinkiewicz P., Lindenmayer A. (1990) *The Algorithmic Beauty of Plants*, Springer-Verlag, Vienna.

Renault O., Magnenat Thalmann N., Thalmann D. (1990) A Vision-Based Approach to Behavioural Animation, *Journal of Visualization and Computer Animation*, Vol.1, No.1, pp. 18–21.

Reynolds C. (1987) Flocks, Herds, and Schools: A Distributed Behavioral Model, *Proc. SIGGRAPH '87, Computer Graphics*, Vol.21, No.4, pp. 25–34.

Reynolds C.W. (1993) An Evolved, Vision-Based Behavioral Model of Coordinated Group Motion, in Meyer J.A. et al. (Eds.), *From Animals to Animats*, Proceedings of the 2nd International Conference on Simulation of Adaptive Behavior, MIT Press, Cambridge MA, pp. 384–392.

Reynolds C.W. (1994) An Evolved, Vision-Based Model of Obstacle Avoidance Behavior, in Langton C.G. (Ed.), *Artificial Life III: SFI Studies in the Sciences of Complexity*, Vol. XVII, Addison-Wesley, Reading MA.

Rohlf J., Helman J. (1994) IRIS Performer: A High Performance Multiprocessing Toolkit for Real-Time 3D Graphics, *Proc. SIGGRAPH '94*, pp. 381–394.

Rosenberg B.G., Langer J. (1965) A study of postural-gestural communication, *Journal of Personality and Social Psychology*, Vol.2, No.4, pp. 593–597.

Rothbaum B., Hodges L., Kooper R., Opdyke D., Williford J., North M. Effectiveness of computer-generated (virtual reality) graded exposure in the treatment of acrophobia. *American Journal of Psychiatry* , Vol.152, No.4, pp. 626–628.

Saji H., Hioki H., Shinagawa Y., Yoshida K., Kunii T. (1992) Extraction of 3D Shapes from the Moving Human Face using Lighting Switch Photometry, in Magnenat Thalmann N., Thalmann D. (Eds.), *Creating and Animating the Virtual World*, Springer-Verlag, Tokyo, pp. 69–86

Schroeder P., Zeltzer D. (1988) Path planning inside Bolio, in Thalmann D. (Ed.), *Synthetic Actors: The Impact of Artificial Intelligence and Robotics on Animation*, Course Notes SIGGRAPH '88, pp. 194–207.

Sederberg T.W., Parry S.R. (1986) Free-Form Deformation of Solid Geometric Models, *Proc. SIGGRAPH '86*, Computer Graphics, Vol.20, No.4, pp. 151–160.

Semwal S.K., Hightower R., Stansfield S. (1996) Closed-Form and Geometric Algorithms for Real-Time Control of an Avatar, *Proc. VRAIS '96*, pp. 177–184.

Shaw C., Green M. (1993) The MR Toolkit Peers Package and Experiment, *Proc. IEEE Virtual Reality Annual International Symposium*, pp. 463–469.

Sheridan T.B. (1994) Musings on telepresence and virtual presence, *Presence: Teleoperators and Virtual Environments*, Vol.1, No.1, pp. 120–126

Singh G., Serra L. (1994) Supporting Collaboration in Virtual Worlds, in Magnenat Thalmann N., Thalmann D. (Eds.), *Artificial Life and Virtual Reality*, John Wiley, Chichester, pp. 211–228.

Singh G., Serra L., Png W., Ng H. (1994) BrickNet: A Software Toolkit for Network-Based Virtual Worlds, *Presence*, Vol.3, No.1, pp. 11–34.

Singh G, Serra L., Png W., Wong A., Ng H. (1995) BrickNet: Sharing Object Behaviors on the Net, *Proc. IEEE VRAIS '95*, pp. 19–27.

Slater M., Usoh M. (1994) Body Centered Interaction in Immersive Virtual Environments, in Magnenat Thalmann N., Thalmann D. (Eds.), *Artificial Life and Virtual Reality*, John Wiley, Chichester, pp. 1–10.

Slater M., Usoh M., Steed A. (1994) Depth of presence in virtual environments, *Presence: Teleoperators and Virtual Environments*, Vol. 3, No. 2, pp. 130–140.

Slater M., Usoh M., Steed A. (1995) Taking Steps: The Influence of a Walking Metaphor on Presence in Virtual Reality, *ACM Transactions on Computer–Human Interaction*, Vol.2, No.3, pp. 201–219.

Slater M., Usoh M., Benford S., Brown C., Rodden T., Smith G., Wilbur S. (1996) Distributed Extensible Virtual Reality Laboratory (DEVRL), in Goebel M., Slavik P., van Wijk J.J. (Eds.), *Virtual Environments and Scientific Visualization'96*, Springer, New York, pp. 137–148.

Smith A.R., Digital Filmmaking, *Abacus*, Vol.1, No.1, pp. 28–45.

Stansfield S., Shawver D., Miner N., Rogers D. (1995) An Application of Shared Virtual Reality to Situational Training, *Proc. IEEE VRAIS '95*, pp. 156–161.

Stephenson N. (1992) *Snow Crash*, Bantam Books, New York.

Steuer J. (1992) Defining Virtual Reality: Dimensions Determining Telepresence, *Journal of Communication*, Vol.42, pp. 73–93.

Stytz M.R. (1996). Distributed Virtual Environments *IEEE Computer Graphics and Applications*, Vol.16, No.3, pp. 19–31.

Taylor R.M., Robinett W., Chi V.L., Brooks F.P. Jr, Wright W.W., Williams S., Snyder E.J. (1993) The Nanomanipulator: A Virtual Reality Interface for a Scanning Tunnelling Microscope, *Proc. SIGGRAPH '93*, pp. 127–134.

Terzopoulos D., Waters K. (1991) Techniques for Realistic Facial Modeling and Animation, *Proc. Computer Animation 1991*, Geneva, Springer-Verlag, Tokyo, pp. 59–74

Thalmann D. (1993) Using Virtual Reality Techniques in the Animation Process, in Earnshaw R., Gigante M., Jones H. (Eds.), *Virtual Reality Systems*, Academic Press, New York, pp. 143–159.

Thalmann D. (1994) Automatic Control and Behavior of Virtual Actors, in MacDonald L., Vince J. (Eds.), *Interacting with Virtual Environments*.

Thalmann D. (1996) A New Generation of Synthetic Actors: The Interactive Perceptive Actors, *Proc. Pacific Graphics '96*, Taipeh, pp. 200–219.

Thalmann D., Çapin T.K., Magnenat Thalmann N., Pandzic I.S. (1995) Participant, User-Guided and Autonomous Actors in the Virtual Life Network VLNET, *Proc. ICAT/VRST '95*, Chiba, Japan, pp. 3–11.

Thalmann D., Babski C., Capin T.K., Magnenat Thalmann N., Pandzic I.S. (1996) Sharing VLNET Worlds on the WEB, *Proc. Compugraphics '96*, Marne-la-Vallee, France.

Thalmann D., Shen J., Chauvineau E. (1997) Fast Human Body Deformations for Animation and VR Applications, *Proc. Computer Graphics International '96*, IEEE Computer Society Press, pp. 166–174.

Tosa N., Nakatsu R. (1996) The Esthetics of Artificial Life: Human-Like Communication Character 'MIC' and Feeling Improvisation Character 'MUSE', *Proc. Artificial Life*.

Tromp J.G. (1995) Presence, Telepresence and Immersion: The Cognitive Factors of Embodiments and Interaction in Virtual Environments, *Proc. FIVE '95*, London.

Tsuji S., Li S. (1993) Memorizing and Representing Route Scenes, in Meyer J.A. et al. (Eds.), *From Animals to Animats, Proceedings of the 2nd International Conference on Simulation of Adaptive Behavior*, MIT Press, Cambridge MA, pp. 225–232.

Tu X., Terzopoulos D. (1994) Artificial Fishes: Physics, Locomotion, Perception, Behavior, *Proc. SIGGRAPH '94, Computer Graphics*, pp. 42–48.

Unuma M., Anjyo K., Takeuchi R. (1995) Fourier Principles for Emotion-Based Human Figure Animation, *Proc. ACM SIGGRAPH '95*, pp. 91–96.

Volino P., Courchesne M., Magnenat Thalmann N. (1995) Versatile Efficient Techniques of Simulating Cloth and Other Deformable Objects, *Proc. SIGGRAPH '95*, pp. 137–144.

VRML (1997) The Virtual Reality Modeling Language, ISO/IEC DIS 14772-1, April 1997.

Watanabe Y., Suenega Y. (1989) Drawing Human Hair Using Wisp Model, *Proc. Computer Graphics International*, Springer, Tokyo, pp. 691–700.

Waters K. (1987) A Muscle Model for Animating Three-Dimensional Facial Expression, *Proc. SIGGRAPH '87*, Vol.21, No.4, pp. 17–24.

Waters K., Terzopoulos D. (1991) Modeling and Animating Faces using Scanned Data *Journal of Visualization and Computer Animation*, Vol.2, No.4, pp. 123–128

Waters R.C., Anderson D.B., Barrus J.W., Brogan D.C., Casey M.C., McKeown S.G., Nitta T., Sterns I.B., Yerazunis W.S. (1997) Diamond Park and Spline: Social Virtual Reality with 3D Animation, Spoken Interaction, and Runtime Extendability, *Presence*, Vol.6, No.4, pp. 461–481.

Watt A. Watt M. (1992) *Advanced Animation and Rendering Techniques*, Addison-Wesley, Reading MA.

Weitz S. (1974) *Nonverbal Communication : Readings with Commentary*, Oxford University Press, New York.

Welch R.B., Blackmon T.T., Liu A, Mellers B.A., Stark L.W. (1996) The Effects of Pictorial Realism, Delay of Visual Feedback, and Observer Interactivity on the Subjective Sense of Presence, *Presence*, Vol.5, No.3, pp. 263–273

Wilhelms J. (1987) Using Dynamic Analysis for Realistic Animation of Articulated Bodies, *IEEE Computer Graphics and Applications*, Vol.7, No.6, pp. 12–27.

Wilson J.R., Brown D.J., Cobb S.V., D'Cruz M.M., Eastgate R.M. (1995) Manufacturing Operations in Virtual Environments (MOVE), *Presence*, Vol.4, No.3, pp. 306–317.

Witten I.H., Neal R.M., Cleary J.G. (1987) Arithmetic Coding for Data Compression, *Communications of the ACM*, Vol.30, No.6, pp. 520–540.

Zeltzer D. (1982) Motor Control Techniques for Figure Animation, *IEEE Computer Graphics and Applications*, Vol.2, No.9, pp. 53–59.

Zeltzer D. (1992) Autonomy, interaction and presence, *Presence*, Vol.1, pp. 127–132.

Zyda M., Sheehan J. (Eds.) (1997) *Modeling and Simulation: Linking Entertainment and Defense*, National Academy Press, ISBN 0-309-05842-2.

Zyda M.J., Pratt D.R., Falby J.S., Barham P., Kelleher K.M. (1993) NPSNET and the Naval Postgraduate School Graphics and Video Laboratory, *Presence*, Vol.2, No.3, pp. 244–258.

Index